# Creative Research in Economics

Researchers are expected to produce original findings, yet nobody explains how original contributions are conceived in economics. Recently there have been calls for more creativity in economic research, yet there is no literature that explores creative research apart from collections of biographical essays. This book aims to address that gap, exploring the process of conceiving and generating ideas for interesting and original research contributions in economics (and potentially other social sciences too).

*Creative Research in Economics* serves both a practical and theoretical purpose. Theoretically it presents a unique way of thinking about the nature of problems and questions in economics and the role of social science researchers in society. As such it offers an interesting way to think about the philosophy of science and methodology in economics, and how new ideas emerge in the discipline. Practically it develops techniques for finding interesting and original research contributions (as opposed to conventional data-gathering research).

Whether you are a graduate student looking for that first interesting question, a novice researcher in search of fresh avenues for research after your PhD, or a seasoned academic looking to teach the philosophy and methodology of economics in more interesting ways, you will find this book of great use.

**Arnold Wentzel** is a lecturer at the University of Johannesburg, South Africa, where he teaches economics, education and research writing across a range of disciplines.

# Routledge Frontiers of Political Economy

*For a full list of titles in this series please visit* www.routledge.com/books/series/SE0345

206. Representing Public Credit
     Credible commitment, fiction, and the rise of the financial subject
     *Natalie Roxburgh*

207. The Rejuvenation of Political Economy
     *Edited by Nobuharu Yokokawa, Kiichiro Yagi, Hiroyasu Uemura and Richard Westra*

208. Macroeconomics After the Financial Crisis
     A Post-Keynesian perspective
     *Edited by Mogens Ove Madsen and Finn Olesen*

209. Structural Analysis and the Process of Economic Development
     *Edited by Jonas Ljungberg*

210. Economics and Power
     A Marxist critique
     *Giulio Palermo*

211. Neoliberalism and the Moral Economy of Fraud
     *Edited by David Whyte and Jörg Wiegratz*

212. Theoretical Foundations of Macroeconomic Policy
     Growth, productivity and public finance
     *Edited by Giovanni Di Bartolomeo and Enrico Saltari*

213. Heterodox Islamic Economics
     The emergence of an ethico-economic theory
     *Ishaq Bhatti and Masudul Alam Choudhury*

214. Intimate Economies of Immigration Detention
     Critical perspectives
     *Edited by Deirdre Conlon and Nancy Hiemstra*

215. Qualitative Methods in Economics
     *Mirjana Radović-Marković and Beatrice Avolio Alecchi*

216. Quantum Macroeconomics
     The legacy of Bernard Schmitt
     *Edited by Jean-Luc Bailly, Alvaro Cencini and Sergio Rossi*

217. Creative Research in Economics
     *Arnold Wentzel*

# Creative Research in Economics

**Arnold Wentzel**

LONDON AND NEW YORK

First published 2017
by Routledge
2 Park Square, Milton Park, Abingdon, Oxon OX14 4RN

and by Routledge
711 Third Avenue, New York, NY 10017

*Routledge is an imprint of the Taylor & Francis Group, an informa business*

© 2017 Arnold Wentzel

The right of Arnold Wentzel to be identified as author of this work has been asserted by him in accordance with sections 77 and 78 of the Copyright, Designs and Patents Act 1988.

All rights reserved. No part of this book may be reprinted or reproduced or utilised in any form or by any electronic, mechanical, or other means, now known or hereafter invented, including photocopying and recording, or in any information storage or retrieval system, without permission in writing from the publishers.

*Trademark notice*: Product or corporate names may be trademarks or registered trademarks, and are used only for identification and explanation without intent to infringe.

*British Library Cataloguing in Publication Data*
A catalogue record for this book is available from the British Library

*Library of Congress Cataloguing in Publication Data*
A catalog record has been requested for this book

ISBN: 978-1-138-69888-8 (hbk)
ISBN: 978-1-315-51801-5 (ebk)

Typeset in Times New Roman
by Out of House Publishing

Printed and bound by CPI Group (UK) Ltd, Croydon, CR0 4YY

To my parents, who inspired me and set me on this path.

# Contents

*List of figures* viii
*List of tables* x
*Preface* xi
*List of logical symbols used* xii

1 The possibility of systematic originality 1
2 Originality in social science research 15
3 The representation of problems in economics 33
4 Originality through questions 60
5 Reasoning towards new ideas 71
6 Rational reconstruction from case studies 91
7 Dealing with authentic economic problems 115
8 An instructional programme 140
9 Next steps 169

*Index* 174

# Figures

| | | |
|---|---|---|
| 2.1 | Typology of novel contributions | 18 |
| 2.2 | Degrees of originality | 21 |
| 2.3 | Einstein's model of scientific discovery | 25 |
| 2.4 | Einstein's approach adapted | 26 |
| 2.5 | Process of conceiving of an original contribution | 27 |
| 3.1 | Process of conceiving an original contribution | 34 |
| 3.2 | Some fundamental trade-offs in economics | 36 |
| 3.3 | Problems as trade-offs call for optimisation | 37 |
| 3.4 | An economic problem as a logical conflict | 40 |
| 3.5 | Mauritius in the 1960s and the 1980s | 45 |
| 3.6 | Mauritius' problem as a logical conflict | 46 |
| 3.7 | Trade-offs shown differently | 49 |
| 3.8 | Meade's Mauritian trade-off | 50 |
| 3.9 | Comparison of logics | 50 |
| 3.10 | Empty boxes | 51 |
| 3.11 | Completed boxes (given a specific state of the economy) | 53 |
| 3.12 | Summary of steps 2–6 | 54 |
| 3.13 | Mauritius' problem as a logical conflict | 55 |
| 4.1 | Process of conceiving an original contribution | 61 |
| 4.2 | Questioning assumptions | 63 |
| 4.3 | Questions designed for synthesis | 65 |
| 4.4 | Relevance relations in a question | 69 |
| 5.1 | Process of conceiving an original contribution | 72 |
| 5.2 | Views of logical versus creative activity | 72 |
| 5.3 | The cross of creative questioning | 84 |
| 5.4 | Simplified grammatical mapping | 85 |
| 5.5 | A question of survival | 86 |
| 6.1 | Simplified grammatical mapping of Coase's question | 108 |
| 6.2 | Cross of questioning based on Coase (1960) | 109 |
| 7.1 | Typology of problems | 119 |
| 7.2 | A conflict about interest rate policy | 127 |
| 7.3 | A Toulmin-like argument structure | 128 |
| 7.4 | Argumentation and the conflict representation combined | 130 |

| 7.5 | Typology of assumptions | 131 |
| 7.6 | Taylor's monetary policy trade-off | 134 |
| 7.7 | The ongoing process of solving wicked problems | 136 |
| 8.1 | The process of instructional design to be followed | 142 |
| 8.2 | Sequence of skills | 147 |
| 8.3 | Unit 1 – Scientific inquiry | 147 |
| 8.4 | Unit 2 – Problem representation | 148 |
| 8.5 | Unit 3 – Question generation | 148 |
| 8.6 | Unit 4 – Idea generation | 149 |
| 8.7 | Unit 5 – Facilitating dialogue | 149 |
| 8.8 | Degrees of originality | 154 |
| 8.9A | Representing the problem | 158 |
| 8.10A | Questions designed for synthesis | 160 |
| 8.11A | Relevance relations in a question | 163 |
| 8.12A | Simplified grammatical mapping of the question | 165 |
| 8.13A | Cross of questioning | 166 |

# Tables

| | | |
|---|---|---|
| 2.1 | Judging originality | 23 |
| 4.1 | Contrast classes and relevance relations | 67 |
| 4.2 | Assumptions derived from Figure 4.4 | 69 |
| 5.1 | Logical structure of an economic problem | 79 |
| 5.2 | Three end points of abductive reasoning | 80 |
| 5.3 | Possible negations | 87 |
| 5.4 | Possible conjunctions | 87 |
| 6.1 | Representing the problem of the liberal paradox | 93 |
| 6.2 | Assumptions that structure the liberal paradox | 94 |
| 6.3 | Questions designed to synthesise | 96 |
| 6.4 | Logical structure of the time-inconsistency problem | 99 |
| 6.5 | Assumptions structuring the time-inconsistency problem | 100 |
| 6.6 | End points derived from the time-inconsistency problem | 102 |
| 6.7 | Contrast classes and relevance relations | 105 |
| 6.8 | Contrast classes and relevance relations in Coase's question | 107 |
| 6.9 | Possible negations | 110 |
| 6.10 | Possible conjunctions | 110 |
| 6.11 | Eliciting assumptions | 111 |
| 8.1 | Conventional view versus constructivist view | 142 |
| 8.2 | Main areas of development in the programme | 145 |
| 8.3 | Prerequisites and evidence | 145 |
| 8.4 | Programme outline | 151 |
| 8.5A | Assumptions that structure the problem | 159 |
| 8.6A | Contrast classes and relevance relations | 162 |
| 8.7A | Assumptions derived from relational analysis | 164 |
| 8.8A | Possible negations | 166 |
| 8.9A | Possible conjunctions | 167 |

# Preface

There is sufficient evidence today that new insight results from analytical thinking. With this book I show that original contributions can be generated systematically by developing a range of analytical tools that can be (and has been) taught to researchers. By the end of this book, you will have been exposed to a variety of techniques that can be used to reformulate problems, expose assumptions, generate interesting questions and discover new ideas in economics, though in my experience, it is also suitable to research in most theory-driven social sciences. Whether you are a graduate student looking for that first interesting question, a novice researcher in search of fresh avenues for research after your PhD, or a seasoned academic looking to teach the philosophy and methodology of economics in more interesting ways, you will find this book useful. Also, through this book I hope to bring the scholarship of creativity *in* economics *within* the discipline itself.

Since the techniques build on each other, it is best to read the chapters in sequence. The book starts fairly abstract in Chapters 1 and 2, but gets into the specifics of the techniques from thereafter. Chapters 3–6 form the core of the book, while Chapters 7–9 explore the extensions of these ideas.

I would like to extend my gratitude to the Universidad Antonio Nariño in Bogotá (specifically Eleonora Herrera-Medina) and Ivan Hernandez from the Universidad de Ibagué, for giving me the opportunity to present the first pilot versions of the instructional programme developed in this book.

# Logical symbols used

Throughout the book, I make extensive use of logical symbols. No prior knowledge of formal logic is needed to understand any of these as they are not used to derive logical theorems. They are merely used as shortcuts: if they were not used, the book would be more lengthy.

For the sake of convenience, the symbols are defined here:

- $\Rightarrow$ is an inferential parameter to set up a logical relationship between two variables. It shows that one variable logically leads to another;
- $\not\Rightarrow$ is the negation of $\Rightarrow$ and implies that a logical relationship does not exist;
- $\rightarrow$ is the conditional operator that sets up an 'if-then' relationship between two variables, e.g. A$\rightarrow$B should be read 'if A then B'. It is a special case of $\Rightarrow$ and sets up a more direct logical relationship;
- $=$ and $\neq$ are used to indicate equality and non-equality, respectively;
- $\wedge$ is the conjunction operator and should be read as 'and';
- $\vee$ is the disjunction operator and should be read as 'or';
- $\neg$ is the negation operator and should be read as 'not'.

# 1 The possibility of systematic originality

**The state of scientific creativity in economics**

Scientific creativity is commonly regarded as the intentional production of original ideas. To be regarded as original, such ideas have to be both novel and meaningful to other scientists (Brodin & Frick, 2011:136; Klausen, 2013:33). Original ideas are valued by economists as evident from Maurice Allais' (1992:36) statement that: "Only through the blossoming of new ideas suggested by creative intuition … can science truly progress." As a recipient of the Nobel Prize in Economics, one would expect he included economics in his view of science.

As in other disciplines, economic research is expected to be original. Originality is what is required to obtain a PhD in Economics and to publish in economics journals. Leading Economics faculties throughout the world emphasise the importance of creative research on their public websites. The following quotes by leading institutions illustrate this: "The dissertation must be based on original research and represent a significant contribution to the body of Economic knowledge" (University of California); "Award of the PhD is dependent on the completion and defence of an original research thesis" (LSE); and, "Throughout the program, there are formal provisions for students to engage in original research work" (MIT). Originality is not only valued in the PhD thesis but also the published scientific paper as both are the product of creative research.

However, since the global financial crisis, the ability of economists to generate truly creative research and new ideas has been questioned. Grieve (2014), for example, argues that the discipline simply cycles between variants of classical and Keynesian ideas. Following the crisis, many calls have been made to rethink the core of the (post)graduate Economics curriculum (for example, Abito *et al.*, 2011). In fact, this issue was already highlighted in 1991 when the American Economic Association's Commission on Graduate Education in Economics (CoGEE) published its report. In this report, twelve leading economists – including Kenneth Arrow, Robert Lucas and Joseph Stiglitz – argued that the early training of graduate students stifled creativity due to the overemphasis on technical skills and analytical tools. Creative research requires not just technical skills, but also the ability to conceive of an original contribution – in the form of posing a new question, reformulating a problem, developing a new model, generating new data or extending techniques. What this report highlighted was that economists were not being adequately developed in the area of conceiving of original contributions (Krueger *et al.*, 1991:1049).

The apparent neglect of clear instruction in how to conceive of original contributions most likely derives from the consensus view amongst economists that it is an art that cannot be reduced to a systematic approach (Ethridge, 2004:30). While creativity is valued, the standard view in the profession about this is close to that of Milton Friedman's (1953:43): "The construction of hypotheses is a creative act of inspiration, intuition, invention ... The process must be discussed in psychological, not logical categories; studied in autobiographies, not treatises on scientific method; and promoted by maxim and example." This view reflects the belief that understanding the origin of new ideas lies outside the scope of economic analysis (Tollison, 1986:909).

Given such a view, one expects that economists would regard instruction in creative research to be futile. The result is that economists spend much of their time developing technical skills in the tools of analysis while leaving the process of conceiving original contributions to serendipity. There appears to be a belief that the generation of new ideas is merely a function of time and analytical skills.

Some economists have tried to offer some guidance by explaining their creative processes in essays, but these are usually brief and autobiographical in nature. From these essays, one gets the impression that creativity comes from new ideas that transpire from interactions with non-economists (Krugman, 1995) and other economists (Colander & Coats, 1989:49; Akerlof, 2003). Some economists' creativity is triggered by problems they experience, either personally (Sen, 1998) or theoretically (Samuelson, 1992:245). Others find that inconsistencies stimulate them to ask new questions (Stiglitz, 2001). All give the impression of creativity in research being innate or something that is triggered by external forces. Colander (2011) points out that even the reports that criticise the lack of attention to creativity in economic education offer little guidance on how exactly the creative capacity of researchers should be developed.

What makes the process of becoming a creative economist even more daunting is that, in most disciplines, the formal undergraduate education that precedes graduate studies hampers this transition. Formal education is a process involving the gradual acquisition of constraints in thinking as the student's mind is disciplined and immersed in disciplines (Gardner, 2000). When this process is completed – usually at the end of undergraduate studies or at the end of graduate coursework – the student is deemed ready to make his/her own contribution to the existing body of knowledge.

The transition from a 'course-taker' to 'independent researcher' is rarely easy: partly because a graduate student is required to challenge and transcend many of the constraints he/she acquired up until that point (Lovitts, 2005). They now face a first 'disorienting dilemma' (Gravett & Peterson, 2009:102) and have to undergo a process of transformational learning, since many of the skills that were effective during their school and undergraduate studies are no longer sufficient to succeed at independent research.

Nowhere is this transformation *of the researcher* more evident than in a PhD (and later in the writing of academic papers) when he/she is required to make an original contribution – something that is not well-defined (Frick, 2011a). PhD candidates and novice researchers are rarely adequately prepared to make such contributions (Trafford & Leshem, 2009:315; Frick, 2010:22). In most cases, the hope is that the student will already have the curiosity to find and produce an original contribution, or will learn to do so through interacting with a supervisor.

Conceiving of an original contribution is the product of a social and creative process that involves questioning or making conceptual leaps beyond one or more of the constraints acquired from the discipline (Brodin & Frick, 2011:138; Klag & Langley, 2013:151). From this, a second disorienting dilemma emerges: a dilemma created by the researcher *for the discipline*. Without such a disorienting dilemma, his/her contribution may be regarded as obvious or irrelevant.

In short, making an original contribution is challenging as it involves a double transformation: that of the researcher and the discipline. The researcher has to undergo a process of transformational learning, while, at the same time, being the agent of transformational learning within the discipline.

Very little of what students learn in their pre-PhD studies adequately prepares them for this daunting task, and some of what they have learned until that point may even undermine their efforts (Lovitts, 2005). Formal graduate education does not help to make the transition to becoming a creative researcher as it offers very little support in helping students to find and conceive an original contribution, and, even when it does, does not offer instruction in any systematic approach. This book takes the view that creative research can be systematic, and consequently, appropriate instruction can, and should, be developed in education programmes in Economics (and other social sciences).

## Can creative research be a systematic process?

The neglect of creativity in research partly stems from the acceptance of Popper's (1965) famous division of scientific work into an act of conceiving new ideas (the context of discovery) and the analysis of such ideas (the context of justification). According to this dichotomy, analysis is a logical process that can be made systematic and improved over time, while the creation of ideas is not a logical process and cannot therefore be reduced to a systematic approach.

## 4  The possibility of systematic originality

This view conflates deductive logic and systematic reasoning. It is correct that new ideas cannot be generated through logical deduction since logical deduction from an unchanging set of beliefs or axioms will always lead to the same ideas. However, deductive logic is but one of three main approaches to systematic reasoning: the other two being inductive and abductive reasoning. Abductive reasoning is the systematic reasoning towards new ideas and a vast body of literature has emerged around it in recent years (cf. Meheus, 1999; Aliseda, 2004; Paavola, 2006; Magnani, 2009). Simply put, the fact that creativity is not deductive does not imply that it cannot be systematic.

Some kind of efficient reasoning that leads to novel ideas, which cannot be reduced to either deduction or induction, does seem to take place in science. This reasoning is not independent of logical analysis, but rather complementary to logical analysis. If the generation of new ideas was entirely "beyond the scope of formal logic", as Keynes (1952:152) also believed, then it would be hard to explain why in hindsight even revolutionary ideas appear logical. If there were no reasoning, it would be even harder to explain how good scientists are able to anticipate that the new hypothesis they are searching for will be of some particular kind, or why many scientists can generate a correct hypothesis after only a few guesses (Kim & Cunningham, 2003). Clearly, there is some reasoning that allows scientists to systematically and efficiently transform doubts into new ideas.

The view that creative research is not systematic has been empirically wrong for some time now, as developments in the field of artificial intelligence suggest. Starting with Economics Nobel Prize winner, Herbert Simon, in a variety of articles since 1966, artificial intelligence researchers have attempted to reduce the mysticism surrounding the process of scientific discovery. Simon (1983) developed a programme called 'BACON' that was able to discover for itself a number of mathematical laws, which were already known to humans, from unorganised raw data.

Simon's work in the computational modelling of creativity eventually led to Lenat and Seely-Brown's (1984) programme, called 'EURISKO', that was able to generate a patentable invention (Boden, 1994). Possibly the most exciting work has been done by Stephen Thaler (1997) whose neural networks have: generated several useful patents; discovered substances unknown to humans; and even created copyrighted works of art. Once trained, these neural networks endogenously generate and evaluate original ideas without being supplied with any external human input. Thaler's mathematical description of the process demonstrated that creative action can be formalised.

Neither abductive reasoning nor the results from artificial intelligence studies rely on a non-logical trial-and-error approach. Trial-and-error could be systematic, but unless it is constrained and guided by some form of reasoning, this type of reasoning is inefficient, given the infinite space to be searched.

Recent experimental research by cognitive scientists, such as Weisberg (2006, 2015) of the actual process by which humans achieve insight, now confirms that the kind of creative thinking that goes into the research process is in fact systematic and reasoned process. In fact, Weisberg (2015:36) concludes that "a sharp distinction between analytic and creative thought processes may not be useful, because analytic thinking can produce novel outcomes".

The ideas of economists, like Milton Friedman and John Maynard Keynes, created the impression that creativity is sharply distinct from analytical thinking, and this may have played a role in the neglect of creativity in the training of researchers in economics. Their ideas were based on the apparently commonsensical understanding of creativity at the time, but not on scientific studies. This book questions their view only to the extent that it contradicts the evidence from cognitive science and artificial intelligence, and argues that there are indeed systematic methods by which to promote creativity in economic research.

The closest economists have come to finding a systematic method by which one can conceive of original contributions resembles a trial-and-error approach. It involves finding the constraints and assumptions of a model, changing one or more, and seeing what happens. McCloskey (1994:137) criticises this as a more or less random "search through the hyperspace of conceivable assumptions" since assumptions are often changed without any epistemological strategy in mind. Without a strategy, this method might just be an exercise in scientific amusement, but there are many cases where the deliberate negation of a carefully chosen assumption has led to major advances. However, without a systematic reasoning strategy to guide the negation of assumptions, this method is difficult to replicate effectively, and it is exactly this possibility that is denied by economists.

## Going beyond existing creativity research

Creativity studies has been a source of useful and widely used techniques, though most of it is difficult to apply to disciplinary scientific research. It is a vast field that has added much to our understanding of creative processes in the fields of: individual creativity and psychology (e.g. Wallas, 1926; De Bono, 1992; Csikszentmihalyi, 1996); advertising (such as Osborn, 1953; Griffin & Morrison, 2010); organisational innovation (for instance, Tanner, 1997; Robinson & Stern, 1998); and engineering (e.g. Savransky, 2000; Fogler & LeBlanc, 2008).

Amabile (1996) argues that creativity is domain-specific so that generic approaches are difficult to transfer from a domain like advertising to one of scientific research. Scientific creativity is closely tied to disciplines and the nature of scientific problems. To be meaningful, a proposed new contribution in a discipline has to *originate and terminate in a particular discipline* and take into account the content, methods and values of that discipline. Hence, a simple application of generic creativity techniques (such as brainstorming) would be less effective in scientific research, and any systematic approach needs to find a way to start and end researchers' creativity within their disciplinary context.

In other words, anyone who wants to find an original research contribution has to start with a strong understanding of their discipline. Any systematic approach to originality should guide the researcher in transforming such an understanding into ideas that are meaningful within the discipline. That is where generic creativity techniques fail – they can be applied regardless of your understanding of your discipline, and are therefore unlikely to produce meaningful results.

There is some research on scientific creativity within a disciplinary context, but it suffers from two problems that limit its usefulness in helping economic researchers conceive of original contributions. First, most of this research has been focused on scientific discovery in the physical and natural sciences (see for example: Hanson, 1961; Holton, 1978; Simon, Langley & Bradshaw, 1981; Darden, 2002; Clement, 2008; Magnani, 2009). There has, however, been a steady trickle of studies focusing on the social sciences, especially in the field of management science (see Weick, 1989; Alvesson & Sandberg, 2011; Cornelissen & Durand, 2014).

While one can learn lessons from the research in the natural sciences, its advice cannot be applied without modification because of the different nature of the reality investigated in the social sciences. In the social sciences, more so than the natural sciences, reality is socially constructed or even 'provoked' (Muniesa, 2014). In a socially constructed reality, new ideas are not so much *discovered* as they are collectively *created* by humans. Though this oversimplifies the differences between the natural and social sciences, it helps to explain why different approaches to promoting research creativity would be effective in these two domains.

A second, and more fundamental, shortcoming is that most of this research is not adapted for more practical pedagogical purposes: it does not aim to elucidate a systematic and rational approach that researchers can follow to increase their chances of conceiving an original contribution. The little literature with pedagogical applicability focuses mainly on: teaching generic creativity techniques (Byron, 2009); offering lists of heuristics (Klag & Langley, 2013; Cornelissen & Durand, 2014); giving general guidelines to the supervisor (Bargar & Duncan, 1982, Frick, 2011b); helping researchers to develop an attitude conducive to inquiry (Muntuori & Donnelly, 2013); or simply by identifying characteristics of those researchers most likely to be original (Dewett, Shin, Toh & Semadeni, 2005). While all of this has advanced our understanding of creative research, none of it offers an approach for systematically reasoning towards an original research contribution.

The research in economics is even more limited. There is much research on the economics of the creative economy (cf. Potts, 2011) and the economic influences on creativity (cf. Galenson, 2010; Menger, 2014). While Paul Romer's (1992, 1994a, 1994b) work on ideas and endogenous growth theory has done much to draw economists' attention to creativity and its role in driving economic growth, the discipline tends to treat creativity as an external phenomenon to be studied, rather than an internal process that can influence its own development.

There have been few attempts (cf. Tollison, 1986; Faulhaber & Baumol, 1988; McKinnon, 2006) to bring economists' own creative activity within the domain of economics. Some of those who attempted to explore creative research in economics suggested that new ideas emerge through creative intuition (Frantz, 2005) or from vision (Schumpeter, 1954). However, as Simon (1983:4569) stated: "We use terms such as 'judgment', 'intuition' and 'creative insight' to name and label ... but labels are not explanations." Labels are often placeholders for that which we do not understand. Labelling the process of scientific discovery merely serves to maintain the psychological mysticism that surrounds it. J.M. Keynes recognised the problem, and, at the height of his creative powers, he regarded the understanding of creative intuition as "the most obscure problem of all in the psychology of original work" (Mini, 1994:164), but did not offer a solution to this problem.

While these studies allow us to superficially analyse the creative work of economists, none of them explore systematic methods to facilitate the creativity of economists. In fact, McKinnon's (2006) review of the literature suggests that no systematic research on the creative work processes of economists exists, and that even biographical accounts (cf. Szenberg, 1992, 1999; Szenberg and Ramrattan, 2004) are scarce relative to what is available in the natural sciences.

One may reasonably expect that the few books on research methods that are actually written for economics researchers would offer something more substantial, but their advice is rather mundane, glancing over the question of how a researcher could produce original research. Greenlaw (2005:2) acknowledges that "research is the creation of knowledge" and nothing more. Ethridge (2004:32) is more helpful. He states that research is creative, but only offers some rather imprecise suggestions such as "do not be afraid to take risks", "exchange ideas with other people" or "challenge assumptions". But, without a systematic approach, it is difficult to know which assumptions to challenge and what to do once you have challenged them. Thomson (2001:2–3) writes for the young academic economist with similar vague advice like "don't forget how you made your discoveries" and "don't forget your errors". None of these authors offer anything close to the kind of specific instruction economics researchers receive in technical areas such as mathematics or econometrics, which are skills that are only required *after* an original contribution has been conceived.

Thomson (2001) does offer something more concrete in recommending that young researchers use the texts of Nobel Prize-winning authors as models. This is probably the most common approach amongst PhD supervisors, hoping that the candidate will somehow absorb an understanding of creative research by being exposed to hundreds of good scientific papers. However, there is one major problem with such papers that make them unsuitable for the teaching of creative research: they all create the wrong impression of the creative process.

Nobelist, Peter Medawar (1991:228), put it most forcefully when he wrote: "The scientific paper may be a fraud because it misrepresents the processes of thought that accompanied or give rise to the work that is described in the paper." After Medawar, many authors made the same claim in a wide range of fields as they argued that the scientific paper only presents the product of creative research, and the product tends to hide the process (Hoffman, 1988; Tobin, 1999; Webster, 2003; Schickore, 2008; Wong & Hodson, 2008; Grinell, 2009). In fact, the product is almost always written in such a way as to hide the mistakes, the dead ends, the wrong turns and the sense of exploration that is integral to the process of creative research.

There is no research which offers researchers an exploration of the *systematic* approach to conceiving of an original contribution *within the discipline* of economics. Admittedly, this act of conception is but a small part of the research process, but it is logically and temporally prior to the use of any analytical technique and a necessary condition for research to be original. Most leading economists have recognised that new ideas precede analytical efforts (cf. Baumol, 1992; Akerlof, 2003) and that progress originates in the discovery or generation of ideas. Technical skills in the analytical tools of economics are of little use if there is no original contribution to develop. And it is exactly this part that is ignored by the research in economics with the result that no instruction can be provided in the skill of creative research.

## Overview of the book

The aim of this book is to make the first steps toward an understanding of creativity in economic research and from that derive an approach that can systematically guide researchers in economics toward an original research contribution in their discipline. To achieve this aim, it will first explore the meaning of originality in the social sciences and develop a theoretical framework that explains how researchers in economics may conceive of original contributions.

This theoretical model will then be applied to cases of seminal research in economics to determine if these enable one to do a rational reconstruction of the possible original thought processes of the authors. Rational reconstruction is common in the philosophy of science as a method to determine a rational explanation for the growth of knowledge as it appears (Lakatos, 1970). My approach to rational reconstruction is best described by Darden (2002:S355) as "compiled hindsight", which is when one tries to draw advice from historical cases of scientific research. In rational reconstruction, one tries to establish whether the patterns observable in the published work – and, where available, the written notes – of scientists can be explained by a particular hypothesis of the scientific process. If the hypothesis is plausible, it should be possible to reconstruct the scientific process that culminated in the published research. Well-known philosophers of the sciences, like Thomas Kuhn (1970) and Imre Lakatos (1976), used rational construction to great effect in astronomy, physics and mathematics to test their hypotheses of the scientific process.

In this book, a rational reconstruction of the following seminal contributions in economics will be done: Sen (1999), Kydland and Prescott (1977) and Coase (1960). Amartya Sen's (1999) capability approach was chosen as the first case since it is an idea with broad application, not only in economics but also in the social sciences. Kydland and Prescott (1977) were chosen for their unusual frankness about their original thought process in their paper, which makes rational reconstruction easier. This frankness is quite useful since economists do not leave 'lab notes', like natural scientists, which help in rational reconstruction. In the absence of such notes, rational reconstruction becomes very difficult because, as Medawar (1991) argued, the structure of the published scientific papers hide the actual creative process that led to the ideas in the paper. Finally, Coase (1960) was selected as a dramatic case of question reformulation in the discipline and because it was for decades the most cited paper in economics.

Finally, the book will take a more practical turn and show how the techniques can be used in a social setting such as one might find in collaborative multi-disciplinary research. Before the book concludes, a programme of instruction will be derived that may be incorporated into a formal graduate programme in Economics or delivered as a short course aimed at developing novice researchers in Economics.

The book proceeds as follows:

- Chapter 2 will refine the concept of originality in scientific research: its definition, kinds and causes. It will argue that such contributions originate from problems and questions.
- Chapter 3 will argue that creativity in research starts with problem representation, which then guides research toward assumptions to challenge and questions to ask. It presents an appropriate approach to problem representation in economics.
- Chapter 4 will present various techniques to generate interesting questions and use these questions to generate new ideas.
- Chapter 5 will review abductive reasoning, which is recognised as the main logical approach for reasoning to arrive at new ideas. It shows how to integrate the techniques from Chapters 3 and 4 with abductive reasoning to generate new ideas.
- Chapter 6 will apply the theoretical framework and techniques of Chapters 2–5 to previous research in economics namely: (1) the capability approach of Sen; (2) the time inconsistency problem of Kydland and Prescott and the research that followed from it; and (3) Coase's theorem.

- Chapter 7 will show how to apply all these techniques to economic problems within a social setting and how to tap into the power of social dialogue to further enhance the ability to conceive of original contributions.
- Chapter 8 will integrate the foregoing chapters into a programme of instruction for (post)graduate students and novice researchers in economics and report on the results from the first pilot programme.
- Chapter 9 concludes.

## References

Abito, J.M., Borovickova, K., Golden, H., Goldin, J., Masten, M.A., Morin, M., Poirier, A., Pons, V., Romem, I., Williams, T. & Yoon, C. 2011. How should the graduate economics core be changed? *The Journal of Economic Education*, 42(4):414–417.

Akerlof, G.A. 2003. Writing the 'The Market for "Lemons" ': a personal and interpretive essay. Available at nobelprize.org, accessed 27 February 2007.

Aliseda, A. 2004. Logics in scientific discovery. *Foundations of Science*, 9:339–363.

Allais, M. 1992. The passion for research. In: Szenberg, M., *Eminent Economists: Their Life Philosophies*, Cambridge: Cambridge University Press, 17–41.

Alvesson, M. & Sandberg, J. 2011. Generating research questions through problematization. *The Academy of Management Review*, 36(2):247–271.

Amabile, T. 1996. *Creativity in Context*. Boulder, CO: Westview Press.

Bargar, R.R. & Duncan, J.K. 1982. Cultivating creative endeavour in doctoral research. *Journal of Higher Education*, 53(1):1–30.

Baumol, W.J. 1992. On my attitudes: socio-political and methodological. In: Szenberg, M. (ed.), *Eminent Economists: Their Life Philosophies*, Cambridge: Cambridge University Press, 51–59.

Boden, M. 1994. Creativity and computers. In: Dartnall, T. (ed.), *Artificial Intelligence and Creativity: An Interdisciplinary Approach*, Dordrecht: Kluwer Academic Publishers, 3–26.

Brodin, E.M. & Frick, L. 2011. Conceptualizing and encouraging critical creativity in doctoral education. *International Journal for Researcher Development*, 2(2):133–151.

Byron, K. 2009. *The Creative Researcher: Tools and Techniques to Unleash Your Creativity*. Cambridge: Careers Research and Advisory Centre (CRAC) Limited.

Clement, A. 2008. *Creative Model Construction in Scientists and Students*. Berlin: Springer.

Coase, R.H. 1960. The problem of social cost. *Journal of Law and Economics*, 3:1–44.

Colander, D.C. 2011. Adding a bit more creativity to the graduate economics core. Paper presented at Allied Social Science Associations, 6–9 January 2011, Denver. https://www.aeaweb.org/aea/2011conference/program/preliminary.php, accessed 19 October 2011.

Colander, D.C. & Coats, A.W. 1989. *The Spread of Economic Ideas*. Cambridge: Cambridge University Press.

Cornelissen, J.P. & Durand, R. 2014. Moving forward: developing theoretical contributions in management studies. *Journal of Management Studies*, 51(6):995–1022.

Csikszentmihalyi, M. 1996. *Creativity: Flow and the Psychology of Discovery and Invention*. New York: HarperCollins.

Darden, L. 2002. Strategies for discovering mechanisms: schema instantion, modular subassembly and forward/backward chaining. *Philosophy of Science*, 69(3):S354–S365.

De Bono, E. 1992. *Serious Creativity*. London: HarperCollins.

Dewett, T., Shin, S.J., Toh, S.M. & Semadeni, M. 2005. Doctoral student research as a creative endeavour. *College Quarterly*, 8(1):1–22.

Ethridge, D.E. 2004. *Research Methodology in Applied Economics*. Ames: Blackwell Publishing.

Faulhaber, G.R. & Baumol, W.J. 1988. Economists as innovators: practical products of theoretical research. *Journal of Economic Literature*, 26(2):577–600.

Fogler, H.S. & LeBlanc, S.E. 2008. *Strategies for Creative Problem Solving*, 2nd edition. Saddle River, NJ: Prentice Hall.

Frantz, R. 2005. *Two Minds: Intuition and Analysis in the History of Economic Thought*. New York: Springer.

Frick, B.L. 2010. Creativity in doctoral education: conceptualising the original contribution. In: Nygaard, C., Courtney, N. & Holtham, C. (eds), *Teaching Creativity – Creativity in Teaching*, Oxfordshire: Libri, 15–32.

Frick, B.L. 2011a. Supervisors' conceptualisations of creativity in education doctorates. *Pertanika Journal of Social Science & Humanities*, 19(2): 495–507.

Frick, B.L. 2011b. Facilitating creativity in doctoral education: a resource for supervisors. In: *Doctoral Education in International Context: Connecting Local, Regional and Global Perspectives*, Serdang: Universiti Putra Malaysia Press, 123–137.

Friedman, M. 1953. *Essays in Positive Economics*. Chicago: University of Chicago Press.

Galenson, D.W. 2010. Understanding Creativity, NBER Working Paper No. 16024.

Gardner, H. 2000. *The Disciplined Mind*. New York: Penguin.

Gravett, S. & Petersen, N. 2009. Promoting dialogic teaching among higher education faculty in South Africa. In: Mezirow, J., Taylor, E.W. & Associates (eds), *Transformative Learning in Practice: Insights from Community, Workplace, and Higher Education*, San Francisco: Jossey Bass, 100–110.

Greenlaw, S.A. 2005. *Doing Economics: A Guide to Understanding and Carrying Out Economic Research*. Boston: Houghton Mifflin.

Grieve, R.H. 2014. 'Right back where we started from': from 'the Classics' to Keynes, and back again. *Real-world Economics Review*, 68(21):41–61.

Griffin, W.G. & Morrison, D. 2010. *The Creative Process Illustrated*. Cincinnati: How Books.

Grinell, F. 2009. *Everyday Practice of Science*. Oxford: Oxford University Press.

Hanson, N.R. 1961. *Patterns of Scientific Discovery*. Cambridge: Cambridge University Press.

Hoffmann, R. 1988. Under the surface of the chemical article. *Angewandte Chemie*, 27, 1593–1602.

Holton, G. 1978. *The Scientific Imagination: Case Studies*. Cambridge: Cambridge University Press.

Keynes. J.M. 1952. *A Treatise on Probability*. London: MacMillan.

Kim, J. & Cunningham, D.K. 2003. A syllogism for formulating hypotheses. *Semiotica*, 144(1/4):303–317.

Klag, M. & Langley, A. 2013. Approaching the conceptual leap in qualitative research. *International Journal of Management Reviews*, 15:149–166.

Klausen, S.H. 2013. Interdisciplinarity and scientific creativity. In: Shin, E. (ed.), *Creativity Research: An Inter-disciplinary and Multi-disciplinary Research Handbook*, New York: Routledge, 31–50.

Krueger, A.O., Arrow, K.J., Blanchard, O.J., Blinder, A.S., Goldin, C., Leamer, E.E., Lucas, R., Panzar, J., Penner, R.G., Schultz, T.P., Stiglitz, J.E. & Summers, L. 1991. Report of the Commission on Graduate Education in Economics. *Journal of Economic Literature*, 29:1035–1053.

Krugman, P. 1995. Incidents from my career. Available at http://web.mit.edu/krugman/www/incidents.html, accessed 18 May 2016.

Kuhn, T.S. 1970. The function of dogma in scientific research. In: Brody, B.A. (ed.), *Readings in the Philosophy of Science*, Englewood Cliffs, NJ: Prentice Hall, 356–373.

Kydland, F.E. & Prescott, E.C. 1977. Rules rather than discretion: the inconsistency of optimal plans. *Journal of Political Economy*, 85(3):473–491.

Lakatos, I. 1970. History of science and its rational reconstructions. *PSA: Proceedings of the Biennial Meeting of the Philosophy of Science Association*, 1970: 91–136.

Lakatos, I. 1976. *Proofs and Refutations: The Logic of Mathematical Discovery*. Cambridge: Cambridge University Press.

Lenat, D.B. & Seely-Brown, J. 1984. Why AM and EURISKO appear to work. *Artificial Intelligence*, 23:269–294.

Lovitts, B.E. 2005. Being a good course-taker is not enough: a theoretical perspective on the transition to independent research. *Studies in Higher Education*, 30(2):137–154.

Magnani, L. 2009. *Abductive Cognition: The Epistemological and Eco-cognitive Dimensions of Hypothetical Reasoning*. Berlin: Springer.

McCloskey, D.N. 1994. *Knowledge and Persuasion in Economics*. Cambridge: Cambridge University Press.

McKinnon, L.A.K. 2006. The social construction of economic man: the genesis, spread and impact and institutionalisation of economic ideas. Doctoral thesis, University of Queensland.

Medawar, P.B. 1991. 'Is the scientific paper a fraud?' In: Medawar P.B., *The Threat and the Glory: Reflections on Science and Scientists*, Oxford: Oxford University Press, 228–233 (based on a BBC interview published in *The Listener*, 12 September 1963).

Meheus, J. 1999. Deductive and ampliative adaptive logics as tools in the study of creativity. *Foundations of Science*, 4:325–336.

Menger, P. 2014. *The Economics of Creativity: Art and Achievement under Uncertainty*. Cambridge, MA: Harvard University Press.

Mini, P. 1994. *John Maynard Keynes: A Study in the Psychology of Original Work*. New York: St Martin's Press.

Muniesa, F. 2014. *The Provoked Economy: Economic Reality and the Performative Turn*. London: Routledge.

Muntuori, A. & Donnelly, G. 2013. Creative inquiry and scholarship: applications and implications in the doctoral degree. *World Futures*, 69(1):1–19.

Osborn, A.F. 1953. *Applied Imagination*. New York: Scribner.

Paavola, S. 2006. On the origin of ideas: an abductivist approach to discovery. *Philosophical Studies from the University of Helsinki*, 15. University of Helsinki.

Popper, K.R. 1965. *The Logic of Scientific Discovery*. New York: Harper Torchbooks.

Potts, J. 2011. *Creative Industries and Economic Evolution*. Cheltenham: Edward Elgar.

Robinson, A.G. & Stern, S. 1998. *Corporate Creativity: How Innovation and Improvement Actually Happen*. San Francisco: Berrett Koehler.

Romer, P.M. 1992. Two strategies for economic development: using ideas and producing ideas. Proceedings of World Bank Annual Conference on Development Economics 1992, 63–91.

Romer, P.M. 1994a. The origins of endogenous growth. *The Journal of Economic Perspectives*, 8(1):3–22.

Romer, P.M. 1994b. New goods, old theory, and the welfare costs of trade restrictions. *Journal of Development Economics*, 43:5–38.

Samuelson, P.A. 1992. My life philosophy: policy credos and working ways. In: Szenberg, M. (ed.), *Eminent Economists: Their Life Philosophies*, Cambridge: Cambridge University Press, 236–274.

Savransky, S.D. 2000. *Engineering of Creativity: Introduction to TRIZ Methodology of Inventive Problem Solving*. Boca Raton, FL: CRC Press.

Schickore, J. 2008. Doing science, writing science. *Philosophy of Science*, 75(3):323–343.

Schumpeter, J.A. 1954. *History of Economic Analysis*. New York: Oxford University Press.

Sen, A.K. 1998. Autobiography. Available at www.nobelprize.org/nobel_prizes/economic-sciences/laureates/1998/sen-bio.html, accessed 18 May 2016.

Sen, A.K. 1999. *Development as Freedom*. Oxford: Oxford University Press.

Simon, H.A. 1983. Discovery, invention, and development: human creative thinking. *Proceedings of the National Academy of Sciences of the United States of America*, 80(14):4569–4571.

Simon, H.A., Langley, P. & Bradshaw, G.L. 1981. Scientific discovery as problem solving. *Synthese*, 47:1–27.

Stiglitz, J.E. 2001. Autobiography. Available at www.nobelprize.org/nobel_prizes/economic-sciences/laureates/2001/stiglitz-bio.html, accessed 18 May 2016.

Szenberg, M. (ed.). 1992. *Eminent Economists: Their Life Philosophies*. Cambridge: Cambridge University Press.

Szenberg, M. (ed.). 1999. *Economists at Work: Passion and Craft*. Ann Arbor: University of Michigan Press.

Szenberg, M. & Ramrattan, L. (eds). 2004. *Reflections of Eminent Economists*. Cheltenham: Edward Elgar.

Tanner, D. 1997. *Total Creativity in Business and Industry*. Des Moines, IA: APTT.

Thaler, S.L. 1997. A quantitative model of seminal cognition: the creativity machine paradigm (US Patent 5,659,666). Online paper available at www.imagination-engines.com, accessed 24 April 2007.

Thomson, W. 2001. *A Guide for the Young Economist*. Cambridge, MA: MIT Press.

Tobin, M.J. 1999. Introducing the 'How it really happened' series. *American Journal of Respiratory and Critical Care*, 160(6):1801.

Tollison, R.D. 1986. Economists as the subject of economic inquiry. *Southern Economic Journal*, 52(4):909–922.

Trafford, V. & Leshem, S. 2009. Doctorateness as a threshold concept. *Innnovations in Education and Teaching International*, 46(3):305–316.

Wallas, G. 1926. The art of thought. In: Vernon, P.E. (ed.), 1970. *Creativity*. Harmondsworth: Penguin Books.

Webster, R. 2003. Let's re-write the scientific paper. *European Journal of Soil Science*, 54(2):215–218.

Weick, K.E. 1989. Theory construction as disciplined imagination. *Academy of Management Review*, 14(4):516–531.

Weisberg, R.W. 2006. *Creativity: Understanding Innovation in Problem Solving, Science, Invention and the Arts.* Hoboken, NJ: John Wiley & Sons.

Weisberg, R.W. 2015. Toward an integrated theory of insight in problem solving, *Thinking & Reasoning*, 21(1):5–39.

Wong, S.L. & Hodson, D. 2008. From the horse's mouth: what scientists say about scientific investigation and scientific knowledge. *Science Education*, 93(1):109–130.

# 2 Originality in social science research

In Chapter 1, scientific creativity was defined as the intentional production of original ideas, that is, ideas that are novel and meaningful to other scientists. But, no idea stands by itself, so simply producing ideas is insufficient. An original idea has to make a contribution to scientists' understanding, and, to do that, it has to be embedded in a system of other ideas familiar to those scientists. So, it is more useful to extend the definition of scientific creativity to be the production of original contributions.

There is a general lack of agreement in the social sciences, of which economics forms part, about what constitutes originality in research, and, surprisingly, little research exists to try and rectify this lack of clarity. There is no single clear definition of originality: in studies where PhD examiners are asked to explain what constitutes an original contribution, it was found that it was judged by very different criteria (Clarke & Lunt, 2014; Edwards, 2014; Frick, 2011). Originality appears to be more of an 'I know it when I see it' phenomenon, so it is usually left up to researchers, supervisors and peer-reviewers to construct their own definition. This vagueness is not adequate for a book such as this one, so before getting into the methods for promoting originality, this chapter will first define and refine the concept of originality in research and explore how it comes about in the social sciences.

## Defining originality

Originality is hard to define. An obvious definition would be the discovery of a new theory, method or phenomenon that never existed before. This view of originality is based on what Hammersley (2011:11–12) refers to as the "discovery model" of science. However, the discovery model's view of originality is too narrow to be used in this book for two reasons: (1) it is based on a naïve understanding of knowledge; and (2) it is not suited to the social sciences.

The naïve view of knowledge thinks of knowledge as resulting from a process of cumulative addition. Original contributions are seen as simply adding something to the base of existing knowledge: they grow the base but do not transform it. The implication of this view is that existing knowledge conveys an essentially correct, but merely incomplete, understanding of the world. All a researcher needs to do is to spot a gap and fill it, so that advances in knowledge simply take the form of filling ever-shrinking gaps. Not only does this lead to the fragmentation of disciplines and rather dull research (Alvesson & Sandberg, 2013), but also makes economists prone to pronouncements, like that of Lester Thurow, who, in 1969, said the following about international economics: "All the great discoveries have been made" (Warsh, 2006:157).

This naïve view of knowledge is not suitable for the social sciences as it is too limiting. Our knowledge about social (and economic) reality does not exist in some discoverable disembodied form: it cannot exist independently from humans because it is collectively constructed by us (Searle, 2010). Social science not only describes reality, but, through research, participates in and transforms this reality. This has been called 'performativity', and many cases has been described in economics (MacKenzie, 2006; Muniesa, 2014) and received reluctant acceptance by some economists in the discipline (Colander, 2008).

Social reality is constantly being transformed, and, thus, a social science that asserts that its understanding is essentially correct is doomed to fail. Indeed, as Weick (1989:524) stated: "The contribution of social science does not lie in validated knowledge, but rather in the suggestion of relationships and connections that had not previously been suspected, relationships that change actions and perspectives." As economic reality is a dynamic social creation, it is more realistic for economists to see their task not simply as adding the finishing touches to a sound intellectual tower, but rather opening up possibilities for questioning and the acquisition of new understanding.

According to Hammersley (2011:11–12), there are two other models of science that may be considered. One is the "construction model" according to which research involves imagining and persuading others of something new. The construction model holds some truth, because it is left to examiners and reviewers to decide whether a contribution is original (Heinze, 2013:928), thus implying that persuasion plays some role in the creation of economic knowledge (McCloskey, 1994, 1998). As a result, a researcher cannot simply present facts, but also has to construct a contribution by appealing to the norms, values and understanding of the scholarly community that decides whether or not to accept such a contribution (Locke & Golden-Biddle, 1997).

But the above view can be taken too far and lead to a solipsistic view of science, where only our rhetorical actions determine what knowledge is. Few economists, if any, hold the view that their research has value only because they can persuade others that it is original and their scepticism is justified. Economists still research a reality that, although collectively created, cannot be changed by the rhetorical actions of an individual. This perception is similar to the idea of institutions propounded by Economics Nobelist, Douglass North (1990), and applied to scientific inquiry (Denzau & North, 1994). Economic research still has to be anchored in an understanding of economic reality that is effectively objective from the perspective of a particular individual.

Both the discovery and construction model lack intellectual humility: we have neither achieved a secure understanding nor is our understanding changeable at will. Economic reality is neither entirely subjective, that is, fundamentally dependent on humans; nor strongly objective, that is, fundamentally independent of humans. Rather, it is what Kastrup (2011:26) calls "weakly objective", in other words: "It can be consistently observed by multiple individuals and ... cannot be independently altered by an individual act of cognition." Yet, without humans, this reality would not exist, and our *collective* understanding continuously shapes this reality, and thus our understanding cannot afford to stagnate.

This leaves us with the third model, what Hammersley (2011:11–12) calls the "hermeneutic model". The hermeneutic model represents scientific research as developing a fruitful, new understanding of the world. The hermeneutic model stands midway between the two other models, in that it recognises that there is a reality outside humans to be understood, but that humans participate in the creation of this understanding. It suggests that it is not sufficient for research to be merely new, as the discovery model assumes; or merely persuasive, as the construction model assumes, but needs to be both. Newness only counts as original when others, besides the author, endow it with such meaning and interpret it as a meaningful contribution to their understanding.

Original research involves the development of a *novel* contribution to knowledge that engages the attention of scientists (other than the researcher) and thereby causes some of them to recognise the contribution as *meaningful*. In the next two sub-sections, these two dimensions of the original contribution are explored.

*Novelty of a contribution*

Within the hermeneutic model, novelty is not the individualistic and artistic idea of "not [being] dependent on other people's ideas" (Edwards, 2014:8), and is also more than the traditional view of simply discovering or revealing the unknown. Rather, novelty emerges from using others' ideas to: raise new questions, reformulate problems, challenge assumptions, make new connections or identify new perspectives (Gordon, 2007:204–206).

By the same token, novelty alone does not imply contribution. It is quite easy to do something new, for example: writing gibberish or just adding one more observation to a prior econometric study. To be deemed a contribution, it also has to be regarded as a meaningful contribution by the intellectual community at whom it is aimed.

## Meaningfulness of a contribution

For a contribution to be meaningful, it has to negotiate the tension between relevant novelty and significant novelty. To be relevant, a contribution has to be judged as being both plausible and having scientific value, and this encourages conformity to existing understanding (Heinze, 2013:928). To be significant, a contribution has to be disruptive enough to have repercussions for the agreed-upon understanding of the intellectual community: the more repercussions, the more significant (Boring, 1927:90). Science Nobelist, Peter Medawar (1979:94), captured this well when he said that: "If research does not hold out the possibility of causing one to revise one's views, it is hard to see why it should be done at all." Significant novelty therefore encourages dissent from the consensus.

Both sides of the tension, if taken too far, will damage science. To ensure that it does not veer too much towards stifling conformity or unbridled chaos, each discipline puts in place certain institutions (such as peer-review, for example) to keep the tension at some desirable level.

## Interesting research

Davis' (1971:309) concept of "interesting" research encapsulates the appropriate balance between relevant and significant novelty. According to him, for research to be interesting, it needs to have practical or theoretical repercussions as recognised by a particular audience in the discipline, without their considering it obvious, irrelevant or absurd. Figure 2.1 summarises the different kinds of novel contributions.

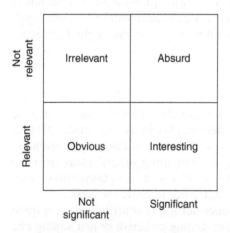

*Figure 2.1* Typology of novel contributions.
*Source*: Derived from Davis (1971).

If a novel contribution is believed to have no scientific value and also has no implications for the discipline, it is irrelevant. If it is relevant, but has no repercussions, then it is obvious. Finally, if it has repercussions that are so disruptive that the result is that of little plausibility, it is regarded as absurd or ahead of its time. Only interesting novel contributions have disruptive repercussions that are also regarded as plausible and valuable.

Davis (1971) offers a simple and powerful way to think about what interesting research is. He states that interesting research takes the generic form of: while a phenomenon appears as α, in reality it is ¬α (not-α), or vice versa. For example, Adam Smith's hidden hand hypothesis was deemed interesting because he argued that while it appears that uncontrolled markets are disorganised; in reality, they produce outcomes that suggest that they are, in fact, highly organised. But this negation of assumptions has to be optimal, that is, it should neither disrupt too little nor so much that the intended audience cannot make sense of it.

Research in artificial intelligence on computer creativity confirms this. Creative neural networks have the ability to generate novelty without human intervention. In this field, Stephen Thaler (1997) found that there is a zone of optimal disruption of the connections in the neural network. Disrupt too little and the neural network continues to produce the expected (the obvious); disrupt too much and it produces completely new gibberish (the absurd). Disrupt just enough, and it creates novelty, but of the kind that can be reconnected to the network.

Lakatos' (1970) methodology of scientific research programmes provides a useful way to think about optimal disruption. A scientific research programme consists of a set of core assumptions that form the theoretical core of the programme. Using heuristics – that is, methods for generating knowledge – researchers do empirical research and this creates a protective belt of theories, which are, in turn, made up of secondary assumptions around the core.

The first conclusion we can draw from this is that scientific knowledge is built on a base of assumptions that we take for granted, of which the mathematical equivalent would be axioms from which theorems are derived. The second conclusion is that the assumption(s) of a research programme is (are) the most efficient place(s) to search for possible disruptions, since this is what the knowledge of the research programme is based on, but that disruptions of the larger protective belt are more likely to be tolerated than disruptions in the core.

Unfortunately, given the lack of instruction on how to produce meaningfully original or interesting research, researchers tend to resort to "gap-spotting" research aimed at just adding to the literature (Sandberg and Alvesson, 2011:23). Interesting research focused on challenging existing understanding takes place in what Alvesson and Sandberg (2013:148) call "path-setting scholarly mode", which is in contrast to "gap-spotting mode". For them the gap-spotting mode involves consensus-seeking development of knowledge through "incremental additions to existing literature" while being unaware of prejudices, and this often leads to formulaic research. They describe path-setting scholarship as development of knowledge by "challenging the assumptions underlying existing literature", and this is more likely to be interesting and influential.

Interesting research is not about disruption for disruption's sake, it is about making real contributions to knowledge. It starts from the recognition that we, as humans, construct knowledge that is limited and biased, as suggested by Alvesson and Sandberg (2013). Interesting research deliberately tries to break out of the self-imposed confines of a discipline and to make our prejudices explicit by putting the disruptive idea in dialogue with the consensus view.

In those social sciences, such as economics, that rely on statistics (and hence on probability) to create knowledge, disruptive ideas may be even more important. Weisberg (2014:11) highlights that statistical probability frames uncertainty only as a quantifiable degree of doubt, while ignoring the ambiguity inherent to the facts and categories being analysed, which is the more qualitative aspect of uncertainty. This brings about an overemphasis on technique, while the hallmark of expertise – the ability to resolve ambiguity – is neglected when training scientists. It is this very unresolved ambiguity that partly explains the long-run ineffectiveness of statistical techniques in the social sciences (Weisberg, 2014:342–345). Ambiguity is only resolved by creating and challenging ideas.

In light of this, when rewarding mainly gap-spotting research in economics, the message being communicated is that creative research is not needed since ambiguity in the discipline has been resolved, and that all that remains is reducing the degree of doubt, which is usually achieved by means of statistical techniques. Thus, the ability to: generate new questions to ask with the aid of data and techniques; discover new problems for which new data may be needed; or precipitate and propagate new ideas to make sense of the data; is relegated to the subjective domain and vaguely labelled 'intuition'. As the quantity of available data rises exponentially, this problem becomes more pressing, because, without new ways to think about the data, little new knowledge can be created since statistical techniques are idea-neutral.

Krugman (1993:25) contrasts the conventional gap-spotting approach to economic research with what he calls the "dare to be silly" strategy of disruption. He explains that it was his willingness to consider new assumptions that allowed him to produce original contributions in trade theory, and contrasts this against the "safe approach" in economics, which is simply to accept old assumptions and extend familiar models. Krugman recognises that the safe approach contributes little to our understanding.

Gap-spotting research does not aim to produce anything interesting, but takes the accepted assumptions for granted. It searches the increasingly narrowed-down problem space for some gap that has not yet been filled by past research; addresses some issue where a particular method has not yet been applied; or covers an area where confusing results have emerged or where some extension or refinement of past research is possible (Sandberg & Alvesson, 2011). It is then just a matter of time before some reputable scientist makes some foolish claim working from a consensus understanding that is thought to be sound at its core.[1]

## Degrees of originality

From the discussion thus far it is clear that the concept of the 'original contribution' is multi-dimensional and a matter of degree. This section will draw some of these ideas together in a continuum of originality. If we remove the 'irrelevant' box of Figure 2.1 and combine it with Lakatos' ideas about research programmes, we have one way to construct such a continuum (Figure 2.2).

To simplify the discussion, the continuum is broken into four discrete ranges demarcated by five kinds of contributions. The contribution labelled 'A' is the only one that possesses no novelty, and is the kind of work one would expect from a talented undergraduate student. Novel contributions within the A–B range simply spot and fill gaps in the existing body of knowledge, and, if they challenge assumptions, usually only minor changes are made, without any epistemological strategy in mind: something McCloskey (2000:235) calls "games in the sandbox". B–C contributions challenge assumptions that are not critical to the identity of a discipline, and, while less significant, are seen as more relevant. Novel contributions in the C–D range challenge core assumptions – such as the premise that all economic agents are preference-driven – and, while these ideas are highly significant, they are less likely to be accepted by the mainstream journals. Contributions that are so disruptive that they cannot be meaningfully connected to existing knowledge appear in the D–E range, so they are unlikely to find an outlet even in the marginal heterodox journals.

Another dimension of originality is feasibility. If a contribution is not feasible either due to the available or potential tools of the discipline or the technical skills of the researcher, the contribution cannot be made relevant to that discipline. Lack of feasibility immediately disqualifies a contribution from

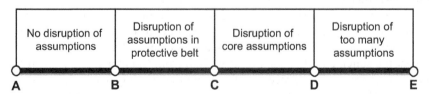

*Figure 2.2* Degrees of originality.

being original, so this dimension need not be considered in determining the degrees of originality.

## What the product of originality looks like

Originality, as explained, is a quality that is socially constructed by an evaluation process. This process involves subject matter experts such as supervisors, examiners or reviewers. As a result, there is great diversity in what is recognised as an original (novel and meaningful) contribution.

One way to make sense of this diversity is to ask evaluators to identify what they look for in the final written product. The most comprehensive such study in the humanities and social sciences is by Guetzkow, Lamont and Mallard (2004). They interviewed 49 subject experts who were panel members in research funding competitions, and collectively evaluated 217 proposals. The interviews led them to categorise original research as follows: (1) original approach; (2) understudied topic; (3) original topic; (4) original theory; (5) original method; (6) original data; and (7) original results.

Combining Guetzkow *et al.*'s (2004) finer distinctions with Figure 2.2 produces Table 2.1. Original but non-interesting research lies within the A–B range of Figure 2.2 and occurs in Alvesson and Sandberg's (2013:148) "gap-spotting mode". It aims at spotting areas within the existing body of knowledge that have been overlooked or under-researched ('neglect spotting'), where existing research may be extended ('application spotting'); or where competing explanations exist ('confusion spotting'). Interesting original research lies within the B–D range and occurs in Alvesson and Sandberg's (2013:148) "path-setting mode". It aims at critically confronting existing ideas, problematising accepted knowledge or generating new ideas.

While it is the ability to produce interesting originality that the systematic approach designed in this book aims to develop, it does not deny the value of non-interesting originality. However, interesting originality is favoured because it is the very ability to produce such originality that is neglected in economics where gap-spotting appears to be prevalent.

Studies that research what originality looks like to evaluators are of limited use, because, by showing only the product, it elides the process. As Locke and Golden-Biddle (1997) explain at length, researchers make it appear as if the opportunity for a contribution existed objectively and they simply spotted it, even though they actually created this opportunity through the use of various rhetorical strategies. Here, the messy creative process is hidden from view. To repeat the statement of Medawar (1991:228) from Chapter 1: "The scientific paper misrepresents the processes of thought that accompanied or give rise to the work that is described in the paper." Except for biographic materials, we are left with little insight into the process of conceiving of an original contribution, which is what we need if we are to develop creative researchers. This is what we turn to in the next few sections.

Table 2.1 Judging originality

| Non-interesting originality | Interesting originality |
|---|---|
| 1 Original approach<br>   *1a: Innovative approach to discipline*<br>2 Understudied area<br>   *2a: Understudied region*<br>   *2b: Understudied period*<br>3 Original topic<br>   *3b: Noncanonical topic*<br>   *3c: Unconventional topic*<br>4 Original theory<br>   *4d: New application of theory*<br>   *4f: Unconventional use of theory*<br>5 Original method<br>   *5b: Synthesis of methods*<br>   *5c: New use of old data*<br>   *5e: Innovative for discipline*<br>6 Original data<br>   *6a: New data*<br>   *6b: Multiple sources*<br>   *6c: Noncanonical data* | 1 Original approach<br>   *1a: New approach*<br>   *1b: New question*<br>   *1c: New argument*<br>   *1d: Approach makes new connections*<br>   *1e: New perspective*<br>3 Original topic<br>   *3a: New topic*<br>4 Original theory<br>   *4a: New theory*<br>   *4b: Connecting ideas*<br>   *4c: Synthesis of literatures*<br>   *4e: Reconceptualisation*<br>5 Original method<br>   *5a: Innovative method*<br>   *5d: Resolve old question/debate*<br>7 Original results<br>   *7a: New insights*<br>   *7b: New findings* |

*Source*: Adapted from Guetzkow *et al.* (2004).

## The disciplinary origin of scientific originality

Based on the discussion thus far, however, we can deduce that an original (novel and meaningful) scientific contribution emerges from within a discipline as its assumptions are challenged. These assumptions are held in the shared mental model of the discipline, and this, in turn, derives from the mental models of the individual mainstream scientists in the discipline.

An individual's mental model is an internal and simplified representation of the world outside that individual, which the individual uses to reason about the world and make sense of new information (Jones *et al.*, 2011). Every individual's mental model is incomplete and contains many assumptions about the world that are wrong or inconsistent.

When individuals want to act together, they need to form shared mental models through communication. Shared mental models allow individuals to tap into a larger reservoir of knowledge and thereby cope with uncertainty and learn faster. In the economy, these shared mental models are found in institutions and ideologies, but they are equally prevalent in science (Denzau & North, 1994). Shared mental models make academic disciplines possible with their various schools of thoughts and institutions (such as universities, peer-review processes, ranking systems, journals and the like). Denzau and North (1994:25) liken a widely held shared mental model amongst scientists to a Kuhnian paradigm.

Shared mental models, like individual mental models, are incomplete and contain many inconsistent assumptions, and these inconsistencies will never be identified or removed. In fact, Cherniak (1984) explains that it would take a computer with the computing capacity of the whole universe more than 20 billion years just to determine if there is logical consistency between 138 *well-defined* statements. Most shared mental models comprise substantially more than 138 statements, many of which are vaguely defined.

Lakatos' (1970) scientific research programme is analogous to the shared mental model of a discipline. Unless there are very few, the assumptions at the core may very well be inconsistent, but they are protected by a much larger layer of secondary assumptions that definitely contains multiple inconsistencies.

Given these inconsistencies, there will always be opportunities to challenge the assumptions of a discipline and thus make original contributions. This shows why the naïve view of knowledge previously discussed is indeed naïve – it holds that the shared mental model is essentially correct, and, as contributions supplement this model, the imperfections (mainly gaps) will gradually be eliminated.

The opportunity for an original contribution therefore originates in the imperfections of the shared mental model of a discipline. For a novel contribution to be meaningful, the researcher needs to understand the shared mental model of the discipline and know where to challenge it, which explains why generic creativity techniques are limited in their applicability to scientific research.

## From shared mental model to original contribution

To illustrate the process of conceiving of original contributions from the perspective of an individual, we can turn to a diagram in a letter written by Einstein in 1952, in which he outlined his approach to making discoveries. With some adaptations, it can describe the process from a social science perspective. The original diagram, translated into English, is shown in Figure 2.3.

Einstein explained that he first needed to break out of his experience ($E$), by making a leap of conjecture ($J$). If the leap is successful, it leads to an axiom ($A$) or a new idea that has not been thought of before. At this stage, the new idea is still vulnerable to criticism as it has not been logically connected to the collective experience yet. The axiom's implications then need to be translated into statements ($S$). In other words, the new idea needs to be connected to other elements to form useful new knowledge. The collection of these statements forms a discovery that has to be tested against experience ($E$). Einstein deliberately left a gap between the arrows and the line representing experience in order to indicate that leaping and testing does not occur in relation to direct experience, but in relation to an imperfect mental model based on experience.

Einstein's model can be adapted to social science by converting $E$ into the discipline's shared mental model from which a researcher needs to break away

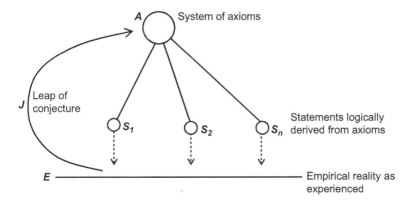

*Figure 2.3* Einstein's model of scientific discovery.
*Source*: Adapted from Einstein's letter to Solovine in Holton (1979:312).

and reconnect. Though not shown, this shared mental model can be envisaged as comprising three layers, each derived from the one below it, with the world outside the discipline at the bottom and the core assumptions and the secondary assumptions on the surface. While the 'leap of conjecture' may still lead to a new axiom, it is better to generalise it to include all forms of potential new contributions. The adapted diagram is shown as Figure 2.4.

The researcher aspiring to an original contribution needs to break out of the shared mental model of the discipline ($E$) by making a 'leap of conjecture' ($J$). The leap is often triggered by a problem or a question, and, if it is successful, it will potentially lead to an original contribution ($A$) that modifies the shared mental model in some way. At this stage, the new idea may be significant but it is not yet relevant, so it needs to be translated into statements ($S$) and reconnected to the shared mental model of the discipline so that its implications can be evaluated.

All four requirements for a successful career in science can be seen in Figure 2.4, these being: knowledge, originality, technical skill and communication (Loehle, 1990:123). A researcher needs to have a strong understanding of his or her discipline's collective knowledge ($E$) in order to identify which assumptions are ripe for challenge. The skill of originality enables the leap to a new contribution ($E$–$J$–$A$). Technical skills now become important as the implications of that new contribution are developed using the analytical techniques of the discipline ($A$–$S$). Finally, the contribution, and its implications, should be communicated to other scientists so that they can evaluate to what degree the contribution should be allowed to modify the shared mental model ($S$–$E$).

The question to be answered in this book is how to engage in the $E$–$J$–$A$ process. Like most creative scientists, Einstein could not explain how someone

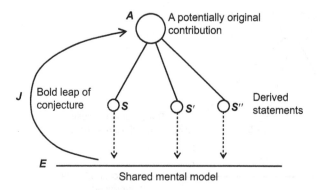

*Figure 2.4* Einstein's approach adapted.
*Source*: Adapted from Holton (1979).

should make leaps of conjecture to original contributions except for stating that it depended on intuition (Holton, 1979).

## How the leap happens

As argued above, any leap to an original contribution starts from the imperfections of the shared mental model of a discipline. These flaws will never be eliminated – unless the mental model consists of only a handful of well-defined statements. Hence, many opportunities for original contributions exist at any time.

There appear to be three things that trigger a researcher to make the leap to an original contribution: problems (Popper, 1972; Hattiangadi, 1978); questions (Bromberger, 1992; Van Fraassen, 1980); and unexpected ideas, usually in response to some implicit or explicit problem or question. Topics and methods are also candidates but they are excluded because they lead to dull research. No interesting research emerges from topic-driven research (Eidlin, 2011). This is due to the fact that such research tends to emphasise gathering information rather than creating knowledge (Jardine, 2000). Research driven by methods tends to favour only a restricted range of questions (White, 2013) and lean towards gap-spotting.

It is interesting to note that, when looking at the finished product of originality (in Table 2.1); methods, topics and ideas feature strongly, while questions and problems barely get any mention. This is another instance of the quandary highlighted by Medawar (1991) asserting that the finished product misrepresents or hides the creative process.

(Auto)biographical accounts of researchers and studies in the philosophy of science leave little doubt that unsolved problems and unanswered questions usually trigger the creative process and thereby lead to new ideas. Of

## Originality in social science research   27

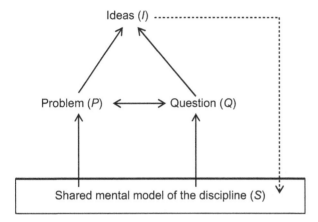

*Figure 2.5* Process of conceiving of an original contribution.

course, the new ideas are integrated into a larger topic, and, although methods and rhetorical devices play a role in this integration, the trigger for the researcher remains the problem or the question.

Figure 2.5 summarises the process of conceiving of an original contribution. Problems and questions signal areas in the shared mental model of the discipline where imperfections reside. If these questions or problems are interesting, they most likely emerge from some inconsistency and will result in at least one assumption being challenged. In the process of solving the problem or question, one or more original ideas will be generated. The $I$–$S$ process in Figure 2.5 is not part of the process, but no original contribution will be regarded as such without it being reconnected to the shared mental model. This is actualised through analytical techniques and writing.

Problems may lead to new ideas ($S$–$P$–$I$) and so can questions ($S$–$Q$–$I$). But problems can also generate new questions, which, in turn, lead to new ideas ($S$–$P$–$Q$–$I$). Questions can also be shown to be problematic so new ideas are needed to solve the problem ($S$–$Q$–$P$–$I$). This book will explore all four of these sub-processes. All of these emerge from the shared mental model, so any systematic approach to conception of original contributions must involve elicitation of the mental model. If the assumptions are not made explicit and brought to the surface, it becomes very difficult (though not impossible) to conceive an original contribution.

## What will be regarded as conceptions?

Figure 2.5 is useful in helping to identify an original contribution before it is converted into a finished product. This is important because the aim of this book is to explore the conception of original contributions in economics.

The five candidates for what may count as an original contribution are: the integrated idea, the initial idea, the problem, the question and the assumptions. I exclude the integration of an idea into the shared mental model since that part of the process mainly requires technical and writing skills and less creativity. The work of Guetzkow *et al.* (2004) in Table 2.1 is therefore not so useful here as it focuses on the perception of the *finished* product, that is, the integrated idea.

All the others – that is, the initial idea, problem, question and assumption – could potentially be conceptions of original contributions. To determine when and why they can be considered relevant conceptions, each one will be defined in turn.

One of the most fruitful definitions of the term 'idea' comes from mathematics, where an idea may be defined as an "organising principle" (Byers, 2007:193). A good idea is one that allows one to easily organise large amounts of knowledge or actions. This is similar to Adam Smith's (1799:58) definition of an idea as being a "connecting principle" that binds "discordant phenomena" together. This suggests that original ideas are rarely new. Instead, they organise or connect previous ideas in a way that open up new ways of thinking. That is why original ideas often appear obvious and logical in hindsight. For example, Friedman himself regarded his revolutionary permanent income hypothesis as "embarrassingly obvious" (Friedman & Friedman, 1998:226). This may create the belief that one only needs logic to be a successful researcher. Logic, however, only plays an evaluative role after the idea has been generated. Unless the original contribution can be deductively connected to previous knowledge, the original contribution will not be regarded as meaningful by the discipline.

The kind of problem that leads to new ideas is what Hattiangadi (1978:348) calls "intellectual problems". These are problems that cannot be solved by merely gathering more data. Intellectual problems contrast with 'gap-spotting' problems that merely require more data for their resolution (Alvesson & Sandberg, 2011:23). This view of problems comes from Popper (1992:8–9) who saw scientific problems as essentially problems in the sphere of existing ideas, though Hattiangadi (1978:352) defines these problems as arising from an inconsistency in beliefs or assumptions. Such inconsistencies create doubts about our ideas, and are impediments to scientific activity (Hattiangadi, 1978:353). Identifying a new problem can therefore open up new possibilities, but sometimes simply reformulating a problem can make solutions appear obvious. Economics contains many examples where the simple act of reformulating a problem itself was an original contribution (cf. Sen, 1970; Kydland & Prescott, 1977).

Erotetic logicians define a question as a range of admissible answers together with a request that an answer satisfies certain conditions (Belnap & Steel, 1976). All questions make assumptions (Collingwood, 1960; Belnap, 1966) and these contain the seeds of new problems in a discipline. Questions do the following in research: direct curiosity; force researchers to clarify ideas;

provoke the development of new methods; and, most importantly, a fruitful question generates more questions (White, 2013). Most researchers do not specify their research questions, and both Jardine (2000) and White (2013) argue that a renewed emphasis on question-led research will reinvigorate the social sciences.

An assumption is any statement taken for granted in a discipline. They may also be regarded as beliefs, presuppositions or axioms. Mental models, problems and questions are all structured by assumptions, and, when challenged, these assumptions have the potential to generate interesting research. Many assumptions are implicit and subconsciously held so that the discipline may not be aware of how these assumptions are confining their reasoning or of the inconsistencies they create. Consider the case of Arrow's Theorem that is made up of four statements that were accepted for decades until Kenneth Arrow finally realised the inconsistency between them (Denzau & North, 1994:26). This triggered a significant amount of new research, much of which suggested new assumptions that were not previously considered. So, a new assumption may itself be an original idea and is evident in disciplines like mathematics. Creative mathematicians very often start with an unproven theorem and exploit ambiguities to work backwards toward a new axiom, which then enables them to prove the theorem (Byers, 2007). This is very different from the way the proofs, as final products, are communicated.

On this basis, this book will take the following as conceptions of an original contribution:

- an original idea that answers an unanswered question or solves an unsolved problem;
- the useful reformulation of an existing problem or the identification of a new problem that is significant to the discipline;
- a new question that opens up new possibilities for research or shows that an old question is problematic;
- identification of a previously unknown, but significant and questionable assumption in the shared mental model of the discipline.

There is some justification for taking all four of the above as conceptions of original contributions in the social sciences. As already argued, there is very little that is entirely new, so novelty by itself is inadequate in defining originality. Significant novelty was shown to be a more important indicator of originality, and this kind of novelty arises from new questions, reformulated problems, challenged assumptions, new connections or shifts in perspectives (Gordon, 2007:204–206). Weick's comment (1989:524) is worth repeating here: "The contribution of social science ... [lies] in the suggestion of relationships and connections that had not previously been suspected." Our knowledge in the social sciences is constantly changing and will never be perfect, so original contributions (of the interesting kind) keep us aware of these changes and imperfections.

## Requirements for a systematic approach

A systematic approach to conceiving of original contributions should enable a researcher to either recognise opportunities for original contributions, called a 'responsive approach', or to create those opportunities, namely a 'provocative approach'. This book favours the provocative approach and will develop techniques in deliberately reformulating problems, problematising and generating new questions and creating new ideas, rather than depending on serendipity. A researcher skilled in provoking opportunities should also be able to recognise them, but the opposite is not necessarily true.

A systematic approach to conceiving of original contributions in economics needs to be consistent with the theory of originality developed in this chapter. Its techniques need to show how original contributions are to be conceived from within the discipline of economics. This approach should offer a systematic way to elicit assumptions from economists' shared mental model and how to convert those assumptions into questions, problems and ideas. Those conceptions should be judged by subject experts as lying in the B–D range of Figure 2.2. And, very importantly, any systematic approach should enable a researcher to start the search for original contributions from within the discipline.

## Note

1 Alan Greenspan's undoubtedly strong grasp of mainstream economic theory led him to testify in 2005 that financial derivatives actually reduced the risk in the financial system, just as a number of non-economists and unorthodox economists were recognising the danger of these instruments. These instruments caused the subprime crisis, but Ben Bernanke's consensus view of monetary policy allowed him to declare in 2007: "At this juncture, however, the impact on the broader economy and financial markets of the problems in the subprime market seems likely to be contained" just as the global financial crisis was about to prove him wrong. See for example: www.thefiscaltimes.com/Articles/2011/12/27/8-Outrageously-Flawed-Economic-Predictions?page=0%2C1 and http://shaundacosta.wordpress.com/2013/06/30/when-economists-get-it-wrong-the-worst-economic-predictions-of-all-time/.

## References

Alvesson, M. & Sandberg, J. 2011. Generating research questions through problematization. *The Academy of Management Review*, 36(2):247–271.

Alvesson, M. & Sandberg, J. 2013. Has management studies lost its way? Ideas for more imaginative and innovative research. *Journal of Management Studies*, 50(1):128–152.

Belnap, N.D. 1966. Questions, answers, and presuppositions. *The Journal of Philosophy*, 63(20):609–611.

Belnap, N.D. & Steel, T.B. 1976. *The Logic of Questions and Answers*. London: Yale University Press.

Boring, E.G. 1927. The problem of originality in science. *The American Journal of Psychology*, 39(1/4):70–90.

Bromberger, S. 1992. *On What We Know We Don't Know*. Chicago: University of Chicago Press.

Byers, W. 2007. *How Mathematicians Think*. Princeton, NJ: Princeton University Press.

Cherniak, C. 1984. Computational complexity and the universal acceptance of logic. *Journal of Philosophy*, 81(12):739–758.

Clarke, G. & Lunt, I. 2014. The concept of 'originality' in the Ph.D.: how is it interpreted by examiners? *Assessment & Evaluation in Higher Education*, 39(7):803–820.

Colander, D.C. 2008. Review of 'Do Economists Make Markets? On the Performativity of Economics', *Journal of Economic Literature*, 46(3):720–724.

Collingwood, R.G. 1960. *An Essay on Metaphysics*. London: Clarendon Press.

Davis, M.S. 1971. That's interesting! *Philosophy of the Social Sciences*, 1:309–344.

Denzau, A.T. & North, D.C. 1994. Shared mental models: ideologies and institutions. *Kyklos*, 47(1):3–31.

Edwards, M. 2014. What does originality in research mean? A student's perspective. *Nurse Researcher*, 21(6):8–11.

Eidlin, F. 2011. The method of problems versus the method of topics. *Political Science and Politics*, 44(4):758–761.

Frick, B.L. 2011. Supervisors' conceptualisations of creativity in education doctorates. *Pertanika Journal of Social Science & Humanities*, 19(2):495–507.

Friedman, M. & Friedman, R.D. 1998. *Two Lucky People: Memoirs*. Chicago: University of Chicago Press.

Gordon, M. 2007. What makes interdisciplinary research original? Integrative scholarship reconsidered. *Oxford Review of Education*, 33(2):195–209.

Guetzkow, J., Lamont, M. & Mallard, G. 2004. What is originality in the humanities and the social sciences? *American Sociological Review*, 69(2):190–212.

Hammersley, M. 2011. *Methodology: Who Needs It?* London: Sage Publications.

Hattiangadi, J.N. 1978. The structure of problems (Part I). *Philosophy of Social Science*, 8:345–365.

Heinze, T. 2013. Creative accomplishments in science: definition, theoretical considerations, examples from science history, and bibliometric findings. *Scientometrics*, 95:927–940.

Holton, G. 1979. Constructing a theory: Einstein's model. *American Scholar*, 48:309–340.

Jardine, N. 2000. *The Scenes of Inquiry: On the Reality of Questions in the Sciences*. Oxford: Oxford University Press.

Jones, N.A., Ross, H., Lynam, T., Perez, P. & Leitch, A. 2011. Mental models: an interdisciplinary synthesis of theory and methods. *Ecology and Society*, 16(1): [online].

Kastrup, B. 2011. *Meaning in Absurdity*. Winchester: Iff Books.

Krugman, P. 1993. How I work. *American Economist*, 37(2):25+ [online].

Kydland, F.E. & Prescott, E.C. 1977. Rules rather than discretion: the inconsistency of optimal plans. *Journal of Political Economy*, 85(3):473–491.

Lakatos, I. 1970. History of science and its rational reconstructions. *PSA: Proceedings of the Biennial Meeting of the Philosophy of Science Association*, 1970:91–136.

Locke, K. & Golden-Biddle, K. 1997. Constructing opportunities for contribution: structuring intertextual coherence and 'problematizing' in organizational studies. *Academy of Management Journal*, 40(5):1023–1062.

Loehle, C. 1990. A guide to increased creativity in research – inspiration or perspiration? *Bioscience*, 40(2):123–129.

McCloskey, D.N. 1994. *Knowledge and Persuasion in Economics*. Cambridge: Cambridge University Press.

McCloskey, D.N. 1998. *The Rhetoric of Economics*, 2nd edition. Madison: University of Wisconsin Press.

McCloskey, D.N. 2000. *How to be Human Though an Economist*. Ann Arbor: University of Michigan Press.

MacKenzie, D. 2006. Is economics performative? Option theory and the construction of the derivatives market. *Journal of the History of Economic Thought*, 28(1):29–55.

Medawar, P.B. 1979. *Advice to a Young Scientist*. New York: Harper and Row.

Medawar, P.B. 1991. 'Is the scientific paper a fraud?' In: Medawar. P.B., *The Threat and the Glory: Reflections on Science and Scientists*. Oxford: Oxford University Press, 228–233 (based on a BBC interview published in *The Listener*, 12 September 1963).

Muniesa, F. 2014. *The Provoked Economy: Economic Reality and the Performative Turn*. London: Routledge.

North, D.C. 1990. *Institutions, Institutional Change and Economic Performance*. Cambridge: Cambridge University Press.

Popper, K.R. 1972. *Objective Knowledge: An Evolutionary Approach*. Oxford: Clarendon.

Popper, K.R. 1992. *In Search of a Better World: Lectures and Essays from Thirty Years*. London: Routledge.

Sandberg, J. & Alvesson, M. 2011. Ways of constructing research questions: gap-spotting or problematization? *Organization*, 18(1):23–44.

Searle, J.R. 2010. *Making the Social World*. Oxford: Oxford University Press.

Sen, A.K. 1970. The impossibility of the Paretian liberal. *Journal of Political Economy*, 78(1):152–157.

Smith, A. 1799. *Essays on Philosophical Subjects*. Basil.

Thaler, S.L. 1997. A quantitative model of seminal cognition: the creativity machine paradigm (US Patent 5,659,666). Online paper available from www.imagination-engines.com, accessed 24 April 2007.

Van Fraassen, B.C. 1980. *The Scientific Image*. Oxford: Clarendon Press.

Warsh, D. 2006. *Knowledge and the Wealth of Nations: A Story of Economic Discovery*. New York: Norton.

Weick, K.E. 1989. Theory construction as disciplined imagination. *Academy of Management Review*, 14(4):516–531.

Weisberg, H.I. 2014. *Willful Ignorance: The Mismeasure of Uncertainty*. Hoboken, NJ: John Wiley.

White, P. 2013. Who's afraid of research questions? The neglect of research questions in the methods literature and a call for question-led methods teaching. *International Journal of Research & Method in Education*, 36(3):213–227.

# 3 The representation of problems in economics

In Chapter 2, four conceptions of original contributions were identified. This chapter looks at the following two conceptions of original contributions in more detail:

- The useful reformulation of an existing problem or the identification of a new problem that is significant to the discipline.
- Identification of previously unknown, but significant and questionable assumptions in the shared mental model of the discipline.

More specifically, it considers how problems should be represented to make fruitful reformulations more likely and enable the elicitation of assumptions. It considers the *S–P* part of the creative process in Figure 2.5, which is reproduced here as Figure 3.1.

In this chapter, I show that economic problems not only matter for creative research, but that the way we choose to represent such problems has a substantial influence over the degree of creativity of economic research. Two possible ways that economists can choose to represent economic problems are discussed here, that is: the common trade-off representation and the conflict representation. This chapter illuminates how the conflict representation is more useful to guide the search for original contributions and concludes on that note. The argument is illustrated from a rather dramatically incorrect prediction made in the field of economics where Nobelist, James Meade, described Mauritius as being "hopeless", just as it was about to become one of the most prosperous African economies. In Chapter 6 more positive applications will be provided, based on the work of Amartya Sen and Kydland and Prescott.

## The importance of problems in science

Without problems there would be no way of knowing whether science matters or whether it is making progress. Viewing science from the perspective of problems offers the most promising way to understand its progress and how scientists can contribute to this progress (Giunti, 1988:439).

## 34  *The representation of problems in economics*

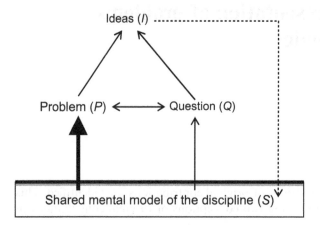

*Figure 3.1* Process of conceiving an original contribution.

Creative scientists are motivated by the need to solve unsolved scientific problems and this drives inquiry as it proceeds from old problems to new ones (Popper, 1972:258). Stigler (1983:535) pointed out that, without unsolved problems science would become sterile since unsolved problems motivate scientists to generate and pursue innovative ideas.

Besides Stigler, other leading economists also regarded the task of the economist as that of solving problems (Simon, Langley & Bradshaw, 1981; Samuelson, 1992; Tinbergen, 1992). For example, Samuelson (1992:245) explains that his scientific activity starts "when a problem is posed". Herbert Simon concurs with this describing scientific discovery as "problem solving" (Simon *et al.*, 1981:1); and Jan Tinbergen (1992:275) described his scientific philosophy as "solving the most urgent problems first".

The word 'problem' is derived from the Greek word *problema*, associated with some kind of impediment (Hattiangadi, 1978:353). The unsolved problems of a discipline cast doubt on its ideas, and so may impede further advances.

Scientific problems are essentially problems in the sphere of existing ideas (Popper, 1992:8–9). Such problems are not mere 'puzzles', which was the term Thomas Kuhn (1970) used to refer to the kinds of problems that scientists investigate when engaging in the gap-spotting research of 'normal' science. Rather, scientific problems are such that they bring the existing body of knowledge into doubt and have the potential to lead to knowledge creation, which is similar to the view that pragmatists such as Dewey (1978) held about problems.

While problems may be undesirable in one way, they are also highly fruitful in another way. Unsolved problems often attract the attention of some theorists and motivate them to generate new ideas that can remove the doubts that impede theoretical progress. So, scientific problems are not only impediments to the advancement of a discipline, but also create incentives for theorists to pursue advances.

## The importance of problem representation

If problems are central to theoretical progress, one would expect gifted economic theorists to be those who have a better understanding of the nature of economic problems. Viner (1937:109), in his survey of trade theory in the "pre-scientific stage" of economic theory, confirmed this: "Such progress as occurred was due almost solely to a small group of capable writers, able to analyse economic problems more acutely and logically than their predecessors."

An understanding of scientific problems makes some researchers more effective than others because the perception of a problem determines how that problem is formulated. Problem formulation is "capable of having spectacular effects on problem solving efficiency" as one of the earliest studies in artificial intelligence found (Amarel, 1968:170). This is partly because problem formulation determines the methods used in solving such problems. In Economics, Nobelist James Tobin (in Minsky, 2008:11) made a similar observation: "The terms in which a problem is stated and which the relevant information is organized can have a great influence on the solution." According to Minsky, this is because problem formulation determines the theory that will be employed, which, in turn, determines the questions asked and the kind of answers that are considered. For this reason, problem formulation is, in itself, seen as an important scientific achievement and the skill of a professional scientist or practitioner is expressed in their ability to formulate the problems in their field (Coyne, 2004:6).

Problem formulation also determines the methods a discipline tends to use when solving its problems. Creative researchers often formulate their problems differently and are likely to focus their efforts by using more appropriate methods for the production of interesting ideas and ground-breaking and original questions.

The formulation of specific problems depends, to a large degree, on the generic structure imposed by every discipline's preferences for representing its problems in general. This generic representation determines what kind of variables and relationships will be used when formulating specific problems, and, to a large degree, dictates how a discipline thinks about its problems and the methods it favours in solving its problems. Problem representation therefore has a strong influence on the ability of a discipline to formulate its specific problems in a fruitful way. In economics, the generic representation of problems, be it graphically or mathematically, is the trade-off.

## Economic problems represented as trade-offs

The discipline of economics derives from its central problem, regarded by many as the problem of scarcity. The original version of the scarcity problem was stated by Lionel Robbins (1952:16) and is worth repeating here: "Economics is the science which studies human behaviour as a relationship between ends and scarce means which have alternative uses." Because means are scarce, choices have to be made between means or between ends. Choice is defined by the act of sacrifice, and economists represent choices as trade-offs, which make the sacrifices clear. Most of the important problems in economics can therefore be represented as trade-offs (Campbell & Kelly, 1994). This is not the only way to represent economic problems, but is a useful way of looking at problems, as long as one assumes that knowledge is unchanged.

From Robbins' definition of the central problem of economics, one can conclude that the most fundamental trade-offs involve: (1) trade-offs between ends; (2) trade-offs between means; and (3) relationships between means and ends (as shown in Figure 3.2).

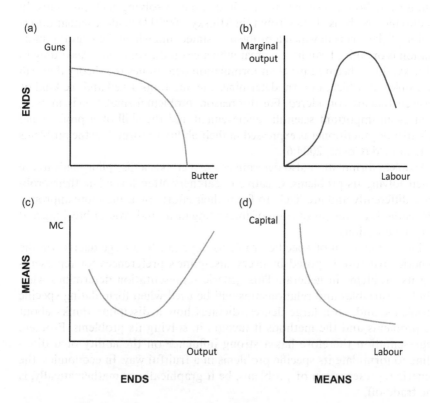

*Figure 3.2* Some fundamental trade-offs in economics.

Figure 3.2(a) shows a trade-off between two desirable ends, in this case the production possibilities frontier which is the best known representation of the scarcity problem. Other well-known end–end trade-offs are the Phillips curve (two undesirable ends) or John Taylor's (1995, 2014) reframing of the monetary policy trade-off and various kinds of indifference curves.

Figure 3.2(d) shows a trade-off between two means (or inputs) and commonly called the 'isoquant'. Other possible means–means trade-offs are the Beveridge (U–V) curve and the Williamson trade-off model of horizontal mergers.

Figures 3.2(b) and 3.2(c) are mirror images of each other, because they both map means against ends, but on different axes. Figure 3.2(b) shows the law of diminishing marginal returns, while Figure 3.2(c) shows the law of increasing marginal cost. Other well-known means–end trade-offs are: offer curves; the risk-return relationship; the Laffer curve, the trade-off theory of capital structure; and various reaction functions.

The representation of a problem suggests which methods are most likely to lead to a satisfying solution. Given problem representations, such as those found in Figures 3.2 and 3.3, the obvious matching solution strategy is that of optimisation.

For example, the monetary policy problem, as represented in Taylor (1995:38) in Figure 3.3(a), is to reach a point on the frontier (moving from inefficient point A to point B). If combined with a social indifference curve (yet another trade-off), the objective would be to achieve the highest social utility. Once the optimum point is reached, then no further net gains are possible and welfare is maximised. This method is also known as 'constrained maximisation' since optimisation is only meaningful when there are constraints. Trade-offs between desired ends are also known as objective functions, but there may also be trade-offs between undesired ends (such as the

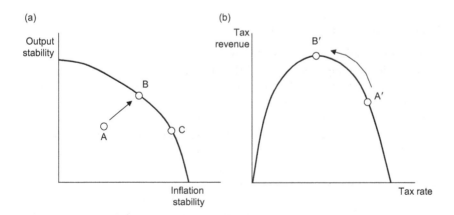

*Figure 3.3* Problems as trade-offs call for optimisation.

Phillips curve). In such cases, we refer to the trade-off as a loss function because finding the optimum will require constrained minimisation.

With the Laffer curve in Figure 3.3(b), it is clear that the problem is also solved through optimisation. The problem is to find the optimum tax rate, that is, the tax rate that maximises tax revenue within the constraints that created the trade-off relationship (shown as moving from A' to the optimum of B').

As Pullen (1982) explains, Malthus was probably the first classical economist to have recognised that economic problems, represented as trade-offs, call for optimisation. Malthus called it the "doctrine of proportions", but it eventually became known as 'optimisation' (Pullen, 1982:270). Wicksell was the first economist to explicitly use the word 'optimum'. Malthus realised that solutions to economic problems could be expressed in the calculus of maxima and minima points. Though he never employed calculus, he applied the thinking behind optimisation to saving, population, wealth distribution, taxation, national debt, public works and various other economic problems.

While Robbins defined the economic problem by its cause (constraints), Malthus defined it by its solution method, which is finding the optimum. Malthus' logic suggested that, due to trade-offs, limits set in after a certain point, and that a kind of give-and-take compromise ultimately becomes the only viable course of action once the optimum is reached. Malthus believed that the source of all erroneous economic reasoning lay in the extremes, which involves neglecting one of the dimensions of a trade-off (Pullen, 1982).

In summary, the most common problem of representation is that of a trade-off in two or more dimensions. When representing a problem as a trade-off, the most appropriate method by which to solve it is optimisation. Scarcity, in its many forms, is the cause of all trade-offs. The next section presents an alternative representation of economic problems: one that is more fruitful than the trade-off representation to direct the conceiving of original contributions.

## Economic problems represented as conflicts

The kind of scientific problems that promote creative research are problems in our understanding, and they call the knowledge, or shared mental model, of a discipline into doubt. Hattiangadi (1978) calls such problems 'intellectual problems'. Due to the doubt they create, intellectual problems impede goal-directed scientific activity and are difficult to solve as they cannot be solved by simply gathering more data. It therefore excludes: Kuhnian puzzles which do not call the paradigm into doubt and are relatively easy for the average competent scientist to solve; as well as most empirical problems, which merely require more data for their resolution and promote gap-spotting research. This exclusion addresses the criticism of some philosophers (Nickles, 1981; Giunti, 1988; Wettersten, 2002) that not all scientific problems fall under Hattiangadi's definition of scientific problems.

It is when our ideas are ambiguous or contradict each other, that we experience the kind of doubts that unsettle our understanding and call for a better understanding. Ambiguity results when a single idea can be perceived in two self-consistent, but mutually incompatible frames of reference. Contradiction is similar to ambiguity, except that the incompatibility is not mediated by some single idea or situation (Byers, 2007). Both ambiguity and contradiction show themselves as a conflict between existing frames of reference. A conflict cannot be solved from existing knowledge alone, because the conflict is caused by it, and it therefore requires new knowledge to address it.

Ideas can only conflict if the beliefs or assumptions from which they are derived are inconsistent, recognised in classical logic as the principle of *ex falso quodlibet* (Tomassi, 1999:120). According to this principle, all statements, even statements that contradict each other, can be deduced from inconsistent assumptions. It suggests that a useful way to represent scientific problems is as a logical conflict arising from an inconsistency. In fact, this is exactly Hattiangadi's (1978) definition of an intellectual problem: a logical conflict or contradiction arising from an inconsistency in beliefs or assumptions. As explained in Chapter 1, the shared mental model of any discipline is likely to contain many inconsistencies, and hence many problems.

Admittedly, original research may sometimes emerge from solving Kuhnian puzzles and empirical problems, and, very often, this kind of research helps to connect other original contributions to the shared mental model of a discipline. However, empirical problems are derived from intellectual problems, so an understanding of intellectual problems must precede an understanding of empirical problems (Nickles, 1981). To see this relationship between the intellectual and empirical, consider Romer's (1994) review of the history of new growth theory. In it, he argued that advances in this field were not hampered so much by the scarcity of data than by the scarcity of ideas, and it is the scarcity of ideas that endogenously creates the scarcity of data.

The inconsistencies that cause intellectual problems therefore mean that such problems can be structured as a logical conflict in the form of a destructive dilemma. The generic representation of a destructive dilemma follows (and uses logic symbols as defined in the list of logical symbols at the start of the book):

$$G \to R \quad R \to A \qquad (3.1)$$

$$G \to R' \quad R' \to \neg A \qquad (3.2)$$

$$\therefore \neg R \vee \neg R' \qquad (3.3)$$

$$\therefore \neg G \qquad (3.4)$$

In the above representation of a problem, $G$, $R$, $R'$, $A$ and $\neg A$ (the negation of $A$) are statements. $G$ is a common objective, $R$ and $R'$ are different

## 40  The representation of problems in economics

requirements that need to be satisfied to achieve the objective, and $A$ and $\neg A$ are apparently conflicting actions to satisfy the requirements. The conditional statement $G \rightarrow R'$ can now be translated as: if goal $G$ is to be achieved, then requirement $R'$ must be satisfied.

All four conditionals will only be plausible if they are supported by certain assumptions. $A$ and $\neg A$ are believed to be logical opposites, so both cannot be true, in other words, $\neg(A \wedge \neg A)$. In the generic representation, if we derive both $A$ and $\neg A$, then either $R$ or $R'$ must be false. Since $R$ and $R'$ are both derived from $G$, and one of them is false, $G$ cannot be true. The existence of a contradiction therefore causes the truth of all statements to be in doubt. When doubt enters, a problem appears, calling for an inquiry into our beliefs (Backhouse, 1998:193–194).

An alternative visual representation will make the logical structure of a problem clearer (see Figure 3.4). This was derived from Goldratt (1994) and its representation is applied to quite an interesting version of a problem that dominates economics: the market versus state debate.

Figure 3.4 implies that there is a common objective in economic science, and that is to find ways to achieve social order ($G$). On the one hand, if this objective is to be achieved, then it is argued that agents need to act collectively ($R$), which, in turn, implies some coercion by the state for the agents' own good. On the other hand, it may be argued that to achieve social order, it is necessary that power be dispersed so that no agent can dominate ($R'$), which necessitates free competition between agents. The result is a problem, because state control ($A$) is in direct conflict with letting the market work freely ($\neg A$).

Figure 3.4 helps to show the role of inconsistent assumptions. Statements $R$, $R'$, $A$ and $\neg A$ are a logical consequence of certain assumptions. The graphic representation makes it easier to locate these assumptions. The assumptions

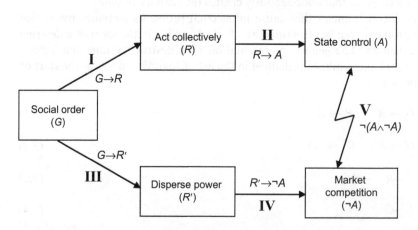

*Figure 3.4* An economic problem as a logical conflict.
*Source*: Derived from Streeck and Schmitter (1985).

are contained in the connectives labelled I–IV, and in connective V, which indicates the existence of the conflict. The assumptions can be made explicit by asking those who agree with each of the conditional connectives (I–IV) to explain why one particular statement follows from another statement. For example, one would state the reasoning of connective IV as: 'To disperse power, it is necessary for free market competition to take place.' To explain and justify this conditional statement, one will need to make further statements, which will, in turn, lead one to find the assumptions underlying connective IV. One may also ask why it follows that state control is in conflict with the free market competition, and so discover the assumptions that maintain contradiction V (e.g. beliefs relating to the nature of freedom and control). Following such a process, it is possible to find twenty or more assumptions that maintain the problem.

Proponents from one competing view will look at one side of such a logical conflict and not agree with the conclusions. For example, some will challenge the statement that state control is necessary to ensure collective action and then proceed to give several reasons for their view. When they do so, they are identifying and challenging the assumptions that underlie the logic of the opposite logical connective II, thereby demonstrating that assumptions are what cause and maintain this problem. A different set of assumptions may resolve this particular problem.

The assumptions cause the problem because they either lead to conflicting statements (connectives I, II, III or IV) or because they lead to the belief that a logical conflict exists (connective V). Assumptions can only lead to a conflict if at least one of them is inconsistent with one other assumption. For example, under connective II, one may draw an assumption that only an authority can possess sufficient knowledge of the economy to direct agents to act collectively for the greater good. However, under connective IV, one may find an assumption that the market mechanism enables individual agents to bring about outcomes as if they possess the collective knowledge of all agents. The two underlying assumptions are therefore inconsistent, and thus lead to contradictory conclusions.

Inconsistencies are constantly created. As new problems are discovered in existing theories and as reality itself changes, the formulation of additional assumptions is necessary. Scientific knowledge and ideas therefore change almost imperceptibly over time and inconsistencies gradually appear in these assumptions. This is compounded when reality changes in response to economic theorists' models and discoveries: for example, when previously known empirical regularities disappear as they are exploited by policymakers (recall Goodhart's Law). It may also happen that the logical consequences of known assumptions conflict with those not yet made explicit, so that inconsistencies may exist without being immediately apparent. Yet another source of inconsistencies in assumptions is when rival theories, with competing views and different sets of assumptions, are developed to address the same problem.

Such inconsistencies are unlikely to be eliminated. Cherniak (1984) estimated that the strongest computer imaginable would need all the time that our universe has existed to determine whether there are inconsistencies between only 138 unambiguous statements. Economists are not supercomputers, so they are likely to struggle with fewer than 138 statements. Even four statements can present some difficulty: consider how long it took the economics profession to even see the logical inconsistency between just four known propositions from which Arrow's Theorem was derived. The body of knowledge in economics consists of more than 138 statements, and many of them are ambiguous. It is inevitable, therefore, that numerous logical inconsistencies exist in the discipline.

Another related way to think about scientific problems is Nickles' (1981:109) definition of a problem as all the constraints on the solution plus a demand that a solution be found that satisfies all the constraints. A problem makes scientific inquiry possible when at least one of its constraints is known, and the more that are known, the better the problem is structured. Problems with inconsistent constraints are over-determined, meaning that it is impossible to find solutions that satisfy all constraints (Nickles, 1981:87). Over-determined problems are solved by discovering the relevant constraints, and then reformulating the problem by adding, rejecting and/or modifying at least one. In the process, the existing state of knowledge is called into doubt and modified.

If something that was previously regarded as a constraint is rejected or modified, it suggests that it was self-imposed and merely an assumption. This is quite common and history shows that there are very few scientific problems with constraints that are beyond question (Simon, 1973:189). Advances in a field often occur when a scientist finds a way to relax an assumption that previously acted as a constraint (Nickles, 1981:95). In other words, this happens when there is a disruption of the assumptional ground on which knowledge is based. For example, Warsh (2006) provides an extensive review of how the assumption of perfect competition, by virtue of not being questioned, acted as a constraint on growth and trade theory. He shows how the growth and trade theory was only able to advance once the assumption was no longer treated as a constraint.

This will also be evident in the case studies used later in this book. For example, prior to Kydland and Prescott's (1977) paper, advances in the practice of monetary policy were impeded by several doubts, including the problem of whether rules or discretion were the best foundation for monetary policy. The theoretical analysis of the competing views was inconclusive (Argy, 1988), thereby hindering further advances. This impediment continued until Kydland and Prescott reformulated the problem as that of time inconsistency and questioned old assumptions and so changed the nature of the debate (Schaling, 1995). With the problem reframed, progress in monetary policy accelerated as the new problem suggested original directions for theoretical and empirical research.

The elimination of logical inconsistencies has motivated much of the pursuit of creative research in economics. Shackle's (1967) documentation of the great advances in economic theory that took place from 1926 to 1939, offers excellent illustrations of the ideas in this chapter. One such illustration is his discussion of the problems that appeared in value theory and their eventual solution (Shackle, 1967:13–60).

Progress in value theory was halted by what came to be known as Sraffa's dilemma. Simply put, the dilemma was that: under conditions of perfect competition, the firm can sell as much as it likes at the prevailing market price, which is set independently of how much the individual firm sells. However, as the quantity that the firm sells increases, its average cost falls so that there is no limit to an individual firm's expansion. If there was no limit to the quantity sold, an individual firm with even a small head start would eventually become a monopoly. There was a contradiction because the theory of perfect competition rules out the possibility that an equilibrium can exist where any firm has market power (Shackle, 1967:13).

The cause of the contradiction was due to assumptions of which no one was aware: that is, that the supply price was the same as marginal cost and that the demand curve was also the marginal revenue curve (Shackle, 1967:15, 24–25). Once it was realised that there was a conceptual separation between the supply price and marginal cost, and between the demand curve and the marginal revenue curve, Sraffa's dilemma was resolved. The solution allowed value theorists – such as Harrod, Robinson and Chamberlin – to introduce a number of new theoretical inventions in the form of the theory of imperfect competition. However, the inventions introduced new dilemmas and problems (e.g. the disappearance of a definite supply curve) and propelled value theorists to make further advances.

In summary, an alternative representation of economic problems is that of a logical conflict caused by inconsistent beliefs, self-imposed constraints or assumptions. Economics, as a dynamic and complex discipline, is populated by a plethora of inconsistencies. It is interesting that the word 'dilemma', which is inherently conflictual, is derived from the Greek words *dis* (meaning twice) and *lemma* (meaning assumption). It suggests that the source of a dilemma is that of inconsistent assumptions which can only occur if there are at least two assumptions that lead to two opposing conclusions.

Representing problems as logical conflicts therefore requires a different method to solving them. Instead of optimisation, it calls for a creative approach to identifying the assumptions in the shared mental model that structure the problem, followed by an attempt to add, modify or reject these in order to remove the conflict. Based on our knowledge of economics, where the phenomena we study are socially constructed, most assumptions are open to debate, and this allows for many possibilities for new ideas to be absorbed into the discipline.

Two possible ways to represent economic problems have now been presented. Both representations are useful depending on the purpose. The next section compares the two representations in order to demonstrate the superiority of the conflict representation for the purpose of guiding creative research.

## Comparing representations

While the trade-off representation is useful when one can safely assume knowledge to be fixed, it is less useful when creative research is needed. As will be shown in this section, trade-offs hide creative possibilities and engender passivity in the face of problems. In contrast, the conflict representation highlights opportunities for new ideas that actually shift or even change the trade-off.

### *James Meade and Mauritius*

In 1961, James Meade, an Economics Nobel Prize recipient in 1977, published the first of two papers on Mauritius, in which he described the island not merely as a disaster waiting to happen, but a disaster that had already happened (Meade, 1961, 1967). He saw a rising population faced with an unproductive agricultural economy, in whose future lay rising poverty, inequality and social conflict. For him, this was an almost insoluble dilemma. He thought that it could be temporarily alleviated through birth control and all the conventional measures – wage restraint, social security, small business subsidies and education – but there was little original thinking in these papers.

From the way he described the issue it was clear that he framed the Mauritian problem as a version of the scarcity problem: as the challenge of how to achieve the highest output from the island's scarce and abundant resources (Meade, 1961:523). For him the ideal solution was to allow for the unfettered operation of the market mechanism to bring about the optimal use of resources. No creative ideas are called for. It is suggested here that one accepts the problem, stands back and lets the market find the optimum.

As a result, one would expect a problem representation in the form of a trade-off, which we indeed find. Meade (1967:250) argued that the island faced a kind of ends–ends trade-off where the rising population would reduce per capita income and either give rise to higher unemployment or greater inequality. This was expressible either as: a loss function (unemployment versus inequality) or an objective function (employment versus equity).

We see the trade-off in another form in Meade (1967:249) where he highlighted that the wage-rate (means) could be used to reduce unemployment (end) or achieve social justice (end), but not both. In other words, Mauritius had to *increase* the real wage to raise incomes and address inequality, but it also needed to *reduce* the real wage in order to stimulate employment. Meade's preference was to reduce the real wage through labour market deregulation.

Meade's representation of the problem is shown visually in Figure 3.5(a). He believed Mauritius to be at point A, and that the best it could do was to

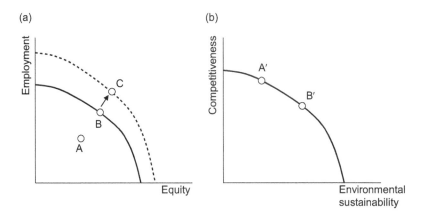

Figure 3.5 Mauritius in the 1960s and the 1980s.

move to a possible optimum point like point B. One gets a sense that he did not believe that the trade-off function could be significantly shifted (B to C in Figure 3.5(a)) or even become irrelevant, that is, transformed perhaps into something similar to Figure 3.5(b). Meade (1961:534) implied that it would be almost impossible when he argued that it would be a "great achievement" if the island could reduce unemployment without reducing the average standard of living.

The trade-off representation of the problem left Meade to passively accept the problem, seeing only solutions that could find an optimum point but left the trade-off intact. However, if economists simply accepted trade-offs there would have been no economic development, which occurs when the trade-off is shifted or transformed. Recall Schumpeter's (1934:64) definition of development as: "Discontinuous change in the channels of the flow, disturbance of equilibrium, which forever *alters and displaces the equilibrium state* previously existing" (emphasis added), which suggests that optimisation alone cannot achieve development since it accepts the constraints that maintain a problem.

Yet this development is exactly what happened in Mauritius, and not by following Meade's advice. By the 1980s, the island reached both full employment and a higher standard of living even as its population continued growing, and was regarded as a role model for other developing economies. In 1961, the island was in desperate need of new ideas, and for that they needed to think differently about their problem. Had Meade employed the conflict representation to formulate the problem (shown as Figure 3.6), he might have been open to other possibilities.

Figure 3.6 shows the common objective to be to increase, or at least maintain, the social welfare ($G$) of Mauritius. On the one hand, if this objective is to be achieved, then an equitable distribution of income needs to be achieved ($R$), which, in turn, implies higher real wages. On the other hand, Meade also

## 46  The representation of problems in economics

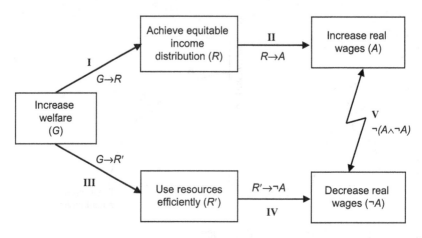

Figure 3.6  Mauritius' problem as a logical conflict.

argued that it is necessary that resources be used more efficiently ($R'$), which necessitates lower real wages. The result is a problem, because the achievement of higher wages ($A$) is in direct conflict with that of lower wages ($\neg A$).

Inconsistent assumptions must exist for such a logical conflict to be possible. This representation makes it easier to see why there is a problem and where opportunities for new thinking lie. It also opens up the logical black box of the trade-off and directs us to the assumptions that maintain the conflict (contained in connectives labelled I–V).

By questioning each connective, asking questions like: 'Is it always necessary for real wages to fall in order to achieve efficiency?'; or, 'Why do we believe that higher wages will achieve an equitable income distribution?'; one can make assumptions explicit. We need to do this, because, by discovering the assumptions that cause the conflict, and then reformulating the problem by adding, rejecting and/or modifying at least one assumption, we may be able to find breakthrough ideas, which is a topic discussed in more detail in Chapters 4 and 5.

Mauritius introduced a number of innovations, such as export processing zones (EPZs), and cleverly exploited the international trade system. The solutions emerged from questioning connective V and finding that it is indeed possible to increase and decrease the real wage at the same time. This is achieved by segmenting the labour market. Subramanian (2009:10) explains that an EPZ allowed for significantly more flexible labour market conditions to prevail in the export sector compared to the rest of the economy. He mentions specifically that it was easier to discharge workers, that no severance allowances needed to be paid and that the minimum wages for women were lower in the EPZs.

As a result, there were effectively two labour markets: one in which real wages could rise, and one in which they could not. It worked: employment in the EPZ sector rose dramatically and the unemployment rate in the late 1980s dropped as low as 3 per cent (Subramanian, 2009).

The idea of segmenting the labour market could not have emerged from the trade-off representation, which hides the logical structure of the problem. Whether used or not, the conflict representation clearly highlights the logical structure and the location of the ideas that Mauritius used. By the late 1970s, the country had shifted the trade-off outwards from B to C in Figure 3.5(a). Matters improved so much that by the late 1980s neither of the two dimensions of that trade-off was as pertinent as before, and Mauritius faced new problems due to its success. The problem had transformed into a trade-off between international competitiveness and environmental sustainability (English, 1998), as indicated by Figure 3.5(b).

## Comparison of the two problem representations

The conflict representation explicitly shows the logical relationships that hold the problem together and provide cues, in the form of the connectives, to find assumptions. Once these are found, real constraints can be separated from questionable assumptions, and inconsistent assumptions can be identified. The questionable assumptions can then direct empirical research that will either confirm the assumptions, or reveal possibilities for invalidating the assumptions, thereby solving the problem. Inherent in the conflict representation of economic problems is the understanding that any economic problem is self-imposed and not permanent. Change is latent because human ingenuity can challenge its own assumptions, solve the problem and create new logical conflicts.

In contrast, the trade-off representation is inherently static. It presents the problem as finding the optimum point or making a choice between the points on the frontier of a given trade-off relationship. This representation offers no obvious way to peer into the problem and the logical relationships that structure the problem, hence offering no handle on solving the problem. The solution strategy consistent with such a static representation is optimisation. If a solution does occur – e.g. when the frontier expands from point B to C in Figure 3.5(a) – it is seen as due to exogenous forces over which economists have little direct influence. Unfortunately, the trade-off representation hides the fact that solutions are in fact often endogenous.

As suggested by Robbins (1952), in the trade-off representation of economic problems, ends are taken as given and means assumed to be governed by natural laws. Both ends and means are regarded as beyond the economist's control. Within this representation, the solution to economic problems is reduced to a search problem, which is to find the optimum point for a specified trade-off relationship.

In summary, the trade-off representation of the economic problem ignores a number of aspects about economic problems that are obvious from the conflict representation:

- Economic problems do not have an objective existence. Problems are self-imposed as a result of the inconsistent assumptions of economic agents and institutions.
- Optimisation is not the ideal solution strategy if creative thinking is needed. One reason is that optimisation does not eliminate the problem, so that progress is limited to searching for a point on the trade-off relationship that is taken as given. Another reason is that it is practically impossible to find the optimum point in real-life trade-offs. Even if the optimum point can be found, it is not stable and can change through the actions, decisions and expectations of economic agents.
- Economic problems cannot be solved simply by getting the valuation right as Robbins (1952:36–37) suggested. Valuation through the market can, at best, help to solve problems by leading us closer to the optimum point on a particular trade-off relationship. The market is a logical system that is unable to operate outside its own constraints. As an abstract and non-thinking entity, the market cannot challenge assumptions and reformulate problems. The best it can do is to: induce incremental innovation through changes in relative prices (Ahmad, 1966; Schmookler, 1966); or balance contradictions via the price mechanism (Nonaka & Toyama, 2002:999).

Again, it has to be noted that the trade-off representation is not undesirable: it is useful in cases where it is appropriate to assume that knowledge is, or should be held, constant. However, it is of little use when trying to create new knowledge.

## How to construct an economic problem as a conflict

This section explains practically how to construct economic problems as conflicts. It takes for granted that the researcher has a problem in mind. It is known that creative researchers are not only good at reformulating problems, but also good at finding problems. This study does not explore problem finding in detail and the reader is referred to the seminal literature in this area (Dillon, 1982). Similar to the act of conceiving original contributions, it is an area in economics that has not yet been systematised and may be the subject of future research.

In disciplines that aim to have some real-world application, studies usually start with a real-world context and problem, followed up by an explanation of the problem in the research or knowledge about the real-world problem. Popper (1978:143–145) distinguished these two kinds of problems by labelling real-world problems as problems in World I, while labelling knowledge and research problems as World III problems. Even though researchers work on World III problems, in disciplines that focus on being useful, such as economics, these problems derive from World I problems.

A useful starting point for constructing an economic problem as a conflict is World I: that is, finding some undesirable effect in the economy or a postulated real-world trade-off or policy dilemma. This section explains how to construct a conflict using these two methods: (1) conversion from a trade-off or dilemma; and (2) conversion from an undesirable effect.

### Convertibility of the two representations

Trade-offs and logical conflicts are not mutually exclusive. Understanding how trade-offs and logical conflicts can be converted into each other will be useful in the next sub-section where a step-wise conversion approach is explained.

Trade-offs in economics are usually between two means (with the ends implied) or between two ends (with the means implied) and this is shown in Figure 3.7. Means$_1$ is employed to pursue End$_1$ and Means$_2$ is employed to pursue End$_2$. Trade-off diagrams usually show the relationship between: Means$_1$ and End$_1$ (A); Means$_2$ and End$_2$ (B); Means$_1$ and Means$_2$ (C); or End$_1$ and End$_2$ (D). The arrow goes from means to end to indicate the direction of causality.

Meade's formulation of the Mauritian problem can therefore be stated as Figure 3.8 and this is quite similar to the conflict formulation in Figure 3.6. The means are the actions ($A$ and $\neg A$) and the ends are the requirements ($R$ and $R'$).

There are two differences between the trade-off formulation in Figure 3.8 and conflict representation formulation in Figure 3.6. These are the fact that the direction of logical reasoning is reversed and that an overarching objective (goal) is added. They are shown side by side in Figure 3.9.

The logic of the trade-off representation in Figure 3.9(a) is that of cause-effect – 'If we employ Means$_1$ then End$_1$ will follow', whereas the conflict representation in Figure 3.9(b) is that of intention and argumentation – 'If we *want* to achieve Goal, then we *must* pursue End$_1$'; and 'If we *want* to achieve End$_1$ then we *must* employ Means$_1$'.

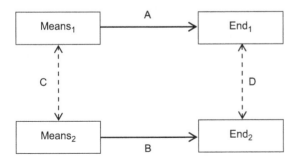

*Figure 3.7* Trade-offs shown differently.

50  *The representation of problems in economics*

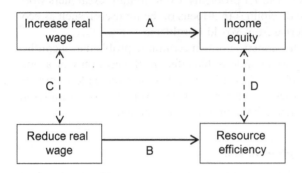

*Figure 3.8* Meade's Mauritian trade-off.

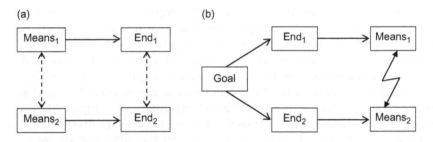

*Figure 3.9* Comparison of logics.

The trade-off representation suggests an almost natural flow of events following the laws of cause and effect, while the logic of the conflict representation emphasises the role of human thought and action in creating and solving economic problems. The logic of the conflict representation is also called 'deontic logic' as it expresses what agents believe must be done and is often used when arguing for a policy.

### *Converting a trade-off or dilemma into a logical conflict*

Since most economists almost naturally define problems as trade-offs or dilemmas, this is arguably the easier approach. The following steps should be followed:

Step 1: Determine if the trade-off is a means–means, means–end or end–end trade-off. Policy dilemmas are means–means trade-offs since they suggest conflicting actions.
Step 2: Insert the dimensions of the trade-off in the appropriate boxes of the conflict shown in Figure 3.10. Figure 3.10 is the original conflict representation superimposed on the trade-off translation of Figure 3.8.

*The representation of problems in economics* 51

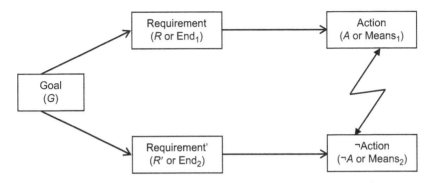

*Figure 3.10* Empty boxes.

- 2a: If the trade-off is an end–end – for example, Taylor's trade-off between price stability and output stability – then place 'maintain output stability' in the Requirement₁ box and 'maintain price stability' in the Requirement₂ box.
- 2b: If it is a policy dilemma which calls for opposing actions – for example, between whether the interest rate should be increased or decreased – then place 'decrease interest rate' in the Action box and 'increase interest rate' in the ¬Action box.
- 2c: If it is a means–end trade-off, it is really just showing one half of the trade-off, so place them on the same level: that is, the means in the Action box and the end in the End₁ box.

Step 3: Derive the other empty boxes from the boxes that are already filled in, as follows:

- 3a: If the ends boxes are filled in, you need to work in two directions. Given both ends, ask yourself what overall objective will be achieved if both End₁ and End₂ are achieved, and fill in the answer in the Goal box. In the case of Taylor's trade-off, one may argue that achieving both price stability and output stability will lead to 'sustained economic growth', or growth that can be maintained over the long run without harming a country's institutions or resources. Moving in the opposite direction, ask yourself what action should be taken to achieve each end. If this is truly a trade-off the actions will be conflicting in some way. To maintain output stability calls for actions like 'employ discretionary monetary policy' (in general) or possibly 'decrease the interest rate' (under specific conditions). To maintain price stability calls for actions like 'follow inflation targeting' (in general) or possibly 'increase the interest rate' (under specific conditions).

- 3b: If the means boxes are filled in, then the reasoning runs in one direction. Starting with each means, ask yourself why we need to take this action and fill in the ends boxes with the answers. Suppose that the economy is currently experiencing stagflation and the opposing actions are to increase or decrease the interest rate. We would then need to 'decrease the interest rate' (Means$_1$) in order to 'maintain output stability' (End$_1$) and to 'increase the interest rate' (Means$_2$) in order to 'maintain price stability' (End$_2$). Given both ends, then ask yourself what overall objective will be achieved if both End$_1$ and End$_2$ are achieved, and fill in the answer in the Goal box. In this case, one may argue that achieving both price stability and output stability will lead to 'sustained economic growth'.
- 3c: If the means and ends boxes are filled in on one side only, then take the action and ask what would be the opposing action in theory or reality. For example, if Means$_1$ is to 'employ discretionary policy', the opposing action would be 'policy rules' and this would then become Means$_2$. Then reason towards End$_2$ and then toward the Goal as in step 3b above.

Step 4: Test the logical flow. Suppose the conflict was constructed for a specific state of the economy – a situation of stagflation as shown in Figure 3.11) – read the boxes from left to right and from right to left.

When reading from left to right, read as follows: 'If we want [G], then we *must* [R], and if we want [R] we *have to* [A]'. Note the use of deontic logic here. When reading from right to left, read as follows: 'If we [A] it will lead to [R], and if [R] it will lead to [A]'. Here, the logic of causality is evident.

If, in both cases, the reading is grammatical and reasonable according to some view of economic reality or theory (even if you don't agree with it) and the actions conflict in some way, then the logical flow is acceptable. Figure 3.11 achieves this. Reading it both ways gives for example: 'If we want sustained economic growth, we must maintain price stability, and, if we want price stability, we have to increase the interest rate'; or, 'If we decrease the interest rate, it will lead to output stability, and, if we have output stability, it will lead sustained economic growth'. Also, increasing the interest rate is in direct conflict with decreasing the interest rate.

### *Converting an undesirable effect into a logical conflict*

When the trade-off is not immediately evident, one has to follow a more roundabout approach. The following steps are derived and adapted from the training material of the Avraham Y. Goldratt Institute (2000):

*The representation of problems in economics* 53

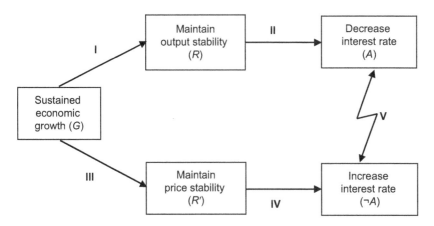

*Figure 3.11* Completed boxes (given a specific state of the economy).

Step 1: State the problem as an undesirable effect relative to some ideal. This undesirable effect can be derived from a question or a narrative of the problem. We therefore start with the everyday conception of a problem as a mismatch between reality and an ideal that is difficult to close (Smith, 1988:1491).

Suppose we take Meade's (1967:250) statement of the problem on Mauritius at the time: "Heavy population pressure must inevitably reduce real income per head ... that surely is bad enough in a community which is full of potential political conflict." The problem may be taken either as: 'real income per head is falling'; or 'political conflict is growing'. Let us suppose that we adopt the first and consider the result.

Figure 3.12 summarises the questions that will be used to construct the conflict in steps 2–6.

Step 2: Your starting point is to complete the first requirement ($R$) by asking the question: 'What need of the system is being jeopardised by the problem?' It has to be expressed as a need, so consider why it is important to solve the problem. What need is not being satisfied due to the problem? Maybe it is something like the possibility that lower real incomes are defeating attempts to make the income distribution more equitable. So, 'achieve equitable income distribution' is filled in inside the $R$-box.

Step 3: The next question goes to the opposing side of the conflict as we ask: 'What action or decision is blocking us from getting rid of the problem?' This has to be expressed as an action or a decision. What action or decision stops us from solving the problem? Maybe it is that the push to decrease real wages will cause incomes to decline and make the problem worse. So 'decrease real wages' is filled in inside the $\neg A$-box.

54  *The representation of problems in economics*

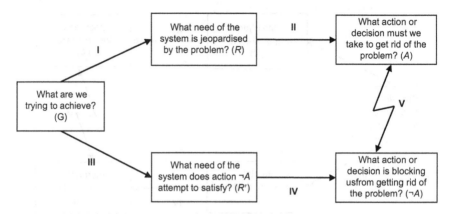

*Figure 3.12* Summary of steps 2–6.

Step 4: To find the opposing action, the next question is: 'What action or decision must you take to get rid of the problem?' Once again, note that it has to be an action or decision. In the Mauritian case, it was simply the opposite approach, that is, to 'increase real wages' and this should be filled in inside the *A*-box.

Step 5: The next question tries to find the reason for the opposing action or decision by asking: 'What need of the system is being satisfied by this action?' This has to be a need. So, why did Mauritius have to reduce real wages? What need would this have satisfied? Since real wages were too high, many resources were not fully employed, so filled in inside the *R'*-box we should have: 'use resources efficiently'.

Step 6: The last question acknowledges that both sides try to achieve the same thing so we should ask: 'What are we trying to achieve overall?' This has to be expressed as a goal. What is the common goal between the two needs? Why do we need both equity and efficiency? Box *G* should then be filled in as 'increase national welfare'.

The result looks like Figure 3.13 (Figure 3.6 reproduced).

Step 7: Test the logical flow by reading the boxes from left to right and from right to left. When reading from left to right, read as follows: 'If we want [*G*] then we *must* [*R*], and if we want [*R*], we *have to* [*A*]'. Again, note the use of deontic logic here. When reading from left to right, read as follows: 'If we [*A*] it will lead to [*R*], and if [*R*] it will lead to [*G*]' (note the logic of causality). *Irrespective of whether you agree with the view or not*, in both cases, the reading is grammatical and reasonable according to some view of economic reality or theory. If the actions conflict in some way then the logical flow is acceptable. Figure 3.13 achieves this.

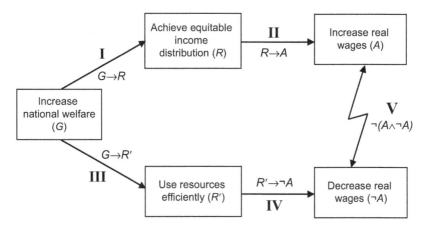

*Figure 3.13* Mauritius' problem as a logical conflict.

There are other ways to approach the construction of a logical conflict. For example, you may start with a question like: 'What action or decision do you complain about?' (becomes box $A$), followed by asking: 'What action would you prefer?' (becomes box $\neg A$). From the action, the requirements can be derived by asking: 'What need are you trying to satisfy with $A$?' (becomes $R$) and, 'What need are you trying to satisfy with $\neg A$?' (becomes $R'$). Then finally ask: 'What is the common objective achieved by $R$ and $R'$?' (becomes $G$).

Once the conflict is constructed, it can be used to elicit the shared mental model. In doing so, we identify the significant assumptions and these assumptions will become the raw material that later goes into the process of generating original contributions. This process is explained in the next chapters.

## Assumption identification

The conflict representation has many uses, and can be used to generate new questions or reason to new ideas. But these two uses presume that the shared mental model can be elicited so that assumptions become clear. As already suggested, the conflict representation makes it much easier to find those assumptions and this section explores this in more detail.

The shared mental model is elicited as assumptions are brought to the surface, and it is demarcated by the problem. The mental models of those whose assumptions collectively create the problem form the shared mental model. The participants may be a very small group in a specialised field of the discipline or a very large group encompassing opposing schools of thought in the discipline. The view of the problem therefore defines whose mental models need to be elicited.

Assumptions make a connective (I, II, III, IV or V in the conflict diagrams) realistic or theoretically plausible given the shared mental model as defined by the problem. Some assumptions act as constraints if agents assume that such assumptions cannot be questioned. A problem is solved by rejecting or modifying one or more of these assumptions, so all innovative solutions violate at least one of the assumptions of the originating problem (Nickles, 1978:139–141).

Every one of the connectives in the conflict problem representation is made plausible by several assumptions. This is to be expected since problems are essentially difficulties with human ideas (Popper, 1992:8–9). These ideas are social constructs that have no objective existence apart from humanity and our social reality (Smith, 1989:965; Dennett, 2003:165).

For a problem to exist as a logical conflict, at least one assumption has to be inconsistent with one other assumption. In other words, at least one assumption is invalid. It is likely that several assumptions are open to questioning provided they are made explicit. Since the conflict representation shows us where the assumptions lie, we find them by interrogating each connective.

Assumptions underlying connectives I, II, III and IV are found by asking two questions:

- Why is it believed, by whomever accepts the validity of the connectives, that: $A$ leads to $R$, $R$ leads to $G$, $\neg A$ leads to $R'$ or $R'$ leads to $G$?
- Why is it believed, by whomever believes in the validity of the connectives, that: for $G$ to happen, we must achieve $R$; for $R$ to be achieved, we must do $A$; for $G$ to happen we must achieve $R'$; and/or for $R'$ to be achieved, we must do $\neg A$?

For example, under connective II, in Figure 3.11, one may find an assumption that central bank interference can have a stabilising influence on the business cycle. However, under arrow IV, one may come across an assumption that interference by the central bank will have no influence on the real economy in the long run. The two assumptions are inconsistent, and thus lead to contradictory conclusions.

The core assumptions in the shared mental model defined by the problem are most likely to be found in connectives I and III. Challenging them can lead to radical new ideas, but these challenges are also more likely to be resisted. Challenges to the assumptions in connectives II, IV and V usually lie in the protective belt and may be more acceptable to the discipline.

Assumptions underlying connective V are found by questions such as:

- Why is it believed that $A$ and $\neg A$ cannot co-exist?
- Why can there be no overlap between $A$ and $\neg A$?
- Why is it believed that we cannot do both $A$ and $\neg A$?

For example, an assumption that one may discover under connective V of Figure 3.11 is: 'There is only one policy rate'. If agents accept this assumption, it will constrain the solution space, and they will not consider policies that suggest a system of multiple policy rates.

Once assumptions are made explicit, they can be questioned. They are challenged in order to generate new ideas or new questions. This is pertinent, as, by bringing a previously unknown and significant assumption to the surface, a researcher may at this point already have conceived of an original contribution.

## Conclusion

This chapter argued that any science needs unsolved problems in order to advance. The way such problems are represented has a major influence on the quality of researchers' creative outputs and the likelihood that new ideas will be generated.

Two ways to represent economic problems were contrasted here: the common trade-off representation and the conflict representation. The trade-off representation assumes stable knowledge, is based on the logic of causality and calls for methods of optimisation; while the conflict representation recognises that problems are socially constructed and is more appropriate when searching for new ideas.

The chapter presented two practical approaches to constructing economic problems as logical conflicts. This is a necessary skill because this representation enables researchers to identify assumptions, which thereafter become the inputs in the systematic approach to finding original contributions for research.

## References

Ahmad, S. 1966. On the theory of induced invention. *The Economic Journal*, 76(302):344–357.
Amarel, S. 1968. On representations of problem reasoning about actions. *Machine Intelligence*, 3:131–171.
Argy, V. 1988. A post-war history of the rules vs discretion debate. *Banca Nazionale del Lavoro Quarterly Review*, 165:147–177.
Avraham Y. Goldratt Institute. 2000. Executive Program (Jonah Program) Course Material.
Backhouse, R.E. 1998. *Explorations in Economic Methodology*. London: Routledge.
Byers, W. 2007. *How Mathematicians Think*. Princeton, NJ: Princeton University Press.
Campbell, D.E. & Kelly, J.S. 1994. Trade-off theory. *American Economic Review*, 84(2):422–426.
Cherniak, C. 1984. Computational complexity and the universal acceptance of logic. *Journal of Philosophy*, 81(12):739–758.

Coyne, R. 2004. Wicked problems revisited. *Design Studies*, 26:5–17.
Dennett, D. 2003. *Freedom Evolves*. London: Penguin.
Dewey, J. 1978. How we think. In: Boydston, J.A. (ed.), *John Dewey: The Middle Works, 1899–1924*, Vol. 6, 177–356. Carbondale: Southern Illinois University Press.
Dillon, J.T. 1982. Problem finding and solving. *Journal of Creative Behavior*, 16(2): 97–111.
English, P. 1998. Mauritius reigniting the engines of growth: a teaching case study. World Bank, Stock No. 37136.
Giunti, M. 1988. Hattiangadi's theory of scientific problems and the structure of standard epistemologies. *British Journal of the Philosophy of Science*, 39:421–439.
Goldratt, E.M. 1994. *It's Not Luck*. Great Barrington, MA: North River Press.
Hattiangadi, J.N. 1978. The structure of problems (Part I). *Philosophy of Social Science*, 8:345–365.
Kuhn, T.S. 1970. The function of dogma in scientific research. In: Brody, B.A. (ed.), *Readings in the Philosophy of Science*, Englewood Cliffs, NJ: Prentice Hall, 356–373.
Kydland, F.E. & Prescott, E.C. 1977. Rules rather than discretion: the inconsistency of optimal plans. *Journal of Political Economy*, 85(3):473–491.
Meade, J.E. 1961. Mauritius: a case study in Malthusian economics. *The Economic Journal*, 71(283):521–534.
Meade, J.E. 1967. Population explosion, the standard of living and social conflict. *The Economic Journal*, 77(306):233–255.
Minsky, H.P. 2008. *Stabilizing an Unstable Economy*. New York: McGraw Hill.
Nickles, T. 1978. Scientific problems and constraints. In: *PSA 1978*, Vol. 1. Hacking, I. & Asquith, P. (eds), East Lansing, MI: Philosophy of Science Association, 134–148.
Nickles, T. 1981. What is a problem that we may solve it? *Synthese*, 47:85–118.
Nonaka, I. & Toyama, R. 2002. A firm as a dialectical being: towards a dynamic theory of a firm. *Industrial and Corporate Change*, 11(5):995–1009.
Popper, K.R. 1972. *Objective Knowledge: An Evolutionary Approach*. Oxford: Clarendon.
Popper, K.R. 1978. Three Worlds. The Tanner Lecture on Human Values, delivered at The University of Michigan, 7 April.
Popper, K.R. 1992. *In Search of a Better World: Lectures and Essays from Thirty Years*. London: Routledge.
Pullen, J. 1982. Malthus on the doctrine of proportions and the concept of the optimum. *Australian Economic Papers*, 21(39):270–285.
Robbins, L.C. 1952. *An Essay on the Nature & Significance of Economic Science*, 2nd revised edition. London: MacMillan.
Romer, P.M. 1994. The origins of endogenous growth. *The Journal of Economic Perspectives*, 8(1):3–22.
Samuelson, P.A. 1992. My life philosophy: policy credos and working ways. In: Szenberg, M. (ed.), *Eminent Economists: Their Life Philosophies*, Cambridge: Cambridge University Press, 236–274.
Schaling, E. 1995. Institutions and monetary policy: credibility, flexibility and central bank independence. Doctoral thesis, Katholieke Universiteit Brabant.
Schmookler, J. 1966. *Invention and Economic Growth*. Cambridge, MA: Harvard University Press.
Schumpeter, J.A. 1934. *The Theory of Economic Development*. London: Oxford University Press.

Shackle, G.L.S. 1967. *The Years of High Theory: Invention and Tradition in Economic Thought 1926–1939*. Cambridge: Cambridge University Press.

Simon, H.A. 1973. The structure of ill-structured problems. *Artificial Intelligence*, 4:181–201.

Simon, H.A., Langley, P. & Bradshaw, G.L. 1981. Scientific discovery as problem solving. *Synthese*, 47:1–27.

Smith, G.F. 1988. Towards a heuristic theory of problem structuring. *Management Science*, 34(12):1489–1506.

Smith, G.F. 1989. Defining managerial problems: A framework for prescriptive theorising. *Management Science*, 35(8):963–981.

Stigler, G.J. 1983. Nobel Lecture: the process and progress of economics. *Journal of Political Economy*, 91(4):529–545.

Streeck, W. & Schmitter, P.C. 1985. Community, market, state-and associations? The prospective contribution of interest governance to social order. *European Sociological Review*, 1(2):119–138.

Subramanian, A. 2009. The Mauritian success story and its lessons. UNU-WIDER Research Paper No. 2009/36.

Taylor, J.B. 1995. Monetary policy guidelines for employment and inflation stability. In: Taylor, J.B. & Solow, R.M. (eds), *Inflation, Unemployment and Monetary Policy*, Cambridge, MA: MIT Press, 29–54.

Taylor, J.B. 2014. Inflation targeting in emerging markets: the global experience. Keynote address at the Annual SARB Conference 'Fourteen years of inflation targeting in South Africa and the challenge of a changing mandate', 30–31 October.

Tinbergen, J. 1992. Solving the most urgent problems first. In: Szenberg, M. (ed.), *Eminent Economists: Their Life Philosophies*, Cambridge: Cambridge University Press, 275–282.

Tomassi, P. 1999. *Logic*. London: Routledge.

Viner, J. 1937. *Studies in the Theory of International Trade*. New York: Harper.

Warsh, D. 2006. *Knowledge and the Wealth of Nations: A Story of Economic Discovery*. New York: Norton.

Wettersten, J. 2002. Problems and meaning today: what can we learn from Hattiangadi's failed attempts to explain them together? *Philosophy of the Social Science*, 32:487–536.

# 4 Originality through questions

What emerged from Chapter 3 is that problems and their representation matter when it comes to increasing the likelihood of conceiving original contributions in economics. The aim of this chapter is to delve into some questioning techniques that can be used to exploit the creative potential of the conflict representation. It will discuss how this representation generates questions that may lead to fruitful, interesting empirical research and new ideas. By looking at the role of questions in more detail, this chapter explores the following two conceptions of original contributions as identified in Chapter 2:

- A new question that opens up new possibilities for research or showing that an old question is problematic.
- Identification of a previously unknown, but significant and questionable assumption in the shared mental model of the discipline.

With reference to the creative process depicted in Figure 4.1, it specifically considers how to generate new questions from the conflict representation of a problem ($P$–$Q$), how a question helps to elicit the shared mental model as defined by that question ($S$–$Q$) and how a question may reveal new problems ($Q$–$P$). This chapter employs some simple illustrative examples, but in Chapter 6 the techniques are applied to the work of Ronald Coase, Amartya Sen and Kydland and Prescott.

## Generating interesting questions

Erotetic logicians define a question as a range of admissible answers together with a request that an answer satisfies certain conditions (Belnap & Steel, 1976). These conditions are set by the researcher who is influenced by the shared mental model of those interested in the question.

Philosophers of science have long recognised that the act of questioning is central to scientific inquiry (Van Fraassen, 1980; Bromberger, 1992). Unfortunately, we again encounter the problem that Medawar highlighted, because the questions that guide research are rarely made explicit in the final

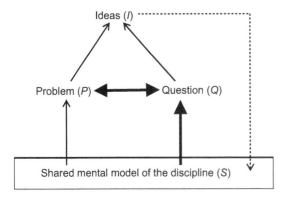

*Figure 4.1* Process of conceiving an original contribution.

published works. As a result, the value of questions is often underestimated (White, 2013).

Sandberg and Alvesson (2011:38–40) suggest that research questions determine the originality of research and that questions that lead to interesting (not gap-spotting) research can be generated in three ways:

- through critical confrontation of a theory or a field by identifying shortcomings such as inconsistencies, lack of perspective or wrong assumptions;
- by finding a new idea that is innovative relative to what has been done before in the field;
- through problematisation, where the logic behind the formulation of a research question is challenged.

Alvesson and Sandberg's (2011:256–260) approach to generating interesting research questions is very similar to the approach followed in this chapter, except that it neglects the step of problem representation. For this reason, their advice is less detailed and this made it difficult for them to develop specific techniques. In brief, their steps are to identify and evaluate assumptions, develop new assumptions that challenge existing ones and assess the meaningfulness of alternative assumptions relative to the intended audience.

This chapter will expand on Sandberg and Alvesson's useful research, and specific techniques will be developed for all three ways of generating interesting questions. In the following sections, a technique for finding questions of critical confrontation will be developed, as well as a technique for generating questions that could lead to new ideas for solving a problem. Finally, I will show how questions can be problematised by eliciting the assumptions of a question using two different techniques.

## Questions of critical confrontation

There are two main approaches to resolving a problem and both aim to collapse the logical conflict (as explained in Chapter 3) through questioning. First, if at least one of the assumptions on either side of a conflict can be shown to be wrong, the conflict may disappear by invalidating the connective which depends on that assumption, and so eliminate the opposing side (explained in this section). Second, a new assumption could be created that reconciles the opposing sides (explained in the next section).

With the aid of the conflict representation, it is possible to locate the assumptions that cause a problem. This is an important step because, as Nickles (1981) explained, advances in a field often occur when a scientist finds a way to relax an assumption that previously acted as a constraint – which means that either it was known and not questioned; or, more perniciously, it was hidden so that it could never be questioned.

If an original contribution involves challenging assumptions, the obvious place to search for questions would be in the assumptions that create a problem. The best questions aim to solve the problem, and, if the problem is created by assumptions, then those assumptions suggest the questions. The act of questioning not only leads to reconsidering assumptions and new ideas, but a new question by itself can also be the idea for original research if it opens the discipline up to possibilities not considered before.

The approach of critical confrontation literally questions each of the assumptions. Simply put, one would list the assumptions, and ask a question that leaves it open to being invalidated. For assumptions found under each connective, one would ask the following:

- Is [the assumption] necessarily so? Do we know this?
- Is [the assumption] true under all conditions? When is it not true?
- Would anything make [the assumption] invalid?

If one of the assumptions is invalidated, then the connective that relies on that assumption is also invalidated. By implication, it then also negates the apparent self-consistent logic of the side of the conflict that relies on that connective. The conflict collapses and the problem is solved.

From Figure 4.2 for example, one may derive the assumption in connective IV that the market mechanism enables individual agents to bring about outcomes as if they possessed the collective knowledge of all agents. The question may then follow: 'Is it always true that a market mechanism enables agents to behave as if they possessed perfect knowledge?' Suppose it is found that this assumption is invalid under current conditions, then the logic of the whole lower side of the conflict fails and becomes irrelevant. When that happens only the upper side remains logically intact, while the lower side becomes logically disconnected, and, as a result, the conflict disappears.

*Originality through questions* 63

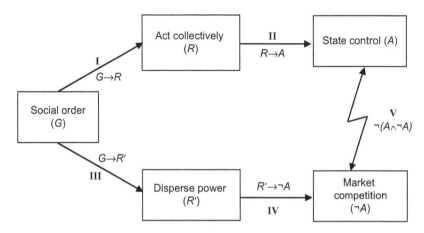

*Figure 4.2* Questioning assumptions.

If one of the assumptions that underlie connective V is invalidated, the conflict collapses, but in a different way. When that happens, the logic that states that $A$ and $\neg A$ are mutually exclusive fails, and the two sides of the conflict become synthesised as they lead essentially to the same action or decision. If it is found that state control and market competition are not really in conflict, the problem is solved by virtue of being a false dichotomy.

Invalidation may occur by confronting an assumption with reality or with a different theoretical perspective. For example, Akerlof's (1970) work on information asymmetry was triggered by a question that emerged from confronting the assumption of perfect information with the reality of the second-hand car market. Most of the field of behavioural economics emerged from questions due to confronting the human rationality assumption with perspectives from artificial intelligence (in the case of Herbert Simon), or psychology (in the case of Kahneman and Tversky's extensive work). Krugman (1993:25) explains that much of his Nobel Prize-winning work was a result of confronting assumptions with reality, which led to "new trade theory", and also other perspectives, which led to the field of "economic geography". He notes that despite the evidence in the real world that economies of scale and imperfect competition called conventional trade theory into question, it was ignored by mainstream researchers. He states that the profession similarly ignored the mass of evidence from geography and regional studies that could have led them to economic geography if they had been willing to engage with different perspectives using a different "language" and approach to research.

Invalidating an assumption may also centre around two inconsistent assumptions. For example, under connective II of Figure 4.2, one may find an assumption that only an authority can possess sufficient knowledge of the economy to direct agents to act collectively for the greater good. However, under connective IV, one may find an assumption that the market mechanism enables individual agents to bring about outcomes as if they possessed the collective knowledge of all agents. The two underlying assumptions are inconsistent, and thus lead to contradictory conclusions, so the question becomes: 'Which system is the best aggregator of knowledge?' If the question is answered, as Hayek (1945) did, the inconsistency is settled and the problem solved.

Assumptions also lead to questions that guide empirical research. If an assumption appears to be accepted, but without strong empirical support, questioning that assumption can lead to research that is ground-breaking should that assumption turn out to be wrong. This is especially likely to occur after dramatic changes in reality or after a period of theoretical disruption in the discipline. Under such conditions, every assumption that structures a problem may be open to question, and turning each of the assumptions into a question can generate a whole research programme for original research.

## Questions in pursuit of new ideas

The second approach to collapsing a logical conflict aims to design questions that synthesise both sides. Again, these questions are easy to find if the problem is represented as a conflict. These synthesising questions do not challenge assumptions as much as they provoke the creation of new ones. This section focuses only on how to generate such questions, while the next chapter will discuss techniques for generating new assumptions (or new ideas) from these questions.

As illustrated by Figure 4.3, there are three main groups of questions that aim to reconcile the opposing sides of a conflict and so generate new ideas or assumptions:

- $R \rightarrow \neg A$: How can agents act collectively by engaging in market competition? This creates a new connective that makes both $R$ and $R'$ lead to a single action ($\neg A$);
- $R' \rightarrow A$: How can agents' power be dispersed through state control? This creates new connective that makes both $R$ and $R'$ lead to a single action ($A$);
- $A \wedge \neg A$: How can both state control and market competition co-exist as coordination mechanisms? This invalidates connective V so that $A$ and $\neg A$ becomes one action.

If any of the three questions lead to new insights, the conflict collapses by leading to the same action ($R \rightarrow \neg A$ and $R' \rightarrow A$) or by combining the two actions into one ($A \wedge \neg A$). In any of these cases, the question by itself would enable a researcher to make an original contribution, since the conflict representation suggests questions most likely to lead to new ideas.

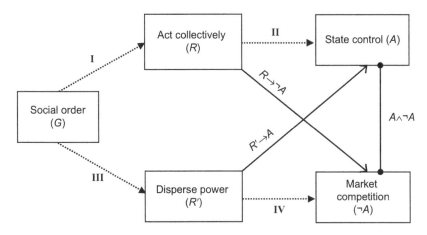

*Figure 4.3* Questions designed for synthesis.

## Problematising questions

Questions give the impression of being open to many answers, when, in fact, all questions impose limits on possible answers. Philosophers of science and erotetic logicians (Collingwood, 1960; Bromberger, 1970; Belnap & Steel, 1976; Van Fraassen, 1980) remind us that all meaningful questions are asked within a framework of presuppositions, which are grouped under the label of 'assumptions' in this study. Belnap (1966:610) explains that a statement is an assumption of a question if the truth of that statement: "is a necessary condition of the question's having some true answer". For example, a question such as, 'How do we alleviate poverty?' presupposes that poverty exists, it is harmful and can be controlled. If, for example, poverty did not exist, the question could not have a meaningful answer.

Bromberger (1970:70) makes a further distinction between p-predicaments and b-predicaments. A p-predicament is a question that a person believes has a correct answer, but the person cannot think of any given his/her background knowledge. A b-predicament has a correct answer but the answer is beyond anyone's mental repertoire. From Bromberger's distinction, one can conclude that predicaments are questions that are unanswerable relative to the prevailing set of concepts and beliefs or assumptions. If a question is unanswerable, it is because people are somehow limited by their own assumptions. This suggests that questions can be problematic and, as with problems, can be answered by adding, changing or rejecting the assumptions imposed by such questions.

Questions can therefore be deceptively limiting, and, when aiming to produce original research, one has to interrogate the questions – even those derived from challenging assumptions (as discussed in the previous section).

## 66  Originality through questions

If one knows how to interrogate even a conventional or common question, original contributions may arise.

Krugman (1993:25) also advises researchers to "question the question". He explained how this helped him to make his own original contributions. He recounts how before 1978 little original research was done on external economies in international trade because researchers limited themselves to the questions suggested by their models, and rarely asking themselves "why ask that particular question?" What Krugman tried to explain was that we may not always be asking the right questions in economics. If we could recognise when our questions are problematic, we would ask new questions that would then lead to original contributions.

To find assumptions imposed by a question is quite difficult in the absence of a systematic approach. What follows are two possible ways to interrogate economic questions: (1) using Van Fraassen's theory of questions; and (2) by relational analysis.

### *Van Fraassen's approach*

Van Fraassen (1980:100–146) expanded on Bromberger's analysis with his theory of why-questions, that is questions that call for explanations. While he applied his theory only to why-questions, Cross (1991) showed it can be applied to any question that calls for an explanation.

Van Fraassen identifies the main elements of a question as being: (1) the topic (what has to be explained); (2) the contrast class (alternative ways to answer, including the topic); (3) the relevance relation (what counts as a relevant answer). This shows that the simple act of asking questions involves making a wide range of assumptions that make up the background knowledge ($K$). At the most basic level, a question assumes that: the topic ($P$) is true; other members of the contrast class ($X$) are false; and there is at least one true and relevant answer ($A$). In other words, given $K$, the following should make sense: $P$ in contrast to $X$ because of $A$. If any of these assumptions are open to question, the question and the background knowledge from which it arises are problematic.

Suppose our core question is: 'Why should the central bank raise the interest rate?' The topic behind asking this core question is then: 'The central bank raises (or can raise) the interest rate.' If this were not true, the question would thus be problematic. It is already at this point where interesting questions can be raised, such as whether the central bank's power to control the interest rate (however defined) is real. It also raises questions about what is meant by 'interest rate'.

Table 4.1 shows some of the contrast classes and relevance relations that may follow from the core question.

The implicit assumptions of a question favour one particular answer over all the others in the same contrast class. A question becomes problematic when current background knowledge ($K$) favours members of the contrast

*Table 4.1* Contrast classes and relevance relations

| | Question | As opposed to: (contrast class) | Answers will focus on: (relevance relation) |
|---|---|---|---|
| 1 | Why should the *central bank* raise the interest rate? | Other institutions | Why the central bank should manage monetary policy instruments |
| 2 | Why should the central bank *raise* the interest rate? | Dropping or not changing the rate | Why the state of the economy requires an upward change of the interest rate |
| 3 | Why should the central bank raise the *interest rate*? | Other policy instruments | Why the interest rate is the preferred policy instrument at the moment |

class other than the one expected. For example, if the intended question is why the central bank should raise – as opposed to drop or not change – the interest rate, and $K$ suggests dropping the rate is what is necessary, then the question becomes problematic.

Selecting one contrast class over the others involves assuming that the other contrast classes are irrelevant, false or constant in some way. As Table 4.1 suggests, there may be a great deal of interesting questions that remain to be asked by simply changing the contrast class. Rethinking a question's contrast class leads to asking a different kind of question. So, looking for contrast classes that have not yet been seriously considered by the discipline can generate new questions that may also generate original contributions.

Depending on the assumptions of the questioner, a single core question may therefore have several contrast classes, with each contrast class containing a relevance relation that describes the kind of answer that is required. The relevance relation is highly contextual, and will change as the context changes, and this adds yet another possibility for finding ideas for original contributions. Changing the context – in terms of time, place or perspective – will change the relevance relation and suggest new questions. Many new and interesting questions may follow if there is reason to believe that the relevance relation of the currently accepted contrast class is incomplete or if another method of investigation might populate the relevance relation differently.

For example, if the intended question is why the central bank, as opposed to other institutions, should raise the interest rate, an economist's relevance relation would rule out an answer like, 'Because it is illegal for other institutions to do so.' Yet, changing the relevance relation so that this answer becomes relevant may well lead to a number of interesting questions that have not yet been adequately researched in the field of economics and law.

This brief summary of Van Fraassen's theory demonstrates how even the simplest of economic questions can be interrogated and potentially problematised. Once problematised, the question can be represented as a logical conflict, which opens up further possibilities. For the sake of brevity, this will not be explained here, but the reader who understands the construction of a logical conflict should have little difficulty comprehending the concept. In the process, a number of original questions or questions that lead to original contributions may emerge.

## *Relational analysis*

Relational analysis involves analysing the relevance relations between the terms in an operational research question. I developed the technique described here as a systematic way for my students to find the assumptions within their research questions. It was intended to help them identify the critical areas they need to cover in a literature review, but I realised later that it is also useful to generate more interesting research questions.

Before this technique can be used, the question needs to be operationalised. This means the question should be defined so well that it meets three conditions: (1) the question itself suggests what information is required to answer the question; (2) the question by itself suggests where and when to get that information; and (3) the question independently suggests by what method to obtain or generate the information. The easiest way to operationalise a question is simply to take each noun, verb, adjective and adverb in the question and define what is meant by each until the question meets these three conditions.

The next step is to break the question up into its key terms. For example, the question: 'How does credit risk management affect bank profitability in South Africa?' may be separated into four terms: (1) credit risk; (2) credit risk management; (3) bank profitability; and (4) South African banks. There is some discretion here and the knowledgeable researcher should know which terms are most relevant.

Since all the terms appear in the same question, the questioner assumes that there is a relevance relation between them. This is then mapped as shown in Figure 4.4.

Each of the pair-wise relevance relations, which are labelled A–F, is then questioned to determine what is assumed about the relationship between each pair of terms in the question. In the case of relation A, one may ask, 'What is the relation between credit risk and its management that is assumed in the question?' One could then emerge with assumptions such as: credit risk is a variable that needs to be managed and credit risk management can reduce credit risk. Each of these assumptions may be questioned and if either of them is not true, the question becomes problematic. Questioning each assumption leads to questions that may not have been considered before.

Some of the assumptions derived from Figure 4.4 appear in Table 4.2. Each one can be converted into a question and some may trigger original research.

Some assumptions – such as C1, D1 and F1– may be so mundane or obvious that they do not need to be questioned. However, if they are indeed questioned, they lead to some very fundamental challenges to the core assumptions

*Originality through questions* 69

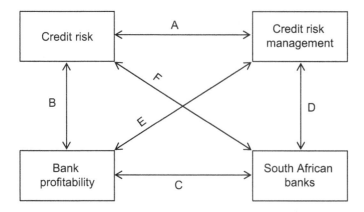

*Figure 4.4* Relevance relations in a question.

*Table 4.2* Assumptions derived from Figure 4.4

| Relation | Assumptions |
|---|---|
| A | A1: Credit risk is a variable that needs to be managed<br>A2: Credit risk management can reduce credit risk |
| B | B1: Credit risk reduces bank profitability |
| C | C1: SA banks need to be profitable |
| D | D1: SA banks employ credit risk management<br>D2: Credit risk management is required in the banking sector |
| E | E1: Credit risk management influences bank profitability<br>E2: Profitable banks need to manage their credit risk |
| F | F1: SA banks experience credit risk |

of the discipline. For example, C1 may lead to the question of whether the private ownership of banks is appropriate. Other assumptions can also be problematised: from E1, a conflict between credit risk management and profitability could arise, which could have the potential to lead to critical confrontation. D2 begs the question of whether credit risk management, as it is currently required, is really appropriate to South Africa or other developing economies. Interesting empirical research can follow from A2, for instance the question: 'When using appropriate indicators and controls, is it really so that credit risk management has been responsible for lower credit risk?'

Again, it becomes clear how apparently uninteresting questions may generate original contributions if the question itself is questioned. It may even be useful to combine this approach with Van Fraassen's theory by analysing the contrast classes of the questions that arise.

## Conclusion

Both the conflict formulation of a problem and Van Fraassen's method of analysing questions expose the assumptional nature of questions and offer ways to identify interesting questions. An interesting question is highly generative in that it suggests new ideas, new methods, and, most importantly, leads to more questions, which, in turn, open up new possibilities for original research.

## References

Akerlof, G.A. 1970. The market for 'lemons': quality uncertainty and the market mechanism. *Quarterly Journal of Economics*, 84(3):488–500.

Alvesson, M. & Sandberg, J. 2011. Generating research questions through problematization. *The Academy of Management Review*, 36(2):247–271.

Belnap, N.D. 1966. Questions, answers, and presuppositions. *The Journal of Philosophy*, 63(20):609–611.

Belnap, N.D. & Steel, T.B. 1976. *The Logic of Questions and Answers*. London: Yale University Press.

Bromberger, S. 1970. Why-questions. In: Brody, B.A. (ed.), *Readings in the Philosophy of Science*, Englewood Cliffs, NJ: Prentice Hall, 66–87.

Bromberger, S. 1992. *On What We Know We Don't Know*. Chicago: University of Chicago Press.

Collingwood, R.G. 1960. *An Essay on Metaphysics*. London: Clarendon Press.

Cross, C. 1991. Explanation and the theory of questions. *Erkenntnis*, 34(2):237–260.

Hayek, F.A. 1945. The use of knowledge in society. *American Economic Review*, 35(4):519–530.

Holton, G. 1979. Constructing a theory: Einstein's model. *American Scholar*, 48:309–340.

Krugman, P. 1993. How I work. *American Economist*, 37(2):25+ [online].

Nickles, T. 1981. What is a problem that we may solve it? *Synthese*, 47:85–118.

Sandberg, J. & Alvesson, M. 2011. Ways of constructing research questions: gap-spotting or problematization? *Organization*, 18(1):23–44.

Van Fraassen, B.C. 1980. *The Scientific Image*. Oxford: Clarendon Press.

Von Krogh, G., Erat, P. & Macus, M. 2000. Exploring the link between dominant logic and company performance. *Creativity and Innovation Management*, 9(2): 82–93.

White, P. 2013. Who's afraid of research questions? The neglect of research questions in the methods literature and a call for question-led methods teaching. *International Journal of Research & Method in Education*, 36(3):213–227.

# 5 Reasoning towards new ideas

The understanding of problems and questions gained from the previous two chapters is useful when generating new ideas. The aim of this chapter is to delve into a rational approach to guide reasoning towards new ideas from problems and questions. It explores the remaining one of the four conceptions of original contributions as identified in Chapter 2: namely, an original idea that answers an unanswered question or solves an unsolved problem. With reference to the creative process in Figure 5.1, it specifically considers how to generate new ideas from the conflict representation of a problem (P–I) and how to do the same from a question (Q–I).

Creative activity, such as idea generation, is believed to be difficult to study and even more difficult to teach, because it is unconstrained. With creative activities, a person might have: an end point (a solution that needs to be reached) with no idea of where to start; or, a starting point (such as a problem), with no idea of what the solution, or end point, might be. In extreme cases, such as in art, one might not know the starting point or the end point. Figure 5.2 illustrates the perceived difference between logical (constrained) and creative activities (unconstrained).

Despite the treatment of idea generation as non-rational, it has been shown that it can be a constrained and reasoned process. This is referred to as 'abduction' or 'abductive reasoning'. Since abduction has a definite logical structure, as will be shown in this chapter, it can turn creative activity into a process of directed reasoning. Similar to logical activity, it can have a clear start point and end point and be guided by constraints.

The key to understanding how creative activity can be constrained and yet generate new ideas, lies in making a finer distinction with regard to constraints, a concept hitherto treated as uniform. Constraints make creative activity more efficient by reducing the possibility space to be searched, thus making creativity more likely. Yet, at the same time, constraints also prevent the perception of possibilities and therefore make creativity less likely. The resolution of this paradox requires that we distinguish between strategic constraints and substance constraints.

Substance constraints are what have thus far been called 'assumptions': they put constraints on the actual content of a mental model defined by a problem, and they differ from problem to problem. In Figure 5.1, substance constraints

## 72  *Reasoning towards new ideas*

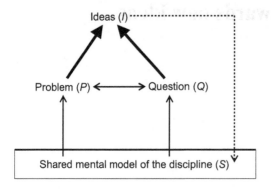

*Figure 5.1* Process of conceiving an original contribution.

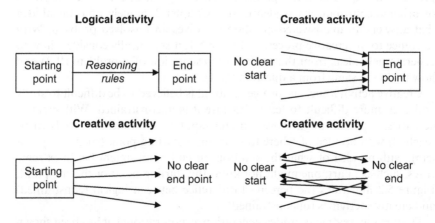

*Figure 5.2* Views of logical versus creative activity.

would dictate what information is relevant in defining the start points and end points. Substance constraints change continuously as knowledge advances.

By contrast, a strategic constraint is a formal concept: such constraints contain no information on the actual content of the start points and end points of reasoning. They are more stable and define the commonly accepted strategies for deriving knowledge from the content of any mental model. For example, strategic constraints may dictate that start points and end points for reasoning must be defined, what form their definitions must take, and the rules for reasoning from one to the other.

New ideas are 'new' because they are not recognised by the prevailing substance constraints (strategic constraints are indifferent by virtue of not dictating any content). Therefore, if new ideas are to be generated, substance constraints need to be open to change so that some of them may be relaxed to allow new ideas. However, without strategic constraints, it would be difficult to know how to modify substance constraints and which new ideas to consider. Strategic constraints make the reasoning more efficient and control the modifications in the substance of start point and end points. Without strategic constraints, very large numbers of implausible ideas may be generated with no efficient way of identifying the best ones except through trial-and-error and relying on serendipity. This is also the essence of abductive reasoning.

Since the ideas can at first be quite difficult to grasp, this chapter will focus on explaining the logical process of abductive reasoning alone using simpler non-economic examples. The application of the process with the aid of case studies from economics will be left to the next chapter.

## Abductive reasoning

Ideas that resolve a problem usually emerge from new assumptions or questions. Deduction does not provide a strategy to generate new assumptions or questions, since it proceeds from given assumptions to conclusions that are predetermined by the given assumptions and rules of deduction. The alternative is abduction, which is more efficient than a random search at finding meaningful new ideas that are not deducible from current assumptions.

Abduction can be described as a rational yet creative process of generating new ideas to explain anomalies or facts that are surprising given existing beliefs. Since it was proposed by the pragmatist philosopher, Charles Peirce, around 1901, abductive reasoning, as a method for generating new ideas, has been substantially improved by researchers in computational philosophy and artificial intelligence (Paavola, 2006). It possesses a clear logical structure and can thus provide a systematic strategy for reasoning towards new ideas.

Aliseda (2003:32) provides one possible structure, which I follow here from (5.1) to (5.3). She explains that it usually starts with a surprising phenomenon ($\varphi$) that cannot be explained by the current background knowledge ($\Theta$):

$$\Theta \nRightarrow \varphi \tag{5.1}$$

An abduced item or new idea ($\alpha$) would explain this surprising phenomenon ($\varphi$), but the new idea has to be meaningful (as explained in Chapter 2), so that $\alpha$ alone should also not be able to explain $\varphi$:

$$\alpha \nRightarrow \varphi \tag{5.2}$$

However, when the new idea ($\alpha$) is used in combination with current knowledge ($\Theta$); it modifies this knowledge and provides an explanation of the surprising phenomenon:

$$\Theta, \alpha \Rightarrow \varphi \tag{5.3}$$

## 74  *Reasoning towards new ideas*

The new idea therefore meets the conditions of meaningful novelty explained in Chapter 2 as it is: relevant, in that it is connected to the existing mental model represented by $\Theta$; and significant since it also modifies $\Theta$.

When looking for original contributions, researchers can either wait for a surprising phenomenon ($\varphi$) to appear, or they can actively trigger the emergence of new ideas ($\alpha$) by deliberately proposing phenomena ($\varphi$) that are either novel or anomalous. A phenomenon is novel if both the phenomenon and its negation are surprising given current knowledge, and it is anomalous if current knowledge can only explain why the surprising phenomenon should *not* occur (Aliseda, 2004:353). Aliseda represents this as follows below:

$$Novelty : \Theta \not\Rightarrow \varphi, \Theta \not\Rightarrow \neg\varphi \tag{5.4}$$

$$Anomaly : \Theta \not\Rightarrow \varphi, \Theta \Rightarrow \neg\varphi \tag{5.5}$$

Waiting for surprising phenomena wastes the creative power of abduction since abduction can be used to generate them. When abduction is used to solve an economic problem, the logical structure of a problem or question can direct researchers in actively proposing the phenomena that may trigger new ideas. As argued in Chapter 2, the provocative approach is preferred to the responsive approach of waiting for opportunities to be creative.

### Abduction, deduction and shared mental models

Abduction, together with deduction, provides the main strategic constraints in idea generation, while the shared mental model contains the substance constraints. This section briefly discusses how they work together.

No new idea is original unless it is meaningful; so abduction cannot operate without deduction. While abductive reasoning guides the process of generating new ideas, it is deductive reasoning that ensures that it is made meaningful by connecting the idea to the shared mental model of the discipline. This is why most new ideas appear logical in hindsight. Even though deductive thinking did not generate the idea, it plays an evaluative role after the idea has been generated. Unless the idea can be deductively connected to the shared mental model of the discipline, it will not be regarded as meaningful by the discipline.

The reverse is also true: deductive rationality cannot exist without abductive reasoning. This is so because, first, before deduction can connect an idea to what is known, that idea has to be created first. A second reason is that all deductive reasoning is based on assumptions. These assumptions themselves exist prior to any reasoning: their source is imagination guided by abductive reasoning.

Abductive reasoning creates an idea that breaks from the shared mental model of the discipline, and deductive reasoning is what integrates the idea back into this mental model. Mental models limit the perception of individuals and whole communities. So, by leaping outside a mental model, one is able to perceive that which has not been perceived before. But no leap of conjecture to a new idea can completely escape the mental model it breaks from. Mental models form the base of the leap and influence the direction and quality of the leap. The mental model's influence returns here by controlling the selection of the ideas that will be allowed to develop (Holton, 1979). Mental models and abductive reasoning are complementary since mental models guide, focus and limit the range of imagination (Von Krogh, Erat & Macus, 2000).

Mental models help to maintain cognitive stability, but an even more important purpose is that they create the conditions required to generate the new knowledge that facilitates abductive reasoning. Since mental models are simplifications and translations of reality, it is common for them to be inconsistent with reality and with other mental models. They are even likely to be internally inconsistent, which, in turn, leads to contradictions (logical conflicts). But, instead of making the knowledge they contain useless (as argued in classical logic), the existence of inconsistencies is, in fact, that which makes a mental model heuristically fruitful as argued by proponents of paraconsistent logic (Da Costa & French, 2002; Nickles, 2002; Berto, 2007). Priest (2002) argues that most empirical scientific activity happens within a situation of paraconsistency, while Bueno (2002) and Van Bendegem (2002) find the same in theoretical fields like mathematics.

Three apparent problems occur as a result of mental models: (1) no researcher's individual mental model is a perfect version of the shared mental model; (2) the shared mental model of the discipline is an imperfect representation of the social reality; and (3) multiple mental models are inconsistent with each other and within themselves. These very problems create the opportunities for original contributions to emerge. If mental models were perfectly externally and internally consistent, there would be no need to create knowledge.

To deal with such inconsistency, agents are forced to examine their mental models and make their assumptions explicit. Implicit assumptions, which Argyris (1980:205) calls "undiscussables", constrain learning and imagination for as long as they are hidden. If someone wants to find an idea for a new contribution, he or she must find the assumptions that reinforce the inconsistency and use these assumptions as a launching pad from which to make leaps of conjecture.

In short then, for a new idea to be meaningful, the researcher needs to *first* understand the shared mental model of the discipline and be able to identify problems within it. If these problems are represented as logical conflicts, it becomes possible to make the inconsistent assumptions, which cause the problems, explicit. By means of abductive reasoning, these assumptions form the raw inputs that can be used to generate new ideas for research contributions. Once these contributions have been created, they have to be logically connected to the shared mental model of the discipline if they are to stand any chance of being accepted by the discipline.

## Mathematical proof and creative reasoning

There are few fields that exhibit so clearly the reasoned, systematic approach toward new ideas as mathematical proof. Mathematical proof consistently leads to new ideas because strategic constraints guide the process of solving proof problems, while it allows substance constraints to be relaxed as long as strategic constraints are met. In economics, mathematics and mathematical proof have been used for their deductive power, but the creative aspect of mathematics is not explored or even recognised in economics.

Creative mathematics may sound like an oxymoron to those familiar only with the Euclidian approach to mathematical proof as taught in school. Mathematical proof is generally regarded as the epitome of objective deductive reasoning from axioms to theorems. It appears to be devoid of creativity since deduction seems to make it unnecessary. Yet, as Byers (2007) reveals, this perception is misleading. Mathematical proof depends as much on creativity, or abduction, as it depends on deduction and can be used as a model for thinking about idea generation.

Mathematical proof involves rigorous and constrained reasoning. As illustrated in Figure 5.2, there is a definite starting point ($S$), a definite end point ($E$) and constant rules of inference for how to logically connect the starting point to the end point ($S \Rightarrow E$). $S$ may be a set of axioms or knowns, and $E$ a theorem or some unknown, while $\Rightarrow$ indicates that $E$ logically follows from $S$. Having to define $S$ and $E$ and follow constant rules of inference supply the strategic constraints since they direct the reasoning process through the infinite space of ideas.

Everything known about a proof can be derived using a few basic assumptions (or axioms) and these form the starting point ($S$). These basic assumptions are therefore sufficient in representing all the knowledge ($K$) relevant to a proof, as long as the proof is unproblematic. If a proof is unproblematic, then $E$ can always be derived starting from $K$, thus $K=S$.

The textbook version of Euclidian geometry offers an illustration of the aforementioned. For a long time, Euclid's proofs appeared unproblematic. All knowledge of Euclidian plane geometry could be derived from five axioms, and these axioms were used as a starting point ($S$) of reasoning. All theorems ($E$) could be consistently derived from the axioms without any need to modify the axioms ($K=S$ so $K \Rightarrow E$). Euclidian proofs are thus unproblematic: at least as conveyed in many introductory textbooks.

A proof becomes problematic when the logical connection between $K$ and some $E$ is not obvious (i.e. $K \not\Rightarrow E$) even though $E$ is desirable or believed to be possible. A knowledge problem now arises as $K$ is questioned because it no longer serves as an adequate $S$ (i.e. $K \neq S$). For example, until the sixteenth century, it was believed that cubic equations were solvable ($E$), but a general solution could not be derived from the existing knowledge ($K$) at the time, so that existing knowledge was problematic ($K \not\Rightarrow E$).

A knowledge problem raises the need to modify $K$ (resulting in $K'$) and to generate a new idea ($\alpha$). Faced with a problematic proof, a creative mathematician often introduces a new element, relation or definition ($\alpha$) that makes $E$ appear to be a logical deduction.

On its own, $\alpha$ should not be so new that it is logically disconnected from the current state of knowledge. It will only be acceptable if it appears logical in conjunction with a modified $K$ (as starting point) to derive $E$ (i.e. $(K' \wedge \alpha) \Rightarrow E$). The new idea should also not be able to exist independently of what is known, so the new idea should not be sufficient to derive $E$ ($\alpha \not\Rightarrow E$). For example, the discovery of complex numbers allowed cubic equations to be solved. Complex numbers were the result of introducing imaginary numbers as the new idea ($\alpha$). Imaginary numbers modified $K$ by first negating the belief that $\sqrt{-1}$ was impossible and then using $\sqrt{-1}$ to extend real numbers. The idea of imaginary numbers alone could not solve cubic equations, but had to be used in conjunction with $K'$ (modified $K$).

The above explanation of mathematical proof may appear strange if mathematical proof is thought of as being the product of logically valid reasoning. Valid logical reasoning is non-ampliative (non-creative) so there is no room for problems or new ideas to emerge. Non-ampliative reasoning means that $E$ stands in a tautological relationship to $S$. Regardless of how often a proof is performed, the same set of axioms should always generate the same theorems. When a proof is presented as a logically valid connection between some $S$ and some $E$, knowledge appears certain, and there is no possibility of surprise, or so it seems.

Yet despite the rigid strategic constraints that govern mathematical proof, it still produces many surprises (Du Sautoy, 2008:114). Surprise often accompanies the best mathematics (Acheson, 2003:9), so there is more room for creativity in mathematical reasoning than one would expect. The process of mathematical proof seems to enable this creativity as many new numbers, functions, methods and theorems have been discovered in pursuit of proofs (Garnier & Taylor, 1996:6). That surprise is expected, and even admired, in mathematics suggests that the substance constraints on $S$ and $E$ are much easier to relax than the strategic constraints.

Strategic constraints are what allow mathematicians the freedom to create ideas that relax substance constraints on $S$ and $E$ without it degenerating into an 'anything goes' approach. A new idea ($\alpha$) usually is, or emerges from the new element, definition or relation introduced in solving a proof problem. After such a proof is completed, one often finds that new knowledge has been created and the problem has been reformulated (Pólya, 1990:46). A proof then is not just the justification or deductive derivation of a new idea; but a *creative* process that generates *new* axioms, concepts and theorems (Lakatos, 1976).

If something new emerges from a proof, ampliative reasoning (of the creative kind) must have occurred; the end result being that the conclusion contains information that was not present in the original premises. When an original contribution is made, it is quite common to find that the premises in the presentation of the proof are different from the original ones.

78  *Reasoning towards new ideas*

Pólya (1990) suggests many ampliative reasoning strategies that are used in pursuing a proof including: introducing (or even imagining) auxiliary elements and auxiliary problems; working backwards; problem reduction; and introducing new elements or relations into a definition. Hamming (1980:86–87) explains that mathematicians often deliberately introduce new concepts or modify axioms in order to prove a theorem.

One needs to distinguish between a proof as a product and as a process to explain why proof requires both non-ampliative (non-creative but deductively valid) and ampliative (creative but deductively invalid) reasoning. Both are essential as the two different kinds of reasoning are complementary.

The communication of a proof as a product should involve only non-ampliative reasoning to ensure that the proof always leads, with certainty, to the same result. As has been suggested above, presentations of proof as a product proceed in an order completely different from that followed in the original process of discovering the proof (Garnier & Taylor, 1996:158). Presenting proofs as the logical derivation of known theorems ($E$) from unchanging axioms ($K=S$) hides the creation of new ideas ($\alpha$), making it appear as if knowledge does not change. Here we encounter the problem highlighted by Peter Medawar (1991) again.

In contrast, the process of proof usually involves ampliative or creative reasoning as new elements are introduced and knowledge modified. Without creative reasoning in the process of discovering a proof, very little new knowledge will be created (Hamming, 1980:87). This is acceptable as long as it generates useful new ideas that can be logically integrated with the current knowledge to solve problems.

## Abduction with the aid of a logical conflict

Like mathematics, economic theory is a product of human creation and the creative proof strategies of mathematics can also be used by economic researchers in search of new ideas. As with proof, creative reasoning starts with a problem to which a solution ($E$) must be found. As has been shown, reframing a problem as a logical conflict makes it easier to uncover the substance constraints on $S$ that prevent $E$ from being reached. Once substance constraints are found, $S$ is appropriately redefined. This modifies the existing state of knowledge and directs creative reasoning towards a new idea that makes $S \Rightarrow E$ logical in hindsight. This process is explained in more detail in the rest of this section.

### *Finding assumptions*

Both the starting point ($S$) and end point ($E$) of creative reasoning depend on the assumptions from which the problem follows. These assumptions can be found by questioning each of the connectives in an economic problem (see Table 5.1).

*Table 5.1* Logical structure of an economic problem

| | |
|---|---|
| Connective I | $Bx(G \to R)$ |
| Connective II | $Bx(R \to A)$ |
| Connective III | $By(G \to R')$ |
| Connective IV | $By(R' \to \neg A)$ |
| Connective V | $Bx(\neg(A \land \neg A))$ |
| | $By(\neg(A \land \neg A))$ |

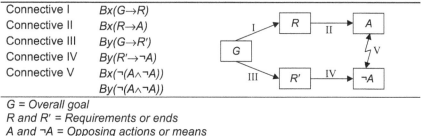

$G$ = Overall goal
$R$ and $R'$ = Requirements or ends
$A$ and $\neg A$ = Opposing actions or means

Table 5.1 shows the already familiar conflict representation of a problem (from Chapter 3) with one addition: it temporarily adds the belief operator $B$ to indicate that not all theorists will agree with both sides of the contradiction. To simplify, $x$ and $y$ are two groups of theorists with competing views and inconsistent beliefs. Group $x$ argues for A and group $y$ argues for ¬A. $Bx$, then stands for '$x$ believes that ...'. The role that belief plays in causing the problem is thereby recognised, acknowledging the possibility that the propositions and their underlying assumptions may be questionable. Since conflicting beliefs could exist within the mind of one theorist, it is possible that $x \cap y \neq \emptyset$.

The assumptions of a problem impose substance constraints on reasoning. If the assumptions are identified, some of them can be relaxed to enable reasoning towards a solution. As indicated earlier, this is what happens when new ideas emerge in the process of mathematical proof. Mathematical proof consistently leads to new ideas because strategic constraints guide the process of solving proof problems.

Strategic constraints dictate that a starting point ($S$) and an end point ($E$) for reasoning must be defined, and that relevant knowledge ($K$) be used to suggest a new idea ($\alpha$) that could make it possible to logically derive $E$. New ideas are generated by relaxing the *substance* constraints on $S$ (or $K$) and $E$, as long as *strategic* constraints are not violated. With strategic constraints in place, creative reasoning is given a clear direction.

The logical structure of a problem, as represented in Table 5.1, and the assumptions that are derived from it, can be used to appropriately redefine $S$ and $E$ and transform a logical conflict into a proof problem. With $S$ and $E$ defined, creative reasoning is guided in the process of trying to prove that $E$ follows from $S$.

## *Deriving the end point* ($E$)

According to Pólya (1990:122), proof problems are easier to solve if one starts with the end in mind. The end point of creative reasoning is a solution to a

## 80  Reasoning towards new ideas

Table 5.2 Three end points of abductive reasoning

| End point | Explanation |
|---|---|
| $R \to \neg A$ | How can R be achieved through $\neg A$? |
| $R' \to A$ | How can R' be achieved through A? |
| $A \wedge \neg A$ | How can both A and $\neg A$ be followed? |

problem. The logical structure of a problem implies that the solution would be an idea that removes the inconsistency. As explained in Chapter 4, this can be done in two ways: by finding an argument that invalidates one side of the contradiction so that it (the side being invalidated) may be ignored; or by finding a synthesis that reconciles the opposing sides. Of the two, synthesis is preferred to invalidation. With invalidation, the information in the opposing side is abandoned, while synthesis aims at maintaining the information contained in both sides.

Three possible ways of creating a synthesis are presented in Table 5.2. It should be noted that the belief operators, though applicable throughout, are dropped for the sake of simplicity. One end point involves directly reconciling the opposing actions, that is, ideas that reconcile $A$ and $\neg A$. The other two end points do so indirectly by letting a specific action ($A$ or $\neg A$) satisfy its opposing requirement. All of them are stated as questions and the end points are the answers to these questions.

The set of three possible end points can thus be stated as:

$$\text{End points}: E = \{R \to \neg A, R' \to A, A \wedge \neg A\} \text{ and } e_i \in E \qquad (5.6)$$

The set of end points that reconcile the contradiction cannot logically be derived from the assumptions that structure the problem, since it is these very assumptions that give rise to the contradiction. In fact, none of the above end points can be derived unless $K$ is somehow modified.

What these end points do is actively trigger the emergence of new ideas by deliberately proposing phenomena (φ) that are either novel or anomalous. Each $e_i$ in (5.6) is surprising since none of them follows logically from $K$.

### *Deriving the starting point* (S)

Because no $e_i$ in (5.6) can be derived given current knowledge about the problem ($K$), it is the case that $K \not\Rightarrow e_i$. $K$ can therefore not be used as the starting point for reasoning to any $e_i$ until $K$ has been suitably modified. $K$ comprises

*Reasoning towards new ideas* 81

all the basic assumptions ($a_1 \ldots a_n$) since everything that is known about the problem can be derived from them:

$$K = \{a_1, a_2, \ldots a_n\} \text{ and } a_i \in K \tag{5.7}$$

To solve this problem, $K$ has to be modified. This can be done by selecting at least one assumption ($a_i$) and negating it ($\neg a_i$).

The choice of $a_i$ is guided by the choice of $e_i$:

- If $R' \rightarrow A$ is chosen as $e_i$, then the most fruitful $a_i$ to negate is most likely to be found in the connectives made redundant by $R' \rightarrow A$, that is connectives I, II and IV. In the case of $R \rightarrow \neg A$, it would probably be connectives II, III and IV.
- If $A \wedge \neg A$ is the end point, then at least one of the assumptions that maintains the belief that $\neg A$ is the logical opposite of $A$ needs to be transformed. Connective V then becomes redundant, and that is where the most fruitful $a_i$ to negate will be found.

To modify $K$, it is necessary to first exclude $a_i$ from $K$:

$$K' = K - a_i \tag{5.8}$$

$K'$ is a diminished version of $K$ so it is insufficient to reach the chosen end point, in other words, $K' \not\Rightarrow e_i$. $K$ needs to be further modified by adding to it the negation of the excluded assumption ($\neg a_i$). The assumption $a_i$ is excluded so that the $\neg a_i$ can be added without causing another contradiction. This modified $K$ creates the need for a new idea and provides a starting point ($S$) for creative reasoning:

$$S = K' \wedge \neg a_i \text{ and } s_i \in S \tag{5.9}$$

If any assumption that underlies one of the connectives is negated, then that connective becomes invalid. When any connective becomes invalid, the logical structure of the problem is disrupted, and it is exactly such a disruption that is needed to solve the problem. As long as the structure of the problem remains intact, the problem will continue to logically lead to a conflict.

A somewhat oversimplified example from astronomy might help to explain the reasons for (5.8) and (5.9). Copernicus realised that certain basic assumptions were the cause of the problem of the movement of the planets. He chose to question one assumption, which was that the sun orbits the earth, and excluded it from $K$. Much of $K$ remained intact: such as the notion that planets orbited in space. The excluded assumption was then replaced by its negation, which was that the sun does not orbit the earth. This modified $K$ brought Copernicus closer to the truth, and provided a

## 82  Reasoning towards new ideas

plausible starting point to reason towards a new idea. It also disrupted the logical structure of the problem sufficiently to create the need for such an idea.

### Abduction that connects S and E

At this point, both *S* and *E* have been defined, and creative reasoning is now clearly directed and focused on finding a way to logically connect *S* and *E*; but something is missing. Taking the example of Copernicus again, it is correct to assume that the sun does not orbit the earth, but this negation reveals what is false, not what is true. A new idea ($\alpha$) must be generated, which, when combined with the modified *K*, logically implies the solution:

$$s_i \wedge \alpha \Rightarrow e_i \qquad (5.10)$$

$\alpha$ is not randomly chosen, but must be related to $\neg a_i$. The new idea reconstitutes *K* by giving meaning to $\neg a_i$ or by transforming $\neg a_i$ into a positive statement. The negation that 'the sun does not orbit the earth' can mean many things. The new idea that 'the earth orbits the sun' *interprets* the negation, so the negation and the new idea are clearly related.

There are several ways to negate $a_i$, so $\alpha$ needs to specify exactly what $\neg a_i$ means. For $\neg a_i$ to be meaningful, the following needs to hold:

$$\alpha \Rightarrow \neg a_i \qquad (5.11)$$

If $\alpha$ is true, then it must follow that $\neg a_i$ would also be true. The new idea introduces new knowledge by transforming $\neg a_i$ into a new assumption. However, there were many ways to negate $a_i$, so the converse does not follow (i.e. $\neg a_i \not\Rightarrow \alpha$).

From (5.6) through to (5.11) a number of interesting points follow. First, it becomes clear that abductive reasoning applied in generating a new idea ($\alpha$) can be described as a directed and systematic process. Second, if $\alpha \Rightarrow \neg a_i$, then it is likely that $\alpha$ can be found by reasoning backward from $\neg a_i$. Abduction through backward reasoning is ampliative and one of the most important strategies used to construct mathematical proofs (Pólya, 1990:227). Third, deriving a new idea from a negation is reminiscent of Lakatos' (1976:93–99) finding that new ideas emerge in mathematical proofs directly as a result of refutations.

### Abduction with the aid of questions

In some cases, it may be difficult to construct a problem as a conflict. For this, I developed a methodology that can guide abductive reasoning from a question alone. It draws on the interplay between convergent and divergent thinking, popularised as brainstorming by Osborn (1953) and Parnes (1992); together with simplified grammatical mapping coupled with Van Fraassen's (1980) theory of questions discussed in the previous chapter.

For a question to lead to new insights, it has to be a problematic question. The discipline should experience the question as a b-predicament (Bromberger, 1970): in other words, it is believed that an answer ($A$) exists, but the available knowledge is inadequate ($K \not\Rightarrow A$). $K$ consists of all the assumptions from which everything that is known about the question can be derived. As stated above (5.7):

$$K = \{a_1, a_2, \ldots a_n\} \text{ and } a_i \in K \tag{5.12}$$

$K$ is inadequate, so it needs to be modified, but, without a conflict representation, it is more difficult to know where the problem lies, and so hard to assess where $K$ should be modified. The assumptions constrain the possible answer, so the key to finding a new insight lies in negating some assumptions while affirming others (keeping them unchanged). As also seen in the previous section, the act of negating assumptions is critical to creativity, for, without it, one would just have the production of the same ideas.

The problem with negation is that there are almost an infinite number of ways to negate something. An analogy might help here: when asked to recount an event, a reasonable person will find that there is usually only one way to tell the truth, but many ways to distort the truth and even more ways to make up complete lies. It is not surprising then that deception has been recognised as a creative act (Hirstein, 2005).

The creative potential of negation needs to be controlled in some way or else it becomes simply overwhelming: having thousands of ideas is not useful unless one knows how to make sense of them and ultimately settle on one. This explosive creative potential can be anchored by affirmation, specifically the affirmation of the assumptions that constrain the possible answers to the question.

Accepting assumptions constrains the possibility space and so makes the creative process more manageable. Assumptions also help to maintain the connection between the familiar and the new, because people are familiar with (if not always aware of) them, and, if new ideas connect to the familiar, they are easier to accept. If a new idea negates every single constraint, people would find it impossible to understand and would describe it as ahead of its time or absurd (Davis, 1971). But, affirming too many assumptions, or affirming the wrong ones, is what causes a problem in the first place, so negation is required to counteract this rigidity. On its own, negation would be useless and affirmation stifling. Negation opens up thinking, while affirmation stabilises it, and thus both are needed. Alex Osborn invented 'brainstorming' to exploit this interplay between the negation of assumptions, which is called 'divergent thinking'; and affirmation of assumptions, which is called 'convergent thinking'.

84  *Reasoning towards new ideas*

As already argued, a systematic creative process needs to have a defined beginning and a defined end. These points need not stay the same throughout the process, but they provide a channel within which exploration can take place. This exploration is provoked by the interplay of negation and affirmation. With this technique, the starting point in creative exploration is a problematic question, the mid-point is a conjunction of an affirmation and a negation, and the end point is a solution that satisfies the conjunction and solves the problem.

The problematic question should have: a noun-phrase (*NP*), containing the subject; a noun-phrase, containing the object; and, a verb-phrase (*VP*), describing the interaction between subject and object. All of them are affirmed and negated. The affirmations and negations are then made to interact in two intersecting channels that resemble a cross, which is shown as Figure 5.3, in its most abstract form. It will be illustrated below by means of a rather simple and non-abstract example that is not from economics before applying it to economics in the next chapter.

An example that is simple but shows how to use this approach is the Mann Gulch disaster. It was made famous in management studies by Weick (1993), and tells the true story of situation where one person escaped death through unconventional thinking. It was found that the escape illustrated an overturning of at least one assumption (Klein, 2013).

In 1949, fifteen smoke-jumpers parachuted into Mann Gulch to bring a forest fire under control. Soon after that, twelve of them were dead after trying to escape the fire that chased them up a steep hill. Only two of them managed to run to safety. The third survivor was the leader, Wagner Dodge, who found an ingenious way to escape and motioned his team to join him. He set a fire ahead of them, which created a safety zone that the pursuing fire could not reach. But everyone in his team thought he was being irrational, and instead

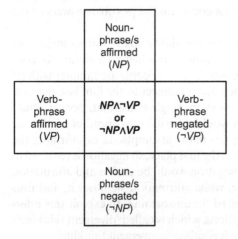

*Figure 5.3* The cross of creative questioning.

*Reasoning towards new ideas* 85

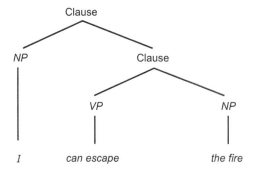

*Figure 5.4* Simplified grammatical mapping.

continued trying to outrun the forest fire that was gaining ground on them. As the rest of his team continued running, Wagner Dodge dived into the ashes of the fire he set and survived as the pursuing fire passed around him.

Wagner Dodge's situation could be expressed as a problematic question: 'How do I survive the fire?' Using Van Fraassen's theory of questions, the topic and various contrast classes will be determined.

The topic of the question – the most basic assumption without which the question would not even arise – is: 'There is a way I can survive the fire.' The subject *NP* is Wagner Dodge ('I'), the object *NP* is 'the fire' and the *VP* is 'survive'. 'There is a way' is not considered as it is implied by the interrogative 'how' and so the simpler topic is: 'I can survive the fire.'

A simple grammatical mapping (Figure 5.4) reveals the structure of the topic. By simple, I mean that we only pay attention to verb and noun phrases and ignore other parts such as prepositions, adjectives, adverbs and coordinators.

The two *NPs* are then placed in the vertical bar of the cross. The affirmation (labelled *NP* in Figure 5.3) is the relation between the two *NPs* as expressed or assumed by the topic, and the negation is simply the opposite of the affirmation (labelled $\neg NP$ in Figure 5.3). As shown in Figure 5.5, *NP* in this case is 'I stay in the fire' and $\neg NP$ is not-('I stay in the fire') or 'I don't stay in the fire'.

The *VP* is placed in the horizontal bar of the cross. The affirmation (labelled *VP* in Figure 5.3) captures the interaction between the subject and object, as expressed or assumed by the topic, and the negation is simply the opposite of the affirmation (labelled $\neg VP$ in Figure 5.3). The verb is 'survive' and this needs elaboration: to survive the fire, the kind of interaction expected is to 'put out the fire'. As shown in Figure 5.5, *VP*, in this case, is 'put out the fire' and $\neg VP$ is not-('put out the fire') or 'don't put out the fire'.

Now the midpoint of the cross can be generated by drawing an affirmation from one bar of the cross and a negation from the other bar of the cross.

86  *Reasoning towards new ideas*

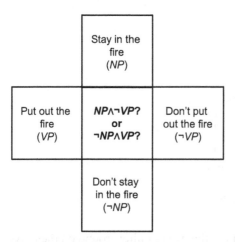

*Figure 5.5* A question of survival.

It makes us search for possibilities that would satisfy one of the following conjunctions true: $NP \wedge \neg VP$ ('stay in the fire' and 'don't put out the fire') or $\neg NP \wedge VP$ ('don't stay in the fire' and 'put out the fire'). These two conjunctions are placed in the middle of the cross. Rephrased as questions, they become: 'How do I stay in the fire and not put out the fire?' or 'How do I not stay in the fire and put out the fire?'

The set of two possible end points can thus be stated as:

$$End\ points: E = \{\neg NP \wedge VP, NP \wedge \neg VP\} \text{ and } e_i \in E \tag{5.13}$$

Neither of these end points follows from $K$. The negations disrupt $K$ and force a search for new assumptions.

To use the creative power of negation, one takes each negation and asks: 'What are the possible forms this negation may take?' What one does when thinking about negation possibilities is populate a contrast class. It was already shown in the previous chapter that contrast classes can be quite generative. For example, to find possible $\neg NP$s, one might ask: 'Stay in the fire as opposed to…?' Table 5.3 shows two possible ways not to stay in the fire and two possible ways not to put out the fire. These negations generate the creative possibilities.

For the creative potential of negation to be utilised, it needs to be constrained by an affirmation. This is done by conjoining the negations on one bar of the cross to an affirmation on the other bar of the cross, as given in Table 5.4.

From Table 5.4, it is clear how negation expands the possibilities, while affirmation limits them. Conjoining the negations in every column with their

Table 5.3 Possible negations

|  | ¬NP: don't stay in the fire | ¬VP: don't put out the fire |
|---|---|---|
| **Negation** | $\neg NP_1$: run away from the fire<br>$\neg NP_2$: run into the fire | $\neg VP_1$: do nothing<br>$\neg VP_2$: make a fire |

Table 5.4 Possible conjunctions

|  | Conjunctions 1–2 (¬NP∧VP) | Conjunctions 3–4 (NP∧¬VP) |
|---|---|---|
| **Negation** | $\neg NP_1$: run away from the fire<br>$\neg NP_2$: run into the fire | $\neg VP_1$: do nothing<br>$\neg VP_2$: make a fire |
| **Conjoin with…** | VP: put out the fire | NP: stay in the fire |

relevant affirmation gives us four possible conjunctions to explore ($\neg NP_1 \wedge VP$, $\neg NP_2 \wedge VP$, $\neg VP_1 \wedge NP$, $\neg VP_2 \wedge NP$). The set of possible end points therefore expands from (5.13) to:

$$End\ points: E = \{\neg NP_1 \wedge VP, \neg NP_2 \wedge VP, \neg VP_1 \wedge NP, \neg VP_2 \wedge NP\}$$
$$and\ e_i \in E \qquad (5.14)$$

We do not conjoin NP and VP because it is this conjunction that describes the status quo. While we could conjoin ¬NP and ¬VP, it is less useful, because, without affirmation to anchor the creative process, all the negations will, in all likelihood, give rise to too many possibilities. This will invariably occur as the number of negation possibilities rises.

The end point of the exploration can be reached by finding an idea ($\alpha$) that makes one of the conjunctions possible and answers the question. To find such an idea, the question's assumptions need to surface. To bring assumptions to the surface, take each one of the elements in each contrast class and ask: 'Why not …?' Take $VP_2$ for example: 'Why not make a fire?' One assumption ($\alpha$) here is that fire will kill you.

Since the new idea will involve disrupting K, it needs to challenge at least one assumption. Take each assumption and ask: 'Is this necessarily true?' For example, one asks: 'If I make fire will it necessarily kill me?' to which one could answer: 'Only if the fire catches up with me, not if it runs ahead of me.' Therein lay the idea that saved Dodge's life: he realised that if he made a fire that would run ahead of him ($\alpha$), then it would not kill him ($\neg a$). In more general terms:

$$\alpha \Rightarrow \neg a_i \qquad (5.15)$$

## 88  Reasoning towards new ideas

If $\alpha$ is true, then it must follow that $\neg a_i$ is also true. The new idea introduces new knowledge by transforming $\neg a_i$ into a new assumption. This modifies the existing knowledge so that:

$$K' = K - a_i \tag{5.16}$$

$K'$ is a modified version of $K$, which, if combined with the new idea, is able to reach one of the end points and answer the question:

$$(K - a_i) \wedge \alpha \Rightarrow e_i \tag{5.17}$$

The conjunction that appeared to have generated the crucial insight was $\neg VP \wedge NP$, and, specifically, $\neg VP_2 \wedge NP$. The question that directs thinking here is whether it is possible to stay in the fire by making fire. The answer was that, by making another fire, Dodge created a safe zone, which the pursuing fire could not reach. Finding a way to satisfy the conjunction ultimately led to his not staying in the dangerous fire nor putting out the fire before it could reach him.

As this section showed, abductive reasoning from a question is similar to abduction from a problem. In the next chapter, this systematic approach will be applied to the question that led to Coase's theorem.

## Conclusion

The approach described in this chapter is a simpler version of the approach that Thaler (1997) uses to transform neural networks into 'creativity machines'. Thaler's approach is to disturb a well-functioning, neural network by deliberately, randomly destroying some of the relations within this network. In the process of trying to restore completeness, the network often generates novelties.

In this chapter, the destruction of relations took place when a particular assumption, within a problem or question, was challenged. Negation fulfils this destructive function but it also opens up creative possibilities. By giving substance to negations, new ideas can emerge that reconstitute the knowledge relations.

While this chapter developed a method to guide creative reasoning in economics, such reasoning is not mechanical. The method directs reasoning, making idea generation more efficient, but much of the process still requires some intuition (when selecting $E$ or $a_i$). However, the method guides reasoning and relies less on serendipity or intuition than a trial-and-error or wait-and-see approach. It is therefore easier to replicate and more likely to suggest fruitful new ideas.

Furthermore, as new ideas eliminate inconsistencies in one place, they also cause disruptions elsewhere, creating a never-ending need for more ideas. As the work of Cherniak (1984) and paraconsistent logic suggest, we are unlikely to ever reach a point where human knowledge is perfectly consistent, and that is exactly what will continue to create the need for original research.

The next chapter takes everything from Chapters 3–5 and applies it to three case studies: Amartya Sen's development of the capability approach; the seminal work of Kydland and Prescott in monetary policy; and Ronald Coase's famous theorem.

## References

Acheson, D. 2003. 1089 and all that: the element of surprise in mathematics. *European Mathematical Society Newsletter*, 49:9–11.

Aliseda, A. 2003. Mathematical reasoning vs. abductive reasoning: a structural approach. *Synthese*, 134:25–44.

Aliseda, A. 2004. Logics in scientific discovery. *Foundations of Science*, 9:339–363.

Argyris, C. 1980. Making the undiscussable and its undiscussability discussable. *Public Administration Review*, May/June: 205–213.

Berto, F. 2007. *How to Sell a Contradiction: The Logic and Metaphysics of Inconsistency*. London: College Publications.

Bromberger, S. 1970. Why-questions. In: Brody, B.A. (ed.), *Readings in the Philosophy of Science*, Englewood Cliffs, NJ: Prentice Hall, 66–87.

Bueno, O. 2002. Mathematical change and inconsistency. In: Meheus, J. (ed.), *Inconsistency in Science*, Dordrecht: Kluwer, 59–79.

Byers, W. 2007. *How Mathematicians Think*. Princeton, NJ: Princeton University Press.

Cherniak, C. 1984. Computational complexity and the universal acceptance of logic. *Journal of Philosophy*, 81(12):739–758.

Da Costa, N. & French, S. 2002. Inconsistency in science: a partial perspective. In: Meheus, J. (ed.), *Inconsistency in Science*, Dordrecht: Kluwer, 105–118.

Davis, M.S. 1971. That's interesting! *Philosophy of the Social Sciences*, 1:309–344.

Du Sautoy, M. 2008. *Finding Moonshine: A Mathematician's Journey Through Symmetry*. London: Fourth Estate.

Garnier, R. & Taylor, J. 1996. *100% Mathematical Proof*. Chichester: John Wiley & Sons.

Hamming, R.W. 1980. The unreasonable effectiveness of mathematics. *The American Mathematical Monthly*, 87(2):81–90.

Hirstein, W. 2005. *Brain Fiction*. Cambridge, MA: MIT Press.

Klein, G. 2013. *Seeing What Others Don't*. New York: Public Affairs.

Lakatos, I. 1976. *Proofs and Refutations: The Logic of Mathematical Discovery*. Cambridge: Cambridge University Press.

Medawar, P.B. 1991. 'Is the scientific paper a fraud?' In: Medawar P.B., *The Threat and the Glory: Reflections on Science and Scientists*. Oxford: Oxford University Press, 228–233 (based on a BBC interview published in *The Listener*, 12 September 1963).

Nickles, T. 2002. From Copernicus to Ptolemy: inconsistency and method. In: Meheus, J. (ed.), *Inconsistency in Science*, Dordrecht: Kluwer, 1–33.

Osborn, A.F. 1953. *Applied Imagination*. New York: Scribner.

Paavola, S. 2006. On the origin of ideas: an abductivist approach to discovery. *Philosophical Studies from the University of Helsinki*, 15. University of Helsinki.

Parnes, S.J. (ed.) 1992. *Sourcebook for Creative Problem Solving*. Buffalo, NY: Creative Education Foundation Press.

Pólya, G. 1990. *How To Solve It: A New Aspect of Mathematical Method*, 2nd edition. London: Penguin.

Priest, G. 2002. Inconsistency and the empirical sciences. In: Meheus, J. (ed.), *Inconsistency in Science*, Dordrecht: Kluwer, 119–128.

Thaler, S.L. 1997. A quantitative model of seminal cognition: the creativity machine paradigm (US Patent 5,659,666). Online paper available from www.imagination-engines.com, accessed 24 April 2007.

Van Bendegem, J.P. 2002. Inconsistencies in the history of mathematics. In: Meheus, J. (ed.), *Inconsistency in Science*, Dordrecht: Kluwer, 43–57.

Van Fraassen, B.C. 1980. *The Scientific Image*. Oxford: Clarendon Press.

Weick, K.E. 1993. The collapse of sensemaking in organizations: the Mann Gulch disaster. *Administrative Science Quarterly*, 38:628–652.

# 6 Rational reconstruction from case studies

The aim of this chapter is to show how the systematic approach developed in Chapters 3–5 can be applied, by means of rational reconstruction, to understanding the conceivable creative processes in the work of economic researchers who produced seminal work. Rational reconstruction is best described by Darden (2002:S355) as "compiled hindsight" in which one tries to establish whether the patterns observable in the published work – and, where available, the written notes – of scientists can be explained by a particular hypothesis of the scientific process. If the hypothesis is plausible, it should be possible to reconstruct the scientific process that culminated in the published research. Well-known philosophers of sciences, like Thomas Kuhn (1970) and Imre Lakatos (1976), used rational construction to great effect in astronomy, physics and mathematics to test their hypotheses of the scientific process.

In this study, a rational reconstruction of three seminal contributions in economics will be done: Sen's (1999) development of the capability approach; the developments in central banking that followed Kydland and Prescott (1977); and Ronald Coase's (1960) work, which became known as 'Coase's Theorem'. It will be used to test whether the techniques developed thus far plausibly describe creative processes that could have led to their contributions.

Kydland and Prescott (1977), though not as radically new as the other two cases, were chosen for their unusual frankness about their creative process in their paper, which makes a rational reconstruction easier. This frankness is quite useful since economists do not leave 'lab notes', like natural scientists, which aid rational reconstruction. In the absence of such notes, rational reconstruction becomes very difficult because, as Medawar (1991) first argued, the structure of the published scientific paper hides the actual creative process that led to the ideas in the paper.

The capability approach was selected because it initiated a truly original way of thinking about a wide range of economic issues. Reconstructing the conceivable creative approach was quite challenging since Sen does not explain how the idea came to him, so this case presented a good test of the descriptive power of the systematic approach developed thus far.

92  *Rational reconstruction from case studies*

The first two case studies start with conflict representation, so I included Coase (1960) to determine if it is possible to rationally reconstruct his original contribution from his question alone by using the cross of creative questioning technique from Chapter 4. Coase's articles are among the most cited in economics.

## Amartya Sen and the capability approach

Amartya Sen received the Bank of Sweden Prize in Economic Sciences in Memory of Alfred Nobel in 1998 for his contributions in the field of social choice. From these contributions, he developed the capability approach, which has become a serious alternative to conventional theories in terms of thinking about economic development, poverty and equity.

First, let us look at a brief summary of Sen's capability approach. Sen (2010:279–282) argues that, when making policy decisions, income and utility offer a poor informational basis because they are limited indicators of the real end of development. The real end is to expand the real freedoms people have to be and do what they value, also called 'beings' and 'doings', and this forms the capabilities of a person or a group. Resources (which are means such as income) are converted into capabilities (ends) and, through choice, a person selects from these capabilities. Such capabilities are then realised in the form of achievements (indicators, such as utility or happiness).

Focusing on income elides the fact that not all people are able to convert inputs like income into capability at the same rate, due to factors such as location or disability; and focusing on achievements obscures the degree of freedom people had in the realisation of those achievements. Overall, the capability approach offers a much richer informational basis for informed policy decisions.

### *Formulating problems*

Sen's research started in the field of social welfare, where he made a breakthrough by reformulating a critical problem. Prior to Sen's work, research in the study of social choice was driven by a number of critical problems, including the problem of Arrow's Impossibility Theorem. This problem hindered further theoretical progress, to the point where discussions of welfare economics resembled "obituary notices" (Baumol, 1965:2).

Sen (1970) did much to create a new sense of possibility, partly because he reformulated the problem as the so-called liberal paradox. With the problem reformulated, research in the field of social welfare accelerated since the new problem suggested original directions for research (Arrow, 1999).

The liberal paradox (Sen, 1970, 1983a) raised the issue of individual freedom in the pursuit of public interest. This paradox was a precursor to the development of the capability approach, and could conceivably have been the source of the ideas that led to the capability approach. This case study does not prove that the capability approach was directly developed from the liberal paradox, only that Sen's way of formulating the impossibility problem made the generation of such new ideas more likely. The clear and simple formulation of the problem as a paradox or logical conflict, made Sen's statement of the problem more powerful than Arrow's statement in the stimulation of new inquiries and ideas.

The liberal paradox suggests that it is impossible to produce a Pareto-optimal society and respect the freedom of individuals. The paradox may arise whenever society needs to make a decision on an issue of public interest where individual rights must be respected. The result of such a decision may either be that: (1) individual rights are respected, but with society as a whole ending at a sub-optimal welfare level; or (2) society decides on a welfare-maximising state, but at the cost of individuals' rights. The paradox reveals that planned economic development will only succeed either if individual rights that are in conflict with development goals are disregarded, or if only those rights that are consistent with development goals are protected.

Unlike Arrow's statement of the social choice problem, the liberal paradox is formulated so that it brings previously implicit assumptions about the meaning of optimality, rights and freedom to the surface (Sen, 2010:311–314). Many of these assumptions and new meanings, in turn, became the foundations of the capability approach and its various insights into freedom, economic development, diversity, poverty, famine prevention, inequality, welfare measurement and the role of the government.

To see how Sen's statement of the problem is different from Arrow's and how it made assumptions explicit, it will help to consider the possible logical structure of the problem presented by the liberal paradox. In Table 6.1, the problem is structured as a set of logical statements.

$G$ represents the common goal of opposing sides, $R$ and $R'$ are the different requirements the opposing sides argue should be met to achieve the goal, while $A$ and $\neg A$ are the contradictory actions that should be taken to meet the

*Table 6.1* Representing the problem of the liberal paradox

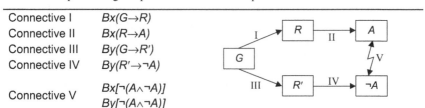

| Connective I | $Bx(G \rightarrow R)$ |
| Connective II | $Bx(R \rightarrow A)$ |
| Connective III | $By(G \rightarrow R')$ |
| Connective IV | $By(R' \rightarrow \neg A)$ |
| Connective V | $Bx[\neg(A \land \neg A)]$ |
|  | $By[\neg(A \land \neg A)]$ |

$G$ = 'Improve well-being of individuals in society'
$R$ = 'Achieve a socially efficient state'
$A$ = 'Restrict choice sets'
$R'$ = 'Agents pursue their own ends without interference'
$\neg A$ = 'Protect individual rights'

requirements. The belief operator, $B$, is added here again as a reminder that humans (groups $x$ and $y$) are putting the propositions forward and that not all of them will agree with both sides of the contradiction.

In Table 6.1, on the one hand, group $x$ believes that if the overall well-being of individuals in society is to be improved ($G$), a socially efficient state needs to be achieved ($R$). Achieving social efficiency would imply that individual choices must be restricted ($A$). On the other hand, group $y$ believes that to improve the well-being of individuals in society ($G$), it is necessary to let agents pursue their own ends without interference ($R'$). To do this, society needs to protect individual rights ($\neg A$). A case for both restricting individual choice sets and protecting individual rights can be argued, but both $x$ and $y$ believe that one contradicts the other given an unrestricted domain. Both views are internally consistent, but inconsistent with each other.

A number of assumptions make the connectives (I, II, III, IV and V) in Table 6.1 plausible to $x$ and $y$, and so give structure to the problem. The assumptions are surfaced by asking what needs to be true to make each of the connectives (as expressed in Table 6.1) plausible. Table 6.2 identifies only some of the assumptions that support each of the connectives.

A logical conflict is generated because the assumptions underlying connectives I and II are inconsistent with the assumptions underlying connectives III and IV in the areas of the nature of rights, role diversity and the need for control. The opposing sides of the contradiction seem logical in isolation given their assumptions, that is, they are self-consistent; but, when juxtaposed, the two sides appear contradictory, that is they are mutually incompatible.

As argued in Chapter 3, the trade-off and conflict representations are convertible into each other. The liberal paradox can be framed as a trade-off between social efficiency and negative freedom. The conflict representation is

Table 6.2 Assumptions that structure the liberal paradox

| | |
|---|---|
| Connective I | Well-being is judged by its utility consequences; differences between individuals are of no consequence; information on individuals and their relations is not required; a Pareto-optimal state can be determined; and utility measures are not biased. |
| Connective II | Existence of authority outside the market mechanism; rights are bestowed; some choices have socially bad consequences; and individuals may make choices inconsistent with social goals. |
| Connective III | Perfect knowledge of the overall system does not exist; freedom to pursue own ends leads to achievement of those ends; market mechanism sufficiently coordinates individual actions; and freedom from interference creates certainty. |
| Connective IV | Rights are inalienable; individual differences may cause conflict; need to create a personal sphere of influence for each individual; and preferences and choices are not equivalent. |
| Connective V | Rights protect negative freedom. |

preferable since it reveals the logical black box of the problem, whereas the trade-off representation conceals it.

*Developing questions*

Once the problem is formulated in a fruitful way, the common practice in research is to search for an inadequacy in the existing research that we would like to address and so derive the research question. However, formulating a problem as a conflict emerging from inconsistent assumptions makes it more likely to find a research question that is more interesting than one that simply spots a gap in the research.

As explained in Chapter 5, there are two approaches to developing interesting questions from a logical conflict: first, questioning to invalidate one or more of the assumptions on either side of a conflict; and, second, questioning to provoke the search for a new assumption that can synthesise the opposing sides. Both of these strategies are evident in this case study.

The first approach of invalidation literally questions each of the assumptions. If the assumption may be negated under certain conditions, then the connective that relies on that assumption is invalidated; and, by implication, it then also negates the apparent self-consistent logic that holds the opposing side together.

It appears that much of Sen's work was directed by the assumptions that were elicited as a result of the liberal paradox: especially assumptions relating to utility measurement, differences between agents and the nature of choices and preferences (mostly in connectives I, II and III). Conceivably, he might have selected the assumption that information on individuals and their relations is not required, and asked: 'Is it really so that information, on individuals and their relations, is not required?' From this might have followed ideas such as Sen's (1983b) conception of absolute and relative poverty.

As a result of Sen's steady questioning, he helped to resolve the logical conflict by invalidating a number of assumptions of the utilitarian approach to social welfare, thus making its existence unwarranted. With the competing view invalidated, only the consistent assumptions of connectives III and IV remained, and the problem seemed to have been solved (at least for a while).

A solution that removes a logical conflict by invalidating the assumptions of one side, leads to a change in beliefs through a reduction of the number of valid beliefs. It is, however, not necessarily the best approach to developing interesting questions due to the loss of information that accompanies it.

The second approach aims to design questions that will reconcile both sides, thereby collapsing the contradiction. Again, these questions are easy to find if the problem is formulated appropriately as shown in Table 6.3. These questions probably led to the most interesting research flowing from Sen's problem formulation.

The conflict representation of the problem clearly shows three groups of questions that may lead to interesting contributions. Each question prompts

*Table 6.3* Questions designed to synthesise

| Question | Explanation in terms of the liberal paradox |
|---|---|
| $R \to \neg A$ | How can a socially efficient state be reached by protecting individual rights (new connective)? |
| $R' \to A$ | How can agents pursue their own ends without interference by restricting choice sets (new connective)? |
| $A \wedge \neg A$ | How can choice sets be restricted while protecting individual rights (collapse connective V)? |

the researcher to search for ways or conditions under which the insights of opposing sides can be synthesised. This is achieved if a requirement of one side can be achieved by the action of the opposing side, or if opposing sides' actions are not necessarily contradictory.

Flowing from Sen's fruitful problem formulation were questions which led to new ideas regarding the nature of freedom, trading of rights and measurements of development. The ideas were derived from the questions emerging from both the invalidation and synthesising approaches.

Sen also employed the synthesising approach by using the $R \to \neg A$ and $A \wedge \neg A$ strategies. Sen (1983a) employed the $A \wedge \neg A$ strategy when he suggested the trading of rights and mutual respect for others' rights – which he preferred – as two possible, but imperfect, ways of directly reconciling the contradiction.

The capability approach could conceivably have emerged from employing the $R \to \neg A$ strategy. A socially efficient state can be achieved through the protection of rights if a right is not simply defined as being able to make choices without interference (negative freedom), but as the capability to control choices (positive freedom). As Sen (1999:3) summarised the essence of the capability approach: "Development can be seen as a process of expanding the real freedom that people enjoy ... freedom is what development advances."

To achieve a socially efficient state by equally protecting the rights of all individuals can also only be achieved if the ideas of rights and efficiency are reconceptualised in a different space where they are not in conflict: Sen used the same strategy in his analysis of absolute and relative poverty.

Efficiency implies a process of converting inputs into outputs, and rights can lead to efficiency if they somehow improve the conversion process. To avoid conflict, the conversion process needs to occur in a space where rights and efficiency are complementary. Through this process, one is forced to look for new meanings and assumptions that make the $R \to \neg A$ expression plausible, and may conceivably have led Sen, and other researchers, to discover: the importance of the conversion rate; 'beings' and 'doings' as the ends of development; and the role of positive freedom in enhancing the capability of individuals to create and control the choices that they value.

The research was, however, not only limited to the work of Sen. He set the scene for a burst of original research. His reformulation of Arrow's Impossibility Theorem as the 'liberal paradox' was surprising to most theorists, and generated a vast amount of literature on the topic, including the famous book by Nozick (1974). Nozick (1974) himself employed the $R' \rightarrow A$ strategy. He argued that the liberal paradox could be resolved by allowing individual rights to restrict the social choice set: that is, only those choices that remain after individual choices have been made should form the final choice set for social choice. Though Nozick's solution was criticised, like most other proposed solutions, his book was one of the many works that created fresh insights into the process of trying to address the liberal paradox.

The impact of the capability approach was felt further in its ability to generate insights that solved other contradictions in the field of social welfare and economic development: for example, the anomaly of famines occurring in the midst of sufficient food supply or the conflict between relative and absolute poverty. The capability approach offered an elegant synthesis of absolute and relative poverty and opened up new insights into poverty measurement and reduction. Sen (1983b:161) neatly summarised it, saying: "Poverty is an absolute notion in the space of capabilities but very often it will take a relative form in the space of commodities." The approach also led to innovations in the measurement of welfare (HDI, GDI, GEM and HPI), as well as revealing insights into fields seemingly unrelated to economics, such as special needs education (Terzi, 2005). Sen (2010) recently extended the capability approach as an alternative to Rawls' Theory of Justice.

The capability approach created its own conflicts which, if approached in the way explained in this book, could direct research into areas that may lead to further breakthroughs. One obvious conflict is the issue of whether the list of capabilities should be predetermined or negotiated depending on the context. As suggested in this book, the most appropriate approach would not be to take sides, but rather to use the inconsistencies within this contradiction in conjunction with abductive reasoning to generate new ideas.

*Conclusion*

A large amount of original research in development economics was generated from a fruitful reformulation of a problem, namely the liberal paradox, which made it easy to identify assumptions, ask interesting questions and find new ideas. Recall that an idea is defined as an 'organising principle' (Byers, 2007), so a good idea is not necessarily new, but one that allows one to organise and connect other ideas in insightful ways. For example, few would argue that Sen's ideas are entirely new, but he was credited with organising some of the knowledge of social welfare issues in such a way that they developed a new way to think about poverty and development. Flowing from Sen's fruitful problem formulation were questions which led to new ideas regarding the nature of freedom, trading of rights and measurements of development. The ideas were derived from the questions emerging from both the invalidation and reconciliation approaches.

## Kydland and Prescott and the ideas of central banking

In the previous section, the emphasis was on problem formulation and question generation. In this section, which draws mainly on Wentzel (2007), the case study goes one step further and reconstructs the abductive reasoning that followed from Kydland and Prescott's (1977) reformulation of the rules-discretion problem in monetary policy as the time-inconsistency problem.

In brief, the time-inconsistency problem occurs when a central bank uses its policy flexibility to achieve short-term employment gains through inflation surprises. For example, a central bank may announce a commitment to low money supply growth, but once agents, who believe the central bank, adjust their nominal wage demands accordingly, it is optimal for the central bank to break its commitment and grow the money supply faster. This inconsistent action over time is done when the central bank tries to exploit a short-run Phillips curve trade-off to push unemployment below its natural rate since high money supply growth pushes up prices, thus reducing the real wage. However, if agents hold rational expectations, this apparently optimal discretionary policy will instead introduce a systematic inflation-bias without reducing unemployment. The conclusion is that consistency in the form of a policy rule would give a central bank the necessary credibility to influence expectations.

### *Formulating problems*

Before Kydland and Prescott (1977) progress in monetary policy theory was impeded by several conflicts, including the problem of whether rules or discretion was the best foundation for monetary policy. Competing views, with inconsistent starting assumptions ($S$), were responsible for the rules versus discretion debate in monetary policy theory. This debate originated in the nineteenth century with the currency and banking schools. The currency school favoured rules, and its ideas were further developed by many theorists, including proponents of rational expectations theory. The banking school, on the other hand, favoured discretion and its views later found support in optimal control theory.

Kydland and Prescott (1977:474) pointed out that assumptions about the role of agents' expectations in shaping outcomes was logically "inconsistent with the assumptions of optimal control theory", thus maintaining the problem. The theoretical analysis of the competing views was inconclusive (Argy,

1988), thereby hindering further advances, until Kydland and Prescott (1977) reformulated the problem as a time-inconsistency paradox and changed the nature of the debate (Schaling, 1995). With the new formulation, progress in monetary policy accelerated as the new problem suggested original directions for theoretical and empirical research.

When there are logical inconsistencies in a set of propositions, a logical conflict will follow. As expected then, it is possible to represent the time-inconsistency problem as such (see Table 6.4).

On the one hand, $x$ believes that if the social objective function is to be maximised ($G$), then, given the current state of the economy ($R$), the best policies must be selected. Selecting such policies would imply the continuous use of discretionary policy ($A$). This side of the paradox assumes that economic planning influences only states of nature. On the other hand, $y$ believes that if the social objective function is to be maximised ($G$), then the best decision must be selected given how agents form expectations and make choices ($R'$). To do this, policymakers need to follow a policy rule ($\neg A$). This side of the paradox assumes that economic planning influences the states of agents. A case for both discretionary policy and a policy rule can be argued given the common goal, but both $x$ and $y$ believe that discretionary policy is in contradiction to a policy rule.

Kydland and Prescott reformulated the problem of monetary policy in such a way that it changed the nature of the rules versus discretion debate. Kydland and Prescott (1977) noted that Friedman's (1948) framing of the monetary policy problem did not succeed in settling the debate, since he accepted a crucial assumption of the competing view: that economic planning is a 'game against nature'. Kydland and Prescott reframed their problem as a paradox (as reflected in Table 6.4), integrating the theoretical developments at the time in the fields of game theory and rational expectations. They showed that the paradox arises because economic planning is, in fact, not only a "game against nature" but also a "game against rational economic agents" (Kydland and Prescott, 1977:473).

Table 6.4 Logical structure of the time-inconsistency problem

| | |
|---|---|
| Connective I | $Bx(G \rightarrow R)$ |
| Connective II | $Bx(R \rightarrow A)$ |
| Connective III | $By(G \rightarrow R')$ |
| Connective IV | $By(R' \rightarrow \neg A)$ |
| Connective V | $Bx(\neg(A \wedge \neg A))$ |
| | $By(\neg(A \wedge \neg A))$ |

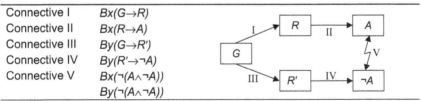

$G$ = 'Maximise social objective function'
$R$ = 'Policy decisions should be based on the current state of economy'
$A$ = 'Use discretionary policy'
$R'$ = 'Policy decisions should take into account the decision-making by agents'
$\neg A$ = 'Follow a policy rule'

Propositions $R$, $R'$, $A$ and $\neg A$ are logical implications that are plausible only if certain assumptions are made. The assumptions are exposed by asking under what conditions the logical implication connectives (I–IV) will explain why one proposition follows from another or under what conditions $A$ and $\neg A$ would be in conflict. Following such a process, it is possible to identify the key assumptions that act as substance constraints and maintain the problem.

Kydland and Prescott's (1977) work was useful, partly because of the clarity with which they made the assumptions of both sides explicit, showed how those assumptions structured the problem, and argued from those assumptions. They surfaced at least twenty assumptions underlying four of the five connectives of the problem and Table 6.5 lists some of the assumptions they identified under each of the connectives. Later, reviews of the rules-discretion debate – such as those of Clarida, Gali and Gertler (1999) – identified further assumptions.

Assumptions can only lead to a contradiction if at least one of them is inconsistent with one other assumption. Some inconsistencies can be seen in Table 6.5. Connective I contains assumptions that mainly support the argument that states of nature affect the social objective function, while connective III contains assumptions that support the conclusion that the states of agents affect the social objective function. The assumptions underlying connective II mainly relate to notions that policy actions are necessary and sufficient to optimise economic performance. Underlying connective IV, are assumptions relating to the shaping role of agents' expectations. The opposing horns of the destructive dilemma seem plausible in isolation given their assumptions, but, when juxtaposed, the two horns present a paradox. This

*Table 6.5* Assumptions structuring the time-inconsistency problem

| | |
|---|---|
| Connective I | There is an "agreed-upon, fixed social objective function" (p. 473); Only the current state of the system determines current outcomes and changes in those outcomes (p. 474); Expectations depend on the past (p. 478). |
| Connective II | Current outcomes and changes in the system depend only upon policy decisions (p. 474); Future policy has no effect on agents' current decisions (p. 476); Agents have given and stable decision rules (p. 481). |
| Connective III | The agreed-upon, fixed social objective function is a function of policies and agents' decisions (p. 475); "Changes in the social objective function ... have an immediate impact upon agents' expectations ... and ... current decisions" (p. 474). |
| Connective IV | Expectations of future policy can influence the current decisions of agents (p. 474); "Expectations are rational ..." (p. 478); The policy rule affects "the optimal decision rules of the economic agents" (p. 474). |

*Source*: Derived from Kydland and Prescott (1977).

logical contradiction exists because the assumptions of connectives I and II are inconsistent with those of connectives III and IV.

By making the assumptions explicit, Kydland and Prescott accelerated the generation of new ideas in the field. Framing the time-inconsistency problem as a logical conflict facilitated the discovery of the assumptions that maintain the problem. Rogoff (1985), Lohmann (1992) and Walsh (1995) reasoned to new ideas in monetary policy as a result of utilising and modifying the assumptions, or substance constraints, visible in Kydland and Prescott's formulation of the problem, and these ideas formed the foundation of what became known as the monetary policy 'consensus' (Goodfriend, 2007:1). The next section shows how abductive reasoning conceivably led to one of these new ideas: that of Rogoff (1985) and his solution to the problem that involved a new role for the central bank.

### Abductive reasoning applied to central bank independence

The assumptions of a problem impose substance constraints on reasoning. If the assumptions can be identified, they can be relaxed to enable reasoning to a solution. Strategic constraints dictate that a starting point ($S$) and an end point ($E$) for reasoning must be defined, and that relevant knowledge ($K$) be used to suggest a new idea ($\alpha$) that could make it possible to logically derive $E$. New ideas are generated as substance constraints on $S$ (or $K$), and $E$ are relaxed as long as strategic constraints are met.

The logical structure of a problem as represented in Table 6.4, and the assumptions that are derived from it, can be used to appropriately redefine $S$ and $E$. With $S$ and $E$ defined, creative reasoning is guided in the process of trying to prove that $E$ follows from $S$.

### Deriving the end point

The end point of creative reasoning is a solution to a problem. The logical structure of a problem implies that the solution would be an idea which removes the inconsistency, either through invalidation or synthesis. Of the two, synthesis is preferred to invalidation. With invalidation, the opposing side's information is abandoned, while synthesis aims at maintaining the information contained in both.

Three possible ways of creating a synthesis of the time-inconsistency problem are presented in Table 6.6. However, the belief operators, though applicable throughout, are dropped for the sake of simplicity. One end point involves directly reconciling the opposing actions (i.e. ideas that reconcile $A$ and $\neg A$). The other two end points do so indirectly by letting a specific action ($A$ or $\neg A$) satisfy its opposing requirement.

The set of three possible end points can thus be stated as:

$$End\ points: E = \{R \rightarrow \neg A, R' \rightarrow A, A \wedge \neg A\}\ and\ e_i \in E \tag{6.1}$$

102  *Rational reconstruction from case studies*

*Table 6.6* End points derived from the time-inconsistency problem

| End point | Explanation in terms of time-inconsistency paradox |
|---|---|
| $R \rightarrow \neg A$ | How can policy decisions be based on the current state of the economy by following a policy rule? |
| $R' \rightarrow A$ | How can policy decisions take the decision-making process of agents into account by using discretionary policy? |
| $A \wedge \neg A$ | How can both discretionary policy and a policy rule be followed? |

The set of end points that reconcile the contradiction cannot logically be derived from the assumptions that structure the problem – some of which appear in Table 6.5 – since it is these very assumptions that give rise to the logical conflict. In fact, none of the above end points can be derived unless *K* is somehow modified.

Rogoff (1985:1169–1170) expressed his desire to solve the problem by finding a synthesis. He stated that rigid rule-based policy is "not generally optimal" while agreeing with those who argue for rules that central bank discretion is ineffective since "private agents anticipate its incentives to inflate". For him, the challenge was to find an idea that would be consistent with the way agents make decisions, while allowing the flexibility of discretion, implying that Rogoff argued towards $R' \rightarrow A$ as the end point ($e_i$).

Many other new ideas that followed Rogoff's work, such as the 'nonlinear' policy rule of Lohmann (1992) and Walsh's (1995) suggestion of optimal contracts for central banks, also had the end point of $R' \rightarrow A$ in mind. Haubrich and Ritter's (2000) interesting contribution was the result of arguing towards $A \wedge \neg A$. They demonstrated that, given certain assumptions, $A$ and $\neg A$ need not be in conflict if they are separated in time. Blinder (1997:12) suggested that $A \wedge \neg A$ is actually used in practice and that it is the assumptions about the meaning of discretion that cause $A$ and $\neg A$ to appear in conflict.

*Deriving the starting point*

Because no $e_i$ in (6.1) could be derived given the current knowledge about the problem (*K*) at the time of Kydland and Prescott, it would have been the case that $K \neq e_i$. *K* could therefore not be used as the starting point for reasoning to $e_i$ until *K* had been suitably modified. Given that economic knowledge is axiomatic, *K* comprises all the basic assumptions ($a_1...a_n$):

$$K = \{a_1, a_2, ... a_n\} \text{ and } a_i \in K \tag{6.2}$$

### Rational reconstruction from case studies 103

The assumptions in Table 6.5 are some of the assumptions that constituted the existing knowledge inherent in the time-inconsistency problem in 1977. To solve this problem, $K$ had to be modified. This had to be done by selecting at least one assumption ($a_i$) and negating it ($\neg a_i$).

The choice of $a_i$ is guided by the choice of $e_i$. If, like Rogoff, $R' \rightarrow A$ is chosen as $e_i$, then the most fruitful $a_i$ to negate is most likely to be found in the connectives made redundant by $R' \rightarrow A$, that is, connectives I, II and IV.

Rogoff's (1985) candidate for negation was Kydland and Prescott's (1977:473) assumption that there is an "agreed-upon, fixed social objective function". To modify $K$, it is necessary to first exclude this assumption from $K$:

$$K' = K - a_i \tag{6.3}$$

$K'$ is a diminished version of $K$, so it is insufficient to reach the chosen end point, in other words, $K' \not\Rightarrow e_i$. $K$ needs to be further modified by adding to it the negation of the excluded assumption ($\neg a_i$) – in this case, the assumption is that: "There is not an agreed-upon, fixed social objective function." The assumption $a_i$ is excluded so that the $\neg a_i$ can be added without causing another contradiction.

This modified $K$ creates the need for a new idea and provides a starting point ($S$) for creative reasoning:

$$S = K' \wedge \neg a_i \text{ and } s_i \in S \tag{6.4}$$

If any assumption that underlies one of the connectives is negated, then that connective becomes implausible. When any connective becomes implausible, the logical structure of the problem is disrupted, and it is exactly such a disruption that is needed to solve the problem. Rogoff's (1985) negation caused a great degree of logical disruption in the problem structure since it is an assumption not only found in connective I, as expected, but also in connective III (refer to Table 6.5). The result was that $G$ became logically severed from both $R \rightarrow A$ and $R' \rightarrow \neg A$.

*Generating an idea by making the connection*

At this point, both $S$ and $E$ have been defined. $S$ is $K'$ combined with the assumption that there is *not* an agreed-upon objective function, and $E$ is that discretionary policy can still be effective in the presence of rational expectations ($R' \rightarrow A$). Creative reasoning is now clearly directed and focused on finding a way to logically connect $S$ and $E$. A new idea ($\alpha$) must be generated, which, when combined with the modified $K$, logically implies the solution:

$$s_i \wedge \alpha \Rightarrow e_i \tag{6.5}$$

## 104  Rational reconstruction from case studies

$\alpha$ is not randomly chosen: it must be related to $\neg a_i$. The new idea reconstitutes $K$ by giving a specific meaning to $\neg a_i$ or by transforming $\neg a_i$ into a positive statement. There are several ways to negate $a_i$, so $\alpha$ needs to specify exactly what $\neg a_i$ means. For $\neg a_i$ to be meaningful, the following needs to hold:

$$\alpha \Rightarrow \neg a_i \qquad (6.6)$$

Rogoff's $\alpha$ was a central banker who "does not share the social objective function [$\neg a_i$], but instead places 'too large' a weight on inflation-rate stabilization relative to employment stabilization" (Rogoff, 1985:1169). So the idea of the conservative central banker emerged. This idea is logically derived from the negated assumption, because the central banker's conservatism means that there is no longer an agreed-upon objective function.

By negating the assumption that there is an agreed-upon, fixed social objective function, Rogoff would have had to explore the meaning of the negation. In doing so, it seems as though Rogoff explored the meaning of the term 'agreed-upon'. If there is disagreement on the social objective function, then there must be at least two groups with different views. Conceivably, the disagreement could be between private agents and the central bank.

The next step would be to explore the nature of this disagreement. As Rogoff indicated, the disagreement would be about the relative weights to be given to inflation and employment stabilisation in the objective function.

The last step would be to specify what the view of each group should be in order to be able to argue his end point, $R' \rightarrow A$. With this in mind, Rogoff might have reasoned that, if one appoints a central banker who puts a larger weight on inflation stabilisation, then $R' \rightarrow A$ becomes logically plausible. The idea of the conservative central banker was thus birthed, and so, according to Blinder (1997), one of the most useful ideas in the theory and practice of monetary policy emerged.

Exploring the meaning of the negation led Rogoff to introduce a distinction between central bankers and private agents. According to Rescher (2001:119), the introduction of distinctions is the prime instrument for removing inconsistency while maintaining the maximum amount of useful information contained in opposing views. It suggests that many useful new ideas in economics may emerge from creating or collapsing categories.

### *Generating questions*

Besides the synthetic questions asked in Table 6.6, there are other ways of generating questions. First, each of the assumptions in Table 6.5 can be converted into a question that can take one of the following forms:

- Is [the assumption] necessarily so? Do we know this?
- Is [the assumption] true under all conditions? When is it not true?
- Would anything make [the assumption] invalid?

*Rational reconstruction from case studies* 105

These questions can guide empirical research that may lead to invalidation of one of the assumptions, and thereby solve the problem. As a result, one of these questions by themselves may turn out to be an idea for an original contribution.

The second way of generating questions is derived from Van Fraassen (1980) as explained in Chapter 3. Suppose the core question is stated as: 'Why should policy rules be preferred?' The topic ($P$) of this core question is: 'Policy rules are preferable.' If this were not true, the question would be problematic. It is at this point already where interesting questions can be raised, such as whether the benefits of following rules outweigh the costs under all conditions. It also raises questions about what is meant by rule-based policy.

Further interesting questions emerge from a deeper analysis of the question. Table 6.7 shows some of the contrast classes ($X$) and relevance relations ($R$) that may follow from it depending on how the question is interpreted.

The questions that followed from Kydland and Prescott's work tended to assume the second contrast class. Selecting one contrast class over the others involves assuming that the other contrast classes are irrelevant, false or unchanged in some way. As Table 6.7 suggests, there may be many more interesting questions that remain to be asked by a simple change in the contrast class.

Rethinking the contrast class leads to asking a different kind of question. Simply looking for contrast classes that have not yet been seriously considered by the discipline can generate questions that generate original contributions. The first contrast class raises questions that touch on issues like free banking, while the third contrast class may take one into issues of the role of a central bank in a democracy.

Each contrast class contains a relevance relation that describes the kind of answer that is required. Many new and interesting questions may follow if there is reason to believe that the relevance relation of the currently accepted contrast class is incomplete or if another method of investigation might

*Table 6.7* Contrast classes and relevance relations

| Core question | As opposed to ... (contrast class) | Answers will focus on ... (relevance relation) |
| --- | --- | --- |
| Why should *policy* rules be preferred? | no central bank intervention at all | the merits of central bank involvement in an economy |
| Why should policy *rules* be preferred? | discretion or constrained discretion | the comparisons between alternatives to policy rules |
| Why should policy rules be *preferred*? | indifference or active dislike | the identity and power of the agent expressing the preference and why it matters |

populate the relevance relation differently. For example, there may be more alternatives than just the two that appear in the second contrast class (rules and discretion).

## *Conclusion*

There are many researchers, such as Blinder (1997) and Forder (2004), who are critical of the time-inconsistency problem. Even so, this formulation of the monetary policy problem was highly generative and led to Rogoff's idea of central banking. This was a concept even a critic, and seasoned central banker, such as Blinder (1997:13), regarded as one of the most useful contributions to the theory of monetary policy. The process of abductive reasoning neatly describes the conceivable creative process from which it resulted.

## Ronald Coase and his Theorem

Ronald Coase won the Nobel Prize in Economics in 1991, for two articles. His 'Nature of the Firm' article started with a problem. His other article became the most cited article in economics, and started with a question. It is this second article that I will analyse here, using two of the question-based techniques from Chapter 4.

Coase's Theorem originated with a problematic question about discouraging externalities. Coase (1960:2) explained that when it comes to externalities where A imposes harm on B, the common question is "How should we restrain A?" However, he questioned this question and believed it to be the wrong question, because externalities often had a reciprocal nature. For him the correct question was "Should A be allowed to harm B or should B be allowed to harm A?" Because of the reciprocal nature of externalities, his view was therefore the problem needed to be reframed as how to minimise overall harm by avoiding the "more serious harm".

I will apply to two techniques of creative questioning to the problematic question that Coase identified. However, given that Coase responded to Pigouvian tax in this article, I will first restate in a way that is more common: 'How should government restrain firms from harming (imposing negative externalities) on others?'

## *Van Fraassen analysis*

The question was, in Coase's (1960:43) view, problematic since he believed that there was a "failure to develop a theory adequate to handle the problem of harmful effects". In other words, he believed that an answer ($A$) to the question could not be derived from the existing knowledge ($K$) so that $K \not\Rightarrow A$.

The topic ($P$) of the core question of: 'How should government restrain agents from harming others?' is: 'Government should restrain agents from

*Table 6.8* Contrast classes and relevance relations in Coase's question

| Core question | As opposed to ... (contrast class) | Answers will focus on ... (relevance relation) |
| --- | --- | --- |
| How should *government* restrain agents from harming others? | other social arrangements | the merits of government intervention |
| How should government *restrain* agents from harming others? | alternatives to restraint measures | reasons why restraint is preferred to doing nothing or allowance of actions |
| How should government restrain agents from *harming* others? | benefitting others | explaining why a focus on negative externalities is more important |

harming others.' Coase (1960:2) argues that this is not the case since it leads to results that are "not necessarily, or even usually, desirable" because it assumes a one-way causation of harm, when, in fact, negative externalities are jointly caused. With the topic of the question refuted, the question becomes problematic.

Another reason the question is problematic is that $K$ should lead to an answer $(A)$ that favours $P$ over other members of the contrast class $(X)$. In other words, given $K$, $P$ in contrast to $X$ because of $A$. Table 6.8 shows some of the possible contrast classes from which Coase could have selected.

Coase's (1960:44) contrast class is the "various social arrangements" for dealing with negative externalities, such as firms or markets. With this contrast class in mind, the question can be restated as: 'How should government restrain agents from harming others (as opposed to other approaches to managing the harm imposed)?' Coase argues that there is no answer that can be derived from economic theory that favours government intervention over markets and firms. In fact, he argues that, in the absence of transaction costs, the market mechanism will be superior, and that, even with transaction costs, it does not follow that government intervention will be superior. Since $K$ favours other members of the contrast class, the question is problematic.

## *Cross of creative questioning*

Given the axiomatic nature of theory, a small number of assumptions $(a)$ make up $K$, and, one or more of them cause the question to be problematic. These assumptions constrain the answers, so the key to finding a new insight lies in negating some assumptions while affirming others, keeping them unchanged. At the same time, accepting assumptions constrains the possibility space and thereby anchors the creative potential of negation in the existing knowledge.

## 108  *Rational reconstruction from case studies*

The cross technique of creative questioning from Chapter 5 can be used to guide the interplay of negation and affirmation and direct the process by defining: the starting point, which is a problematic question; the mid-point, a conjunction of an affirmation and a negation; and the end point, which is a solution that satisfies the conjunction and solves the problem.

The topic of the problematic question should have: a noun-phrase (*NP*), containing the subject; another noun-phrase, containing the object; and a verb-phrase (*VP*), describing the interaction between subject and object. This topic is a compound sentence, which complicates matters because it allows for more than one way to set up the cross diagram. There is an inner sentence, which is: 'Agents harm others', with a subject *NP* ('agents'), an object *NP* ('others') and a *VP* ('harm'). Around this is an outer sentence where the subject *NP* is 'government', the *VP* is 'restrain' and the object *NP* is: 'Agents harm(ing) others'. Figure 6.1 shows the simple grammatical mapping that helps to clarify the analysis.

In this case, the two *NP*s that are of the inner sentence are placed in the vertical bar of the cross. The affirmation, labelled *NP* in Figure 6.2, is the relation between these two *NP*s, and the negation is simply the opposite of the affirmation (labelled ¬*NP* in Figure 6.2). As shown in Figure 6.2, the *NP*, in this case, is 'Agents harm others' and the ¬*NP* is: 'Agents don't harm others.'

The *VP* is placed in the horizontal bar of the cross. The affirmation, labelled *VP* in Figure 6.2, captures the interaction between the subject ('government') and object ('the inner sentence') and the negation is simply the opposite of the affirmation, labelled ¬*VP* in Figure 6.2. The verb is 'restrain' and this needs elaboration: the kind of restraint implied is government restraint of agents.

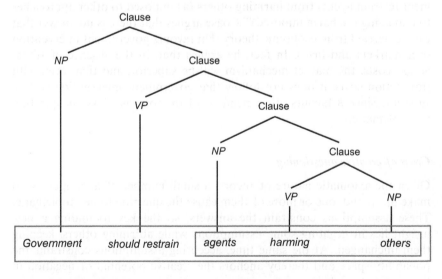

*Figure 6.1* Simplified grammatical mapping of Coase's question.

Rational reconstruction from case studies 109

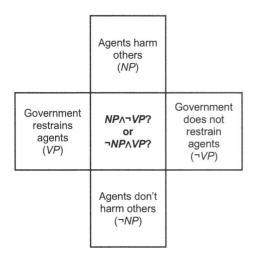

*Figure 6.2* Cross of questioning based on Coase (1960).

As shown in Figure 6.2, the *VP*, in this case, is: 'Government restrains agents'; and ¬*VP* is: 'Government does not restrain agents.'

Now the midpoint of the cross can be generated by conjoining an affirmation from one bar of the cross and a negation from the other bar of the cross. It makes us search for answers to the question: 'How could *NP*∧¬*VP* or ¬*NP*∧*VP* be true?' The set of two possible end points for abductive reasoning can thus be stated as:

$$End\ points: E = \{\neg NP \wedge VP, NP \wedge \neg VP\} \text{ and } e_i \in E \tag{6.7}$$

Neither of these end points follows from *K*, which means that $K \not\Rightarrow e_i$. All these end points are deliberate provocations of anomalies aimed at disrupting *K* and force a search for new assumptions.

To use the creative power of negation, one should take each negation and ask: 'What are the possible forms this negation may take (and so populate the contrast classes)?' Table 6.9 shows three possible ways for agents not to harm others and five possible ways in which government does not restrain others. These negations generate the creative possibilities.

For the creative potential of negation to be utilised, it needs to be constrained by an affirmation. This is done by conjoining the negations on one bar of the cross to an affirmation on the other bar of the cross, as given in Table 6.10.

Conjoining the negations in every column with their relevant affirmation gives us eight possible conjunctions to explore. While we could conjoin ¬*NP* and ¬*VP*, it is less useful, because, without affirmation to anchor the creative process, all the negations together will very likely give rise to too many

110  *Rational reconstruction from case studies*

*Table 6.9* Possible negations

| | ¬NP: Agents don't harm others | ¬VP: Government does not restrain agents |
|---|---|---|
| Negation | ¬NP₁: Agents do nothing to others<br>¬NP₂: Agents benefit others<br>¬NP₃: Others harm themselves | ¬VP₁: Government does nothing<br>¬VP₂: Government allows agents<br>¬VP₃: Government encourages agents<br>¬VP₄: Others restrain agents<br>¬VP₅: Others don't restrain agents (i.e. neither government nor others do any restraining) |

*Table 6.10* Possible conjunctions

| | *Conjunctions 1–3 (¬NP∧VP)* | *Conjunctions 4–8 (NP∧¬VP)* |
|---|---|---|
| Negation | ¬NP₁: Agents do nothing to others<br>¬NP₂: Agents benefit others<br>¬NP₃: Others harm themselves | ¬VP₁: Government does nothing<br>¬VP₂: Government allows agents<br>¬VP₃: Government encourages agents<br>¬VP₄: Others restrain agents<br>¬VP₅: Others don't restrain agents |
| **Conjoin with** | VP: Government restrains agents | NP: Agents harm others |

possibilities (an additional fifteen in this case). The set of possible end points therefore expands from (6.7) to:

*End points:* $E = \{\neg NP_1 \wedge VP, \neg NP_2 \wedge VP, \neg NP_3 \wedge VP, \neg VP_1 \wedge NP,$
$\neg VP_2 \wedge NP, \neg VP_3 \wedge NP, \neg VP_4 \wedge NP, \neg VP_5 \wedge NP\}$
and $e_i \in E$ (6.8)

Since the core question is problematic, one would expect one or more of these end points to be true. If abductive reasoning is directed at them, it is more likely to lead to a new idea that solves the problem inherent in the core question.

The end point of the exploration can be reached by finding an idea (α) that makes one of the conjunctions possible. To find such an idea, the question's assumptions need to be surfaced and negated, because, as previously explained, a new idea follows from the negation:

$$\alpha \Rightarrow \neg a_i \qquad (6.9)$$

To surface assumptions, take each one of the conjunctions and ask: 'Why not?' All five of the ¬VP∧NP conjunctions make assumptions about the absence of alternative social arrangements and about impediments, such as

Table 6.11 Eliciting assumptions

| Why not? | Because (assumptions) ... |
|---|---|
| $\neg VP_1 \wedge NP$: Why should government not *do nothing as agents harm others*? | it is the government's responsibility to address market failure. Government has the most effective instruments to manage such harm (tax, regulation, prohibition). |
| $\neg VP_2 \wedge NP$: Why should government not *allow agents to harm others*? | if harm is allowed, it will continue. Only coercive measures are effective when trying to minimise harm. |
| $\neg VP_3 \wedge NP$: Why should government not *encourage agents to harm others*? | if encouraged, harm will increase since agents benefit from the harm they impose. Perpetrators of harm do not consider the effect they have on others. |
| $\neg VP_4 \wedge NP$: Why shouldn't *others restrain the agents harming them*? | there is no benefit for agents to make arrangements among themselves. There are barriers to such arrangements (e.g. the prior allocation of rights). |
| $\neg VP_5 \wedge NP$: Why shouldn't *alternatives (beside others and government) be used to restrain agents*? | there are no alternatives. Alternatives (firms, non-governmental sectors) are unable, unwilling or ineffective in managing harm for which they are not responsible. |

transaction costs, to such arrangements. Taking each one in turn, some key assumptions emerge in Table 6.11.

Some of the assumptions overlap between conjunctions: for example, all five have a fixed conception of harm being one-directional. This would also have been evident from questioning $\neg NP_3 \wedge VP$ by asking: 'Why should government not restrain others (victims) from harming themselves?' One assumption is the harming happens only in one direction, which is an assumption which Coase made explicit. The reasoning would be something like this: 'Government intervention is not necessary because victims do not harm themselves, but have it imposed on them by other agents.' Coase also argued that this assumption is invalid since harm is reciprocal.

Since the new idea will involve disrupting $K$, it needs to challenge at least one assumption. Take each assumption and ask, 'Is it necessarily true that ...?' or 'Under what conditions may it be false that ...?' Given Coase's preference for free markets, he would have favoured questioning the assumptions that emerged from the $\neg VP \wedge NP$ conjunctions in Table 6.11. For example, with $\neg VP_4 \wedge NP$, he challenged the assumption that the prior allocation of rights can be a barrier to mutual arrangements.

A new idea ($\alpha$) emerges that makes the negation of the assumption true. Coase showed that, under conditions of no transaction costs, the trading of rights will lead to an optimal outcome regardless of the prior distribution of rights. The idea of zero transaction costs transforms $\neg a_i$ into a new assumption. This modifies the existing knowledge by removing the negated assumption and adding the new idea. $K$ is modified and combined with a new idea that is able to reach one of the end points and answer the question:

$$(K - a_i) \wedge \alpha \Rightarrow e_i \tag{6.10}$$

The conjunction $\neg VP_4 \wedge NP$ seems particularly fruitful as it offers another way to reason to Coase's Theorem. With this conjunction, the question that directs thinking is: 'Why would others not restrain those who harm them?' The answer is that victims can actually benefit from not restraining the perpetrators if frictionless market functioning enables them to trade the right to harm. Finding a way to satisfy the conjunction ultimately leads to a socially efficient state where there is mutual benefit due to bargaining between agents.

But Coase regarded this situation of no transaction costs as a special case and found $\neg VP_5 \wedge NP$ more interesting to explore. He showed that, with positive transaction costs, alternative institutions, like firms, are likely to be formed and that they are expected to be more socially efficient than government, on condition that government allows them to operate freely.

Posner (1993) credited Coase's questioning of the question as instrumental in starting the 'law and economics' movement within economics and also contributing to the emergence of 'new institutional economics'. Coase's article (1960) was one of the most generative in the discipline, sparking much productive criticism (Baumol, 1972; Usher, 1998; Baffi, 2007). In addition, it precipitated further refinements and explorations into the other conjunctions that he neglected (Calabresi & Melamed, 1972; Shavell, 1983; Cooter, 1984).

## Conclusion

The approaches to the systematic generation of new ideas reconstructed in this chapter are just that: reconstructions in hindsight. I do not propose that this is actually how the new questions were raised and new ideas generated, nor do I suggest that these contributions would have been inevitable had my approaches been used. What this chapter shows is that that the approaches developed in Chapters 3–5 fit the conceivable creative process and can therefore be used to guide the development of an instructional programme.

The approaches developed and illustrated thus far are but a few of many, and are especially appropriate for subject areas in economics, where trade-offs and disagreements between opposing views are abundant. Methodological and empirical research, aimed at gap-spotting, would require a different approach, though it may benefit from these approaches.

There is no guarantee of originality, but the approaches outlined in this chapter make it more likely. It guides researchers away from gap-spotting towards finding the non-obvious areas for future research. Unfortunately, it does not make the work of finding an original contribution that much easier, but it does help to direct such efforts. This is preferable to the trial-and-error or random search approach of talking to others and reading as much as possible.

This is not to say that the researcher following this approach will not have to talk to others and to read extensively. It may very well lead to more reading and more talking, though this may take on a different quality than before. In fact, the first step of formulating the problem often requires an intense immersion in the literature. It also encourages searching for literature outside the expected areas, thereby leading to a greater engagement with different ideas. This engagement is critical if writing is to take on the argumentative quality that is so often missing from novice researchers' work.

## References

Argy, V. 1988. A post-war history of the rules vs discretion debate. *Banca Nazionale del Lavoro Quarterly Review*, 165:147–177.

Arrow, K.J. 1999. Amartya K. Sen's contributions to the study of welfare. *Scandinavian Journal of Economics*, 101(2):163–172.

Baffi, E. 2007. The problem of internalisation of social costs and the ideas of Ronald Coase. MPRA Paper No. 7277.

Baumol, W. 1965. *Welfare Economics and the Theory of the State*. Cambridge, MA: Harvard University Press.

Baumol, W.J. 1972. On taxation and the control of externalities. *American Economic Review*, 62(3):307–322.

Blinder, A.S. 1997. What central bankers could learn from academics. *Journal of Economic Perspectives*, 11(2):3–19.

Byers, W. 2007. *How Mathematicians Think*. Princeton, NJ: Princeton University Press.

Calabresi, G. & Melamed, D. 1972. Property rules, liability rules, and inalienability: one view of the cathedral. *Harvard Law Review*, 85(6):1089–1128.

Clarida, R., Gali, J. & Gertler, M. 1999. The science of monetary policy: a New-Keynesian perspective. *Journal of Economic Literature*, 37(4):1661–1707.

Coase, R.H. 1960. The problem of social cost. *Journal of Law and Economics*, 3:1–44.

Cooter, R. 1984. Prices and sanctions. *Columbia Law Review*, 1523–1560.

Darden, L. 2002. Strategies for discovering mechanisms: schema instantion, modular subassembly and forward/backward chaining. *Philosophy of Science*, 69(3):S354–S365.

Forder, J. 2004. The theory of credibility: confusions, limitations and dangers. In: Arestis, P. & Sawyer, M.C. (eds), *Neo-Liberal Economic Policy: Critical Essays*, Cheltenham: Edward Elgar, 4–37.

Friedman, M. 1948. A monetary and fiscal framework for economic stability. *The American Economic Review*, 38(3):245–264.

Goodfriend, M. 2007. How the world achieved consensus on monetary policy. NBER Working Paper No. 13580.

Haubrich, J.G. & Ritter, J.A. 2000. Dynamic commitment and incomplete rules. *Journal of Money, Credit and Banking*, 32(4):766–784.

Kuhn, T.S. 1970. The function of dogma in scientific research. In: Brody, B.A. (ed.), *Readings in the Philosophy of Science*, Englewood Cliffs, NJ: Prentice Hall, 356–373.

Kydland, F.E. & Prescott, E.C. 1977. Rules rather than discretion: the inconsistency of optimal plans. *Journal of Political Economy*, 85(3):473–491.

Lakatos, I. 1976. *Proofs and Refutations: The Logic of Mathematical Discovery*. Cambridge: Cambridge University Press.

Lohmann, S. 1992. Optimal commitment in monetary policy: credibility versus flexibility. *The American Economic Review*, 82(1):273–286.

Medawar, P.B. 1991. 'Is the scientific paper a fraud?' In: Medawar P.B., *The Threat and the Glory: Reflections on Science and Scientists*. Oxford: Oxford University Press, 228–233 (based on a BBC interview published in *The Listener*, 12 September 1963).

Nozick, R. 1974. *Anarchy, State and Utopia*. Blackwell: Oxford.

Posner, R.A. 1993. Nobel laureate: Ronald Coase and methodology. *The Journal of Economic Perspectives*, 7(4):195–210.

Rescher, N. 2001. *Philosophical Reasoning: A Study in the Methodology of Philosophizing*. Malden, MA: Blackwell.

Rogoff, K. 1985. The optimal degree of commitment to an intermediate monetary target. *Quarterly Journal of Economics*, 100(4):1169–1189.

Schaling, E. 1995. Institutions and monetary policy: credibility, flexibility and central bank independence. Doctoral thesis, Katholieke Universiteit Brabant.

Sen, A.K. 1970. The impossibility of the Paretian liberal. *Journal of Political Economy*, 78(1):152–157.

Sen, A.K. 1983a. Liberty and social choice. *The Journal of Philosophy*, 80(1):5–28.

Sen, A.K. 1983b. Poor, relatively speaking. *Oxford Economic Papers*, 35(2):153–169.

Sen, A.K. 1999. *Development as Freedom*. Oxford: Oxford University Press.

Sen, A.K. 2010. *The Idea of Justice*. London: Penguin.

Shavell, S. 1983. Liability for harm versus regulation of safety. NBER Working Paper No. 1218.

Terzi, L. 2005. Beyond the dilemma of difference: the capability approach to disability and special education needs. *Journal of Philosophy of Education*, 39(3): 443–459.

Usher, D. 1998. The Coase theorem is tautological, incoherent, or wrong. *Economic Letters*, 61:3–11.

Van Fraassen, B.C. 1980. *The Scientific Image*. Oxford: Clarendon Press.

Walsh, C.E. 1995. Optimal contracts for central bankers. *American Economic Review*, 85(1):150–167.

Wentzel, A. 2007. A method for theoretical innovation in economics. Economic Research Southern Africa, Working Paper No. 66.

# 7 Dealing with authentic economic problems

Thus far, it was assumed that the economic researcher in search of an original contribution is working in isolation and on problems that can be neatly defined. In reality, economic problems involve Knightian uncertainty, diverse stakeholders and political complications which make them difficult to research and resolve. It will be demonstrated in this chapter that, by using the approach developed thus far, a researcher can harness these apparent difficulties to generate new questions and ideas.

While one must recognise that researchers working in isolation on well-defined problems have made original contributions in economics, it is in policymaking where the value of such contributions is tested. It is in economic policy problems that we really confront the problems that matter. Such economic problems are more authentic than those captured in an economic model, but they are also embedded in a reality that is not nearly as well-behaved as that described by such models.

For ideas to create real economic change, they must be converted into actions. One such conversion mechanism is economic policymaking. Without an understanding of the nature of policies and the policymaking process, theorists will find it difficult to get policymakers to put their ideas into practice (Colander, 2001; Edwards, 2002).

This understanding starts with grasping the nature of economic policy problems. I argued in Chapter 3 that economic problems are best represented, not as trade-offs, but as logical conflicts. In the messy world of policymaking, the trade-off representation creates the impression of economic problems as well-defined, and is unable to offer guidance on creative ways to adequately address such problems. In that same chapter, we saw how Meade's trade-off thinking hampered his ability to see the creative possibilities later explored by Mauritius.

This chapter will explain that authentic economic policy problems are not well-defined and inherently socio-political in nature. The conventional approach is to screen out these complications for the sake of expediency with a resulting loss of opportunities for innovation and learning. I will show that the tools developed thus far can be adapted to find original contributions even when faced with the complications that make authentic economic problems so difficult to solve. The ideas will be illustrated with examples drawn from monetary policy, and South African monetary policy in particular.

## The problem of authentic economic problem solving

Most economic policy problems, such as underdevelopment or poverty, remain stubborn despite the efforts of generations of economic theorists to solve them. Other problems seem to get solved, then recur in another form or at another time, only to be re-solved. For example, just before the global financial crisis of 2007/8, authors such as Goodfriend (2007) and Mishkin (2007) created the impression that the problems of monetary policy were largely solved, only to be embarrassed when it appeared that many problems arose as a result of the pre-crisis consensus (Borio & Zhu, 2008; Disyatat, 2008; Galbraith, 2008; Goodhart, 2010). This case is only the most recent and dramatic example of economists' inability to permanently solve economic problems. And, to date, only a few economists (such as Tuma, 1981) have tried to grapple with the reasons for this.

Theorists may rationalise such failures of economic theory to provide permanent solutions to economic problems by questioning the realities of policymaking, laying the blame on: irrational behaviour by the agents involved; bad policies; or the poor implementation of good policies. What is peculiar though is that many theorists assume away the very thing on which they lay the blame by basing their solutions on the assumption of rational agents with consistent beliefs. Even more puzzling are the many cases where apparently 'bad' policies, from the perspective of orthodox economic theory, had good results in solving problems (Chang, 2010:242–251), and cases where the correct implementation of 'good' policies created even more problems (Fox, 1997:49–52; Stiglitz, 2001:518–519).

This dearth of new ideas for effective policy derives from a mistaken view of economic problems and policies. The criticism goes beyond pointing out the shortcomings of the trade-off representation of economic problems. It extends further into showing that the social and political complexities of such problems are usually underestimated, which severely impoverishes the creative processes of economists.

## The social nature of economic problems

As previously argued, problems are essentially difficulties with human ideas and assumptions. They emerge from inconsistencies in the beliefs and assumptions within a shared mental model. Problems cannot be regarded as objective since they are social constructs that have no existence apart from humans and their social reality (Smith, 1989; Dennett, 2003; Harris, 2013).

As argued in earlier chapters, the boundary of a shared mental model is determined by a judgement made on whose assumptions are relevant in creating the problem. Until now, this boundary was assumed to be determined by academics: from a very small group in a specialised field of the discipline with fairly homogenous beliefs to larger groups encompassing opposing schools of thought in the discipline. However, economic problems are not merely created by the assumptions of academic economists, and therefore, defining shared mental models along narrow academic lines is a vast oversimplification.

A much wider range of agents, beyond policymakers and academics, are affected by any economic policy problem. It is to be expected that they will also want their beliefs to be considered. If one includes their beliefs into the shared mental model of a problem, even more logical inconsistencies will appear. These inconsistent beliefs lead to logical conflicts; and, within a logical conflict, all possible policy conclusions can be argued and so impede the achievement of desired ends.

For example, a set of inconsistent beliefs about monetary policy will, at most times, generate contradictory conclusions even when considering a group of economists with fairly similar views (as will be shown later in this chapter). Taken as a collective, it is not uncommon to find all possible policy recommendations among them: to increase the interest rate; to decrease it; or to keep it constant. At best, this leads to indecisiveness and movement between extremes, and, at worst, to actions that aggravate the problem.

The broader social nature of economic policy problems is clear even when considered from the trade-off perspective. Economic problems, from a trade-off perspective, are defined as gaps between a current state (perceived to be non-optimal) and an ideal state of optimality, as defined by given values.

When there is a policy problem, it means that there is a gap between a *perceived* current state that lies below the frontier and a *normatively valued* state that lies on the frontier. Optimality in the economic sphere can therefore have no meaning apart from economic agents, their values and perceptions. Since perceptions and values change and are different between humans, not everyone will believe at all times that a problem exists. For example: what was an optimal state in monetary policy in 1960 is not believed to be an optimal state in 2010; and, what is believed to be optimal in Ukraine will not be deemed optimal in Sierra Leone. Economic problems are therefore mismatches that are not *discovered* as much as they are *created* by human actions and beliefs.

## The political nature of economic problems

The extra-academic and social nature of economic policy problems introduces complexities that are aggravated when these problems become issues of public debate and political power struggles, as they often do. This affects all spheres of economic policymaking. For example, the power struggles in monetary policy may range from the discreet (between commercial banks and the central bank) to the combative (between trade unions and the central bank). In such cases, problems will also take on a political dimension as different groups with different beliefs will compete for the power to determine the direction of policymaking.

The politics is evident in so-called "policy games" where agents interact to influence how the problem is defined (Van Bueren, Klijn & Koppenjang, 2003:195). All role players who share a problem will have an interest in trying to solve that problem to their advantage. If their beliefs are different, they will compete in order to have their beliefs accepted.

The agent whose definition of the problem is accepted, is the agent whose beliefs will dominate and have the power to dictate what information is relevant and what policy alternatives are to be considered (Hisschemoller & Hoppe, 1995:46). Since the interests of agents play a critical role in the understanding of economic problems, agents will self-select different data or interpret the same data differently, in order to support their beliefs (Mitroff & Mason, 1980:335). Beliefs are intimately tied up with interests and power, and this provides an incentive for agents not to change them. This political aspect of policy problems makes beliefs resistant to empirical tests so that the inconsistencies remain.

More data does not eliminate inconsistencies in beliefs (Barberis and Thaler, 2003:1063–1067). As recorded in the research of various experimental and behavioural economists (Cartwright, 2011), systematic biases appear when humans form beliefs and such biases often remain constant even if contradictory data emerge. This world with real people – who have limited capabilities and conflicting beliefs, engage in power struggles and exhibit diverging interests – not only guarantees that the collective understanding of any economic issue will be rife with inconsistencies, but also that these inconsistencies will be impervious to data.

This is of course reminiscent of Hattiangadi's (1978) definition of intellectual problems as logical inconsistencies in beliefs that cannot be eliminated simply by gathering more data. If these problems appear in academia, one should not be surprised to encounter them when considering economic problems where a diverse range of stakeholders want their beliefs to influence the solutions.

## The unstructured nature of authentic economic problems

The social and political nature of the authentic economic problems found in the sphere of policymaking alerts one to the fact that such problems are not well-structured. A well-structured problem can be solved by search and computation alone, since there is no disagreement about the ends or the means for achieving those ends. Agents are assumed to have the knowledge and cognitive capacity to do the computations, so that there is no need for them to form beliefs to compensate for any doubts and uncertainties. The problem space is taken to be constant and that it is possible to know when the best solution has been reached. Well-structured problems exist in an ideal world (Simon, 1973:181–187) and it is similar to what Rittel and Webber (1973:155) called "tame" problems.

In reality, authentic problems are characterised by conflict, disagreement and confusion amongst agents. In fact, the basic characteristic of problems that are not well-structured is the existence of inconsistencies due to stakeholders' different perceptions of problems (Mitroff & Mason, 1980).

Problems that are not well-structured fall into the class of problems Herbert Simon (1973:185) labelled "ill-structured". Ill-structure in problems results from uncertainty and a lack of knowledge about goals, heuristics and the problem space itself. Attempts to solve ill-structured problems have unintended consequences, so that the problem is continuously redefined (Simon, 1973). Ill-structured problems have no known algorithm that can be used to determine if the correct solution exists (Nickles, 1981), because there is no given means–ends structure for an efficient solution search. This is attributed to the fact that the means are perceived to be uncertain or the ends are disputed. The means–end structure provides a simple typology of problems, in which well-structured problems are a special case, as seen in Figure 7.1.

Figure 7.1 shows that when both means and ends are certain, one has a well-structured problem, such as the majority of theoretical problems in economics. While policymakers prefer well-structured problems, many of those involved in the implementation of policies are aware that ends are disputed by agents and that means are uncertain (i.e. unstructured problems). To gain some perceived leverage on the problem, such unstructured problems may be reduced to problems that are either ill-structured by means (by assuming that there is consensus about ends) or ill-structured by ends (by assuming that the means to solve the problem are certain).

Most authentic problems are unstructured since structure is usually imposed by those with an interest in simplifying the problem. Rittel and Webber (1973:160) expanded the concept of unstructured problems with

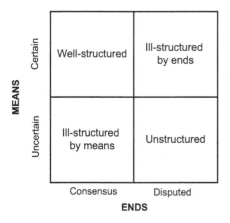

*Figure 7.1* Typology of problems.
*Source*: Adapted from Khisty (2000:106).

their idea of "wicked" problems. A wicked problem is an unstructured problem that will never be eliminated: it cannot be solved, but only continuously 're-solved'. As evident from the problems of monetary policy for example, economic problems are often solved, only to reappear at another time in a different form.

The wickedness of economic problems emerges from agents' inconsistent beliefs and conflicting preferences, values and perceptions about ends and means. Rittel and Webber (1973:161–166) explain how this produces the characteristics of wicked problems:

- Diverse agents will *not be able to settle on a definitive formulation of the problem* that affects them all.
- Without a definitive formulation of the problem, numerous explanations will be offered for the existence of the problem *without any rule for determining the correct explanation*.
- Without a clear explanation of the problem, it is *not possible to know when the correct solution has been reached, no way to know when to stop searching for the solution, and no specified set of solutions or operations to reach a solution*.
- Judgements about solutions differ amongst agents, so *solutions cannot be true or false, only better or worse* given agents' goals and values.
- Every problem is uniquely situated in an open system; causally connected to other problems in an open system. This means *every problem is both a symptom and a cause of other wicked problems, so any solution will have waves of real and irreversible consequences*.

The diversity of goals means that a true aggregate measure of welfare cannot be determined. Any optimal solution to a wicked problem is likely to be only one agent's version of the problem (Rosenhead, 1992). Pareto-optimal solutions to wicked economic problems therefore do not exist, since there is no measure to optimise; and any policy solution will make at least one group worse off (Rittel and Webber, 1973).

Wicked problems are difficult, if not impossible, to solve. At the core is the difficulty to define problems as a result of the diverse and inconsistent beliefs of agents. If economic problems did not affect humans, or affected only homogenous agents with consistent beliefs, so that only a single uncontested version of these problems existed, they would not be wicked. Unfortunately, economic problems affect a wide range of agents, so that all significant economic problems are likely to be wicked (Coyne, 2004).

## Conventional ways of dealing with wicked problems

Few policy problems are well-structured, yet economists find the concept of wicked problems much too pessimistic. In fact, besides Batie (2008), one is unlikely to come across a journal article in economics that even considers it relevant. Instead, economists deploy authoritative problem-solving strategies that enable them to avoid confronting the wickedness of their problems.

*Authoritative problem-solving strategies*

Structure needs to be imposed on economic problems if the analytical tools of the discipline are to work. This requires that ends appear as agreed-upon even if they are disputed, or that means appear as certain even if they are uncertain – or most likely both. Converting wicked problems into well-structured problems allows the policymaking process to be faster and ostensibly more predictable, and helps to make the process appear objective and apolitical (Hisschemoller & Hoppe, 1995).

Only authority can achieve this excision of uncertainty and dispute by imposing its clear problem definition and limited range of policy alternatives. If power is concentrated, a single agent (like the central bank) can impose its beliefs despite disagreement about ends or means (Roberts, 2000). Such authoritative problem-solving strategies solve an unstructured problem by fiat, reducing and simplifying it to a soluble structured problem.

Within an authoritative problem-solving strategy, innovative thinking is not required. When a problem is well-structured, one is already assumed to be in the interior of a well-defined solution space and all that is required is to find the global optimum. Problems in this view can be solved mainly by gathering and processing data.

The process of generating policy solutions involves collecting data to establish the current state, preferences and available means. An expert – or group of experts who are usually economists – then develops a model in which the trade-offs and the interactions between them are represented mathematically or statistically. The data are entered into the model and alternative courses of action are tested. The course of action that achieves the optimal state is then presented as the policy solution. This linear process is known by some policy scientists as the Rational Planning Model (RPM) (Khisty, 2000). The RPM can only succeed if the problem to be solved is a well-structured or a so-called 'tame' problem (Rittel and Webber, 1973).

Policies, in this view, are rational solutions to objective and well-structured problems, and the result of a mainly deductive and inductive technical (non-participative) process. Due to consensus among role players, well-structured problems can be approached within a control paradigm, and, if the policy fails, it is believed to be the result of random noise, unpredictable external shocks, irrational behaviour and bad implementation, all of which one essentially expects to find in reality.

One can see this logic at play in most policymaking. In South Africa, for example, monetary policy is approached as a well-structured problem in a manner similar to the RPM. Every second month, a group of experts feed the available data into a model and communicate this to the Monetary Policy Committee (MPC). They do not disagree on what means are available and the

MPC usually reaches consensus on a course of action, usually with regard to the level of interest rate, that will ensure the achievement of a predetermined end, that is, the inflation target.

Such authoritative strategies involve denying the social and political nature of problems by introducing two biases to the process. The first bias denies the social aspect of economic problems by reducing the number of agents allowed to participate in the policy process. The second bias denies the political aspect by limiting the range of arguments allowed in the process (Hisschemoller & Hoppe, 1995:44). The biases disguise the complexity of the problem, without changing the causes of the complexity, and make it likely that policymakers will address the wrong problem with the wrong techniques. Such biases in economic policymaking have been documented by Edwards (2002:19–24) in Australia and Willets (1987) and Rosenhead (1992:297–298) in the UK. These authors point out how policymaking is often based on caricaturised versions of the complexities of economic theory (Coats, 1989).

Both biases are also observed in monetary policymaking in South Africa. The central bank allows for no discussion outside of a group of employees who already agree on the end, the means and what data are relevant. Most academics, economists and other interest groups are excluded from participating, and the range of arguments is implicitly restricted by a set of accepted economic theories and the derived inflation forecasting model. As one central banker said, "We hear, but we don't listen" (Anon, 2006:7) though this may often be simply for pragmatic reasons.

### *Taming wicked economic problems*

Increasing the structure of unstructured wicked problems so that they resemble well-structured problems is called "taming" (Churchman, 1967:B141). Taming involves denying the very aspects that make real problems problematic, namely: beliefs, imperfect knowledge, power struggles, social interaction and uncertainty. Wicked problems can be tamed using one or more of the strategies explained below (Conklin, 2001:11).

The first taming strategy is to fix the problem definition to fit a particular discipline's view of it. An economist researching crime would, most likely, exclude cultural and psychological aspects of the problem and reduce it to a problem of finding the right set of sanctions and incentives.

This results in a second strategy, which is to act as though there are only a limited set of alternative solutions, and focus efforts on choosing one from this set. During times of self-imposed austerity in fiscal policy, governments argue that their choices are limited to cutting government spending and raising taxes, despite the existence of a larger range of alternatives.

A third strategy is to assume that the problem does not exist and declare it solved. For example, the theory of the vertical Phillips curve was used for many years to deny the possibility of a trade-off in monetary policy. This was aided by the theory of rational expectations. Another Nobel Prize winner,

Thomas Sargent's description of the foundations of the rational expectations theory makes it clear how the problem was simply assumed away. Amongst other things he (Sargent, 1993:6) mentions that rational expectations describe agents' maximising behaviour subject to "constraints perceived by everybody in the system [to be] *mutually consistent*" (emphasis added). He explains that this "*imposes consistency* of those perceptions across people ... individual rationality and consistency of beliefs" (emphasis added) and that is was this assumption that made rational expectations such a "powerful hypothesis". Note that while the role of perceptions and beliefs is acknowledged, it is *assumed* that they cannot be inconsistent. There can be no problem except for computing the optimal achievement of an agreed-upon end with known means. No trade-off or logical conflict can result in such a system, so that the course of action is always clear.

The fourth strategy is to reduce the problem to one that was solved before by screening out certain complications. Stiglitz illustrates this strategy in some detail, within the context of his Nobel Prize-winning research and his work in developing countries, where economic theorists are often blind to the unique trade-offs in developing countries. In denying certain trade-offs at work in developing countries, economists have often exacerbated the trade-offs, and created additional problems (Stiglitz, 2001).

A fifth taming strategy is to specify the measurement of success so that what is not measured can absorb the real problem. This turns attention away from the problem towards the question of measurement. The problems created from this strategy are evident in the measurement of economic growth. Pursuing economic growth, as measured by GNP, means that economists feel no compunction to pay attention to factors that are harmed by such a pursuit, but not measured in the GNP (Stiglitz, Sen & Fitoussi, 2009).

The last taming strategy is to decompose the problem, and to solve only that part that can be structured, leaving the untamed part up to someone else. This strategy is often a particular frustration to those who have to live with the solutions. It involves neglecting the interrelations that make the larger problem unstructured. When these interrelations appear after implementing the policy solutions, unintended consequences cause these policies to degenerate as they are patched up over time with often conflicting solutions (Simon, 1973). This happened recently as theorists excluded the financial stability complications from the problems of monetary policy, which then had to be addressed with macroprudential policy.

Taming economic problems therefore means diminishing the information content inherent in such problems. Taming strategies are attempts to convert an unfamiliar, unique problem into a known problem so that known solutions can be found. Because the nature of a problem is changed during the taming process, it is virtually certain that researchers will solve a problem that is different from the real one, applying inappropriate methods and implementing solutions that are more detrimental than the problem.

Applying solutions designed for well-structured problems to wicked problems will always leave residual demands that have not been met (Smith, 1988).

The residual demands may be in the form of unintended consequences, a residue of unsolved problems or additional problems created. Stiglitz (2001) explains that economists are particularly guilty of this. It can also take the shape of "intractable social controversies" (Hisschemoller & Hoppe, 1995:44) as a result of excluding affected parties from the solution-generating process. When agents are excluded from engaging with problems that affect them, there is a tendency for them to harden their positions, and resort to processes other than reasoned argument.

Even so, there may be circumstances where taming is acceptable, if not ideal. Such circumstances would include cases where the unintended consequences are benign relative to the consequences of not 'solving' the problem within a limited period of time.

*Conclusion*

Treating authentic economic problems as well-structured does not encourage the generation of new questions and ideas, it tries to limit them instead in order to tame such problems. This is usually attained with the aid of authoritative strategies that impose problem definitions and assumptions. Authoritative strategies, by restricting the problem-solving process, limit the possibilities for learning and innovation in a particular policy issue.

A researcher in search of original contributions needs to follow an approach that not only accommodates, but also relies on the existence of diverse and inconsistent beliefs that lead to contrasting views. As previously argued, the representation of economic problems as logical conflicts fits this description, although it needs to be expanded in order to be useful in a participative social and political process that facilitates learning through new questions and the generation of new ideas.

## A participative approach to original contributions

The source of the wickedness of economic problems is the social nature of such problems, which makes it difficult to define such problems. Wicked problems therefore require a social process of collaboration (Roberts, 2000). By combining basic argument theory with the tools developed thus far, this section will propose how this might be done. Instead of economic researchers approaching a problem as individuals in a purely cognitive way, this combination will enable economists to collaborate in a social process of argumentation that opens further opportunities for original contributions.

Collaboration does not mean searching for consensus, though there needs to be some common ground in the form of an agreed-upon process with the purpose of finding breakthroughs and learning from each other. This is similar to abductive reasoning, where complying with strategic constraints allows the substance constraints to be relaxed without the process becoming chaotic.

*Dealing with authentic economic problems* 125

To enable a collective process of learning and innovation, the agreed-upon methodology must enable diverse agents with inconsistent beliefs to reason together about a particular problem and its definition. Any such approach has to recognise that problems are created by sets of inconsistent assumptions, emerging from the beliefs of diverse and purposeful individuals. To make progress, policy solutions must be found that reconcile the conflicting beliefs by creating a change in the beliefs of agents, which, in turn, leads to learning and innovation. Authoritative strategies do not facilitate a change in beliefs, but, because they impose beliefs, may instead bring about polarisation and solutions that are similar to past solutions.

The process, that will act as the strategic constraint, starts with group selection followed by the elicitation of each group's mental model. The assumptions of each group are then made explicit and used to generate questions and ideas. It draws on the insights of Ian Mitroff and his many collaborators with regard to treating policy problems as social arguments (Mitroff, Emshoff & Kilmann, 1979; Mitroff & Mason, 1980, 1982; Mitroff, Mason & Barabba, 1982).

## *Group selection and preparation*

Assumptions are what create a problem, so, to address the problem, the crucial assumptions have to be brought to the surface. To expose as many assumptions as possible, agents must be divided into two groups with maximally different views of the problem. Their assumptions should lead to policy recommendations ($A$ and $\neg A$) that are clearly in opposition from the perspective of both groups. For example, at a given time, labour unions may argue for lower interest rates ($A$), while the central bank argues for higher rates ($\neg A$).

Next, the groups should find their common ground, which is an overall objective ($G$) that is suitably ambiguous so that both groups can agree with it. For example, the common ground between labour unions and the central bank may be to achieve economic stability or sustained economic growth. This ambiguity hides many assumptions, which will surface later in the process. At this point, however, it is important that some common ground exists as a foundation for collective reasoning. As explained in Chapter 4, creativity emerges from the interplay of affirmation (the common ground in this case) and negation (of opposing groups' assumptions).

The greater the degree of difference between the two groups, the easier they will find it to identify and question assumptions that the other group takes for granted. Assumption identification is, as should have been clear from preceding chapters, critical to the creative process. Collectively, groups that hold maximally different views, identify more assumptions than individuals that favour one side of a logical conflict. It is this identification of assumptions that is the next step.

### Mental model elicitation

Each group will have a particular view of the relevant economic reality as captured in their mental model. If each group's mental model can be elicited, their assumptions will be made explicit. Within each of the groups, there will be small differences in the mental models of individuals. This does not matter as long as each person's individual mental model is not so different as to make him or her doubt the group to which they should belong.

#### Elicitation by means of the logical conflict

The logical conflict created when each group's reasoning is interrogated is, as shown in Chapter 3, a useful tool to elicit each group's mental model. Each group will be asked to reason from their recommended policy action to the overall goal, and, in doing so, construct their branch of the conflict diagram separately. The two groups' separate branches together will create the conflict diagram (as shown later).

Taking the policy action ($A$ or $\neg A$) into consideration, each group is asked which need of the economic system is fulfilled by their preferred policy action alone, and this results in either $R$ or $R'$. Each group is then asked if they agree that if this need is fulfilled, then the overall goal ($G$) will be achieved. After they reach an agreement, they are asked to test their logic by applying deontic reasoning. This is done by reading their branch of the conflict diagram as follows:

- if $G$, then we must have $R$, and to have $R$, we must do $A$ (that is, the group constructing the upper branch of the conflict); or
- if $G$, then we must have $R'$, and to have $R'$, we must do $\neg A$ (that is, the group constructing the lower branch of the conflict).

Groups make adjustments until members within each group agree on the deontic reasoning. The two branches are then brought together into a single conflict diagram so that the process of mental model elicitation can start. Figure 7.2 shows a possible result if the two groups were labour unions (the upper branch) and a strict inflation targeting central bank (the lower branch) at a time of stagflation. $R$ and $R'$ also constitute the two axes of Taylor's monetary policy trade-off (shown in Figure 7.6).

For the sake of convenience, the two groups will henceforth be labelled the 'upper group', arguing for connectives I and II; and the 'lower group', proposing connectives III and IV. Both the upper and lower groups argue for connective V (that $A$ and $\neg A$ are in conflict).

Each group is already predisposed to being against the arguments of the other group, so they will be more inclined to notice the assumptions that the opposing group is making. Using an approach already described in Chapter 3, each group takes the connectives of the opposing group and questions them in order to produce and record a list of assumptions under each connective.

*Dealing with authentic economic problems* 127

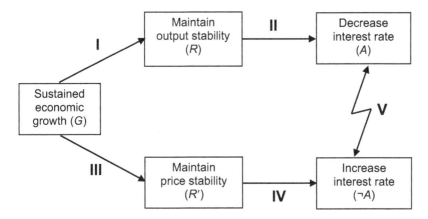

*Figure 7.2* A conflict about interest rate policy.

Both groups are brought together, and are made to question the assumptions of connective V (as described in Chapter 3 as well). This is then added to the list of assumptions.

Here, not all groups will agree on the assumptions. It is this very disagreement that will be harnessed to provoke dialogue between them and highlight possible areas for research and innovation.

*Mental model exploration through argument construction*

It has already been established that policymaking occurs in a contested space where diverse agents argue about whether a problem exists, and, if so, the reasons for its existence and how it should be defined. Economic problems are therefore arguments, and, by extension, so are the policies designed to address them.

The argumentative nature of economic problems and policies offers a second procedure for bringing assumptions to the surface. In some cases, this procedure is useful if groups find it difficult to identify the opposing group's assumptions. This is a lengthier procedure because it combines the conflict diagram with argument construction.

A well-known way to construct an argument was developed by Toulmin (1958), as shown in an adapted version as Figure 7.3. It is more complex than the classic syllogism and was developed by Toulmin to better handle the intricacies of actual human reasoning.

Any argument can be structured in the form of Figure 7.3. A policy, for example, is the consequence of a complex argument that results in a claim (*C*) about reality that is neither certain nor complete. The claim is a statement about the state of reality and the action that should be taken to transform this into a more ideal state.

128  *Dealing with authentic economic problems*

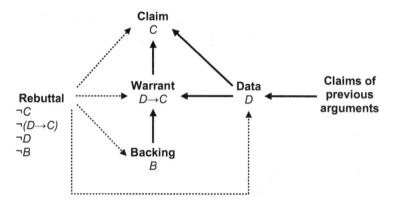

*Figure 7.3* A Toulmin-like argument structure.
*Source*: Adapted from Mitroff and Mason (1980:337).

The data (*D*) provide both the objective and subjective evidence supporting the claim, and are the result of the claims of previous arguments. Data need not be quantitative: anything that is not questioned and taken as given is regarded as data by those making the argument. The warrant (*W*) contains the reasons or assumptions that justify why the data can be interpreted as support for the claim. Those assumptions entitle one to state that if the data are true, then the claim will follow. The backing (*B*) is the background of often ideological beliefs about truth and reality that make the warrant believable. Backing can be found in the theoretical stance (monetarist, neo-classical Keynesian, Marxist, etc.) that influences how an economist would interpret data. The complex argument is rebutted by others who: deny the background beliefs ($\neg B$); believe that the data are incorrect ($\neg D$); consider the warrant unreasonable ($\neg(D \rightarrow C)$); or believe the claim to not be legitimate ($\neg C$) (Mitroff & Mason, 1980:334–335).

The way any group constructs an argument reveals much about its mental model. The assumptions it makes determines: what claims it considers worth making (*C*); which data are seen as relevant and selected in support (*D*); how the data are interpreted (*W*); and the kind of warrants that are seen as acceptable (*B*).

As often happens with economists, even if there are similar ideological views (*B*), it is possible that groups will make different claims. Bisseker (2006:22–26) provided a case study of such a situation that will also be used here to illustrate the Toulmin model of argumentation.

She interviewed ten economists, with fairly similar ideological stances and access to the same economic data, on monetary policy in South Africa in mid-2006. It is quite rare to have the reasoning of economists exposed so clearly, and see how they came to opposing policy recommendations: half

*Dealing with authentic economic problems* 129

believed that interest rates should be reduced or stay constant, while the other half argued for a rate increase.

Given the assumptions that surfaced through the interviews, an argument to reduce interest rates appeared to be as follows:

- C: Reduce interest rates;
- D: An inflation rate of 3.7 per cent that is well within the target of 3–6 per cent;
- D→C: If the inflation rate is within the target range, then the central bank should reduce interest rates because the inflation outlook is positive;
- B: The central bank should maximise social welfare; inflation harms social welfare; inflation targeting is an appropriate monetary policy framework.

All of these were rebutted by the other five economists. Rebuttals came from those who argued, from different premises, for a rate decrease and those who advocated a rate increase. The following rebuttals are just a list of these and not a coherent argument in support of the negations:

- ¬C: Increase interest rates;
- ¬D: One needs to consider inflation expectations and forecasts of inflation and other data need to be considered that might undermine the economy in the future, such as: the current account deficit, household savings, rising house prices and credit growth;
- ¬(D→C): The inflation outlook is not necessarily good if the current inflation rate is well within the target range as, since some forecasts show a high probability of inflation exceeding the target, an increase of the interest rate might reinforce the central bank's credibility;
- ¬B: It is more important for the central bank to be credible rather than maximising current welfare; actions by government counteract the efforts of the central bank.

Assumptions also become visible in the rebuttals: the negations of the different elements. The group performing the rebuttal not only reveals the assumptions of the opposing group, but also illuminates its own assumptions.

When combining argument construction with the conflict representation of economic problems, we can see there would be five arguments. The claims are: the requirements (R and R') that follow from G, the actions (A and ¬A) that follow from the requirements and the claim that the actions are in conflict. Four arguments constitute the reasoning that leads to conflicting policies (G→R, R→A, G→R' and R'→¬A) and the fifth argument is that A and ¬A are incompatible.

Figure 7.4 shows the combination visually. Each group draws on different backing (B and B') and different data (D and D'). Since the core assumptions of a mental model are most likely located in connectives I and III, one would expect the backing to exercise a strong influence on the warrants ($w_1$

## 130  Dealing with authentic economic problems

and $w'_1$), which logically connect the overall goal to the requirements, and a weaker influence on reasoning ($w_2$ and $w'_2$) from the requirements to the policy actions. Data are more important to warrants $w_2$ and $w'_2$. Together, the backing and data of both groups lead them to argue that their recommended policy actions are in conflict.

With this procedure of eliciting mental models, each group is asked to elaborate on their own reasoning. They should identify the data and warrant, and, if they can, the backing for each of the two connectives on their branch.

This is presented to the opposing group, who is then asked to counteract the argument by explaining: why the data are incomplete or inappropriate; why the claim is not warranted; or why the backing is wrong or inadequate. The group who is refuting the other thus reveals the assumptions contained in the argument and this is recorded. However, the group suffering the rebuttal is asked to identify assumptions that the rebutters themselves are making as a result of their counterarguments and this is also recorded.

### Preparation of mental model content

Many assumptions will now have been produced, and should be prepared to guide dialogue within and between the groups. Assumptions are prioritised by their perceived importance and certainty. Those that are perceived as certain or viewed as obvious truths by all agents will act as substance constraints that are not to be questioned and will not be the object of inquiry. If any of the groups doubt the certainty of any assumption, it is classified as uncertain.

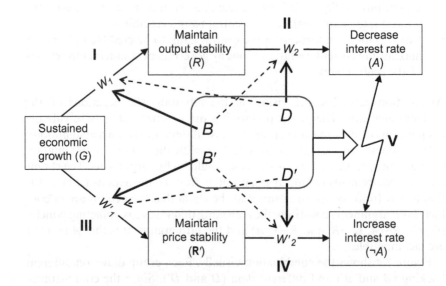

*Figure 7.4* Argumentation and the conflict representation combined.

*Dealing with authentic economic problems* 131

Assumptions that, if negated, will not materially change a policy are considered insignificant, and are also given low priority, as per the method of Mitroff *et al.* (1979:587–588). If a group argues that any assumption is significant to them or to the opposing group, it is classified as important. The result will be a typology (as exhibited in Figure 7.5). When completing the typology, it is useful, for later purposes, to identify the source of each assumption by the connective (I, II, III, IV or V) from which it originated.

Those assumptions that are recognised as significant and least certain are the critical assumptions around which dialogue will revolve. The purpose of the dialogue is to create an understanding of the role of assumptions in the conflicting problem perspectives and to challenge those assumptions either for the purpose of: (1) persuasion through new arguments; or (2) the generation of new ideas.

Assumptions are entered in the relevant cell of the typology. Those in the 'seeds of dialogue' cell will be the basis of dialogue between the groups. As a result of the dialogue, any of the groups may rethink the perceived certainty or significance of an assumption, so the content of the typology is likely to change over time.

*Creative dialogue*

Dialogue will center around the assumptions identified as seeds of dialogue. If executed well, this dialogue will lead to learning and innovation in the form of new questions to guide empirical research and new ideas for policy solutions. There are two approaches to dialogue: the confrontational-empirical

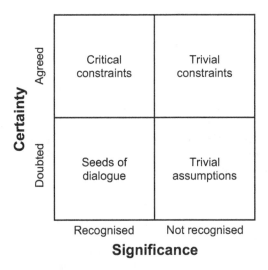

*Figure 7.5* Typology of assumptions.

132  *Dealing with authentic economic problems*

approach, which aims at producing new questions; and the synthetic-abductive approach, which aims at producing new ideas.

*Confrontational-empirical dialogue*

The first approach to argumentation is more confrontational since it involves questioning opposing perspectives by challenging connectives I, II, III and IV. For example, connective IV in Figure 7.2 is based on assumptions regarding the monetary policy transmission mechanism. The upper group may argue that the important channels of the transmission mechanism break down under current conditions, and, if they could convince the lower group that this is indeed the case, the conflict would be resolved.

Since the assumptions that form the seeds of dialogue are not regarded as certain, the groups can structure their dialogue around the kind of empirical research that would settle the ontological status of the assumption, that is, supposing previous research was unable to do so. Research may be guided by any of the following three questions:

- Is it necessarily so that [assumption] is true?
- Is [the assumption] true under all conditions?
- What actions will make [the assumption] invalid?

Dialogue may also lead to questions about data. If it is agreed that data are not available or inadequate to answer these questions, it indicates areas where primary research would be most fruitful.

If any of the connectives is successfully challenged, this results in one group learning from another, but does not necessarily lead to new ideas. The generation of new ideas is the focus of the next approach.

*Synthetic-abductive dialogue*

Confrontational dialogue may lead to new directions for empirical research and learning, but is likely to be resisted by the group whose assumptions are being challenged. For this reason, a synthetic approach, where opposing sides are reconciled, may be more acceptable. This approach involves generating new ideas through abductive reasoning (as explained in Chapter 5). This approach would lead to breakthrough ideas or new questions that can then be supported by all agents.

Once the new ideas are developed, both groups engage in an unfolding argument. Such an argument ideally leads to a change in beliefs on both sides, (learning) as the innovation is refined and a synthetic position is developed.

A policy innovation occurs when a new set of synthetic assumptions can be found to support a new policy idea that is acceptable to all groups. Given a contradiction, such as that represented by Figure 7.2, breakthrough ideas occur when the critical assumptions underlying connective V are invalidated (direct reconciliation), or when a new idea creates the possibility to connect the two opposing sides though $R \rightarrow \neg A$ or $R' \rightarrow A$ (cross synthesis).

Direct reconciliation involves the same three questions posed in the confrontational approach, but applied to connective V. For example, its validity depends on the assumptions that: only one relevant interest rate could exist; the inflation target should be fixed by the central bank; or that this interest rate can only be changed in one way, that is, by official announcement. With direct reconciliation there is no opposition, so, in order to successfully challenge any of these assumptions, both sides need to work together to develop new ideas.

Both direct reconciliation and cross synthesis involve replacing a negated assumption with an assumption or idea that is new to both sides. The procedure for abductive reasoning being applied to this new idea ($\alpha$) was explained in detail in Chapter 5 and will therefore not be repeated here. The new idea itself will likely trigger new questions that will provoke further original research and learning on both sides.

Returning to the case study, some of the participating economists attempted cross synthesis, such as: requesting the Minister of Finance to change the inflation target; adopting more than one relevant interest rate; or for the central bank governor "to talk tough so he doesn't have to act tough" (Bisseker, 2006:23).

Each of the aforementioned suggestions has weaknesses and is based on other assumptions, but they illustrate synthetic thinking. For example, if the Minister of Finance widens the inflation target, it becomes possible for the central bank to pursue price stability (now with a redefined meaning) without increasing the interest rate. A critical assumption underlying this suggestion is that the central bank's independence will not be questioned. This also demonstrates that semantic meanings, which are created by beliefs, maintain problems (Wettersten, 2002) and that synthesis often occurs when the meanings of concepts are challenged and redefined.

Based on my limited experience, I have observed three ways in which synthetic positions come about. First, they materialise through semantics, as illustrated above and by Rogoff (in Chapter 6) when he redefined 'discretion' as something that could be constrained. This raises the often neglected issue of the role of language in economics and its power to limit or open up our thinking (McCloskey, 1998). Second, synthetic positions come about through segmentation, as was seen in Chapter 3 when Mauritius solved its problem by segmenting the labour market. The final way these positions often manifest is through variation of the time horizon. The prime example is when Japanese firms solved the cost-versus-quality trade-off by recognising that high quality is not really costly if one factors in the savings and gains that materialise over a longer period of time.

Whichever way it is done, if synthesis is achieved, it could be represented on Figure 7.6(a) as a movement to a new frontier intersecting at point C. The movement to this previously impossible region constitutes progress, and will

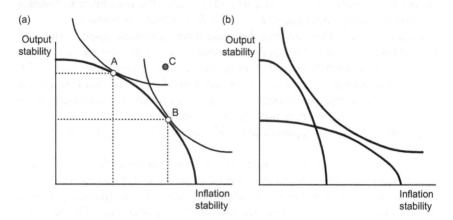

*Figure 7.6* Taylor's monetary policy trade-off.

only be achieved if the existing knowledge is improved on through learning and/or innovation.

It should be noted that these approaches are not the only ones. The appendix to this chapter presents an alternative approach which places more emphasis on argumentation and less on assumptional analysis.

*Infertility of the trade-off for dialogue*

While being more time-consuming, the approach explained in this chapter is preferred to taming strategies. Taming strategies not only prevent learning and innovation but also lead to a loss of information. The suggested approach results in learning and innovation as agents change their beliefs and open up more possibilities for original research.

Returning to an issue raised in Chapter 3, it can once again be seen that how a problem is represented is crucial if a group of diverse agents are to be engaged. An appropriate representation would facilitate a systematic approach to collective knowledge elicitation and creation. The trade-off representation and the derived mathematical equations suffer from weaknesses in this regard. Mathematical equations, due to their unfamiliarity to most agents, are of little use in a participative process (Rosenhead, 1992). Equations also fix the dimensions of a trade-off, and, as purely deductive phenomena, cannot generate (innovative) solutions outside their own constraints.

The trade-off representation, while easy to understand, fails similarly. It does not provide cues (e.g. in the form of statements or connectives) that facilitate the surfacing of assumptions around which dialogue can take place. In fact, the trade-off representation hides or denies the role of assumptions, giving the impression that they must be accepted as given, rather than their having been constructed through social and political processes. Within absolute constraints, there is little room for expanding the problem space through innovation, and the problem is reduced to one of optimisation.

Figure 7.6 exhibits the kinds of dialogue likely to emerge around a trade-off. Figure 7.6(a) shows two inconsistent views of the social indifference curve (hence the intersecting curves) with labour unions arguing that society prefers point A, while the central bank asserts that society prefers, or should prefer, point B. Figure 7.6(b) reflects a debate about the slope or shape of the possibility frontier. Labour unions will argue for a steep concave curve, where the pursuit of inflation stability involves increasing sacrifices of output stability, while a central bank may prefer the flat or even the convex curve.

However, even though it may be more pragmatic, this kind of dialogue will not be as creatively productive since it accepts the trade-off. It does not question the trade-off itself or how to jointly create the knowledge that will allow point C to be reached.

The conflict representation and derived approaches, on the other hand, provide obvious cues that enable one to locate the assumptions from which the problem emerges by recognising that it is socially and politically constructed. Only this recognition can enable a creative process that may lead to a change in beliefs, and, by extension, turn the problem into one of innovation and human ingenuity. The conflict representation implies that agents have the power to change the problem as they engage with it, and is open to the possibility that any change will create new problems.

*Continuing the process*

As mentioned above, Rittel and Webber (1973) argued that, due to their social nature, wicked problems can never be solved. Any solution creates new problems elsewhere, and therefore the participative process described above will need to continue (as shown in Figure 7.7).

The process starts by representing an economic problem as a logical conflict, and this representation enables us to make the assumptions that maintain the conflict explicit. These assumptions trigger new questions and guide abductive reasoning to new ideas. The new questions are answered through research and the new ideas are explored in research and consultation with affected parties. This results in new policy ideas that add to our collective knowledge and are then implemented. Through implementation, the policy ideas will produce results in the real world which will reveal new problems. The brand-new knowledge acquired also modifies the mental models of the participants which then have to be made explicit by confronting the new problems created.

By acknowledging the nature of economic problems and their role, economists can enable a continuous social learning process rather than restrict it. The economy is dynamic and opportunities for creative research can therefore never be exhausted.

136  *Dealing with authentic economic problems*

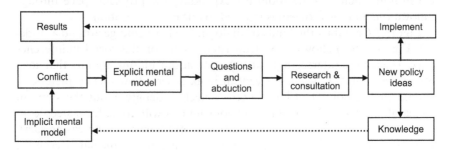

*Figure 7.7* The ongoing process of solving wicked problems.
*Source*: Adapted from Wentzel (2006).

## Conclusion

Economic problems, for which policies need to be developed, are not well-structured optimisation problems. In reality, economic problems have a wicked nature. Wicked problems are unstructured problems caused by the inconsistent beliefs of agents and can never be solved permanently. Many people are affected by wicked problems, so it is impossible to settle on a single correct definition of the problem. As long as there is no definition, there is no way to know when one has found a solution. Every such problem is unique, and, concomitantly, part of an interlocking set of problems. So, even if a solution is tried, it will create other wicked problems and have unintended consequences.

Wicked economic problems require a different set of tools from those that economists are used to. The most important mindshift economists and policymakers have to make in approaching wicked problems, is to recognise the social and political nature of such problems. Agents affected by a wicked problem need to be engaged in a social process, which would generate more interesting questions and new ideas if facilitated in the participative way explained in this chapter.

To solve wicked problems, the inconsistent beliefs of all affected agents must be surfaced and challenged so that new knowledge can be developed. Economists should be participants in such collective learning processes. Assumptions are the basic tools of economists as model-builders, and they are likely to play a significant role in such processes by applying their skill in identifying assumptions.

Unfortunately, the language and tradition in dealing with such problems do not exist in economic theory, and prevent economists from making original contributions to the solution of wicked problems. Solving wicked problems with the tools suited to well-structured problems leads to solutions that aggravate the problem. Econometric and mathematical models alone cannot capture the social complexity of economic problems and cannot generate innovative policies that will change perceptions and satisfy the greatest number of groups.

## Appendix: a less confrontational approach

The approach developed in Chapter 7 involves critical confrontation and questioning, which, in turn, results in the rejection or modification of inconsistent assumptions. However, there is a systematic approach to generate new ideas for policies that does not require rejecting inconsistent assumptions. In their seminal work in modal logic, Rescher and Manor (1970) created the concept of the maximally consistent subset (mcs) that enables agents to derive conclusions from inconsistent beliefs. The mcs is the largest set of statements that can be conjoined without contradiction, so that policies can be derived from an mcs.

With the aid of this concept, Mitroff *et al.* (1982) developed a methodology for deriving policies from the inconsistent assumptions that structure a Toulmin-like argument. The complete set of maximally consistent sets is first derived from the argument and inconsistent sets discarded. For example, from Figure 7.3, one can derive eight maximally consistent sets: $\{B, D, D \rightarrow C, C\}$ or $\{\neg B, D, \neg(D \rightarrow C), \neg C\}$. Neither of these two sets contains logical inconsistencies.

This is followed by determining the logical consequent of each mcs. From the set $\{B, D, D \rightarrow C, C\}$, one derives the logical consequents $B \& D \& C$; while from the mcs $\{\neg B, D, \neg(D \rightarrow C), \neg C\}$, one derives $\neg B \& D \& \neg C$. The conjunction of the logical consequents of each mcs then forms an argument for a policy proposal.

The last step is to rank each mcs according to plausibility, choosing the policy derived with the highest plausibility. The research conducted by Mitroff and Mason (1982) provides a method for measuring the plausibility of maximally consistent sets on an interval scale and, given certain plausibility constraints, transforming the choice of the most plausible mcs into a linear programming problem. Mitroff and Mason (1982:346–348) also demonstrate how agents can develop synthetic positions (where $C$ and $\neg C$ are true) by relaxing particular plausibility constraints.

No information is lost by treating a wicked problem as a complex argument. The inconsistent assumptions are used to create knowledge and promote learning, especially if synthetic positions are developed. In fact, it would not be possible, through argument or innovation, to develop a synthetic position without the inconsistent beliefs of diverse agents. If beliefs were consistent, there would only be one argument, from which only one set of policies would be derived repeatedly, and thus innovation would not occur at all. So, if policymakers deny the social nature of economic problems, they also preclude innovation.

## References

Anon. 2006. Pursuing the objective of price stability. *Finweek*, Survey: The South African Reserve Bank, 21 September.

Barberis, N. & Thaler, R. 2003. A survey of behavioral finance. In: Constantinides, G., Harris, M. & Stulz, R. (eds), *Handbook of the Economics of Finance*, Amsterdam: Elsevier, 1052–1118.

Batie, S.S. 2008. Wicked problems and applied economics. *American Journal of Agricultural Economics*, 90(5):1176–1191.
Bisseker, C. 2006. Tito's too tight. *Financial Mail*, 2 June, 22–26.
Borio, C. & Zhu, H. 2008. Capital regulation, risk-taking and monetary policy: a missing link in the transmission mechanism? BIS Working Paper No. 268.
Cartwright, E. 2011 *Behavioral Economics*. London: Routledge.
Chang, H.-J. 2010. *23 Things They Don't Tell You About Capitalism*. London: Penguin.
Churchman, C.W. 1967. Wicked problems. *Management Science*, 14(4):B141–B142.
Coats, A.W. 1989. Economic ideas and economists in government: accomplishments and frustrations. In: Colander, D.C. & Coats, A.W. (eds), *The Spread of Economic Ideas*, Cambridge: Cambridge University Press, 109–118.
Colander, D.C. 2001. *The Lost Art of Economics: Economics and the Economics Profession*. Cheltenham: Edward Elgar.
Conklin, E.J. 2001. Wicked problems and fragmentation. Cognexus White paper. Available from www.cognexus.org, accessed 12 May 2005.
Coyne, R. 2004. Wicked problems revisited. *Design Studies*, 26:5–17.
Dennett, D. 2003. *Freedom Evolves*. London: Penguin.
Disyatat, P. 2008. Monetary policy implementation: misconceptions and their consequences. BIS Working Paper No. 269.
Edwards, L. 2002. *How to Argue with an Economist: Reopening Political Debate in Australia*. Cambridge: Cambridge University Press.
Fox, J.W. 1997. What do economists know that policymakers need to? *The American Economic Review*, 87(2):49–53.
Galbraith, J.K. 2008. The collapse of monetarism and the irrelevance of the new monetary consensus. The Levy Economics Institute of Bard College Policy Note 2008/1.
Goodfriend, M. 2007. How the world achieved consensus on monetary policy. NBER Working Paper No. 13580.
Goodhart, C.A.E. 2010. The changing role of central banks. BIS Working Paper No. 326.
Harris, S.R. 2013. Studying the construction of social problems. In: Best, J. & Harris, S.R. (eds), *Making Sense of Social Problems: New Images, New Issues*, Boulder, CO: Lynne Rienner Publishers, 1–9.
Hattiangadi, J.N. 1978. The structure of problems (Part I). *Philosophy of Social Science*, 8:345–365.
Hisschemoller, M. & Hoppe, R. 1995. Coping with intractable controversies: the case for problem structuring in policy design and analysis. *Knowledge & Policy*, 8(4):40–61.
Khisty, C.J. 2000. Can wicked problems be tackled through abductive inferencing? *Journal of Urban Planning and Development*, 126(3):104–118.
McCloskey, D.N. 1998. *The Rhetoric of Economics*, 2nd edition. Madison: University of Wisconsin Press.
Mishkin, F.S. 2007. Will monetary policy become more of a science? NBER Working Paper No. 13566.
Mitroff, I.I., Emshoff, J.R. & Kilmann, R.H. 1979. Assumptional analysis: A methodology for strategic problem solving. *Management Science*, 25(6):583–593.
Mitroff, I.I. & Mason, R.O. 1980. Structuring ill-structured policy issues: Further explorations in a methodology for messy problems. *Strategic Management Journal*, 1(4):331–342.

Mitroff, I.I. & Mason, R.O. 1982. On the structure of dialectical reasoning in the social and policy sciences. *Theory and Decision*, 14:331–350.

Mitroff, I.I., Mason, R.O. & Barabba, V.P. 1982. Policy as argument – a logic for ill-structured decision problems. *Management Science*, 28(12):1391–1404.

Nickles, T. 1981. What is a problem that we may solve it? *Synthese*, 47:85–118.

Rescher, N. & Manor, R. 1970. On inference from inconsistent premises. *Theory and Decision*, 1:179–217.

Rittel, H.W.J. & Webber, M.M. 1973. Dilemmas in a general theory of planning. *Policy Sciences*, 4:155–169.

Roberts, N. 2000. Coping with wicked problems. Paper presented at the 3rd Bi-Annual Research Conference of the International Public Management Network, 4–6 March.

Rosenhead, J. 1992. Into the swamp: the analysis of social issues. *Journal of the Operational Research Society*, 43(4):293–305.

Sargent, T.J. 1993. *Bounded Rationality in Macroeconomics: The Arne Ryde Memorial Lectures*. Oxford: Clarendon Press.

Simon, H.A. 1973. The structure of ill-structured problems. *Artificial Intelligence*, 4:181–201.

Smith, G.F. 1988. Towards a heuristic theory of problem structuring. *Management Science*, 34(12):1489–1506.

Smith, G.F. 1989. Defining managerial problems: A framework for prescriptive theorising. *Management Science*, 35(8):963–981.

Stiglitz, J.E. 2001. Autobiography. Available at www.nobelprize.org/nobel_prizes/economic-sciences/laureates/2001/stiglitz-bio.html, accessed 18 May 2016.

Stiglitz, J.E., Sen, A.K. & Fitoussi, J.-P. 2009. Report by the Commission on the Measurement of Economic Performance and Social Progress.

Toulmin, S. 1958. *Uses of Argument*. Cambridge: Cambridge University Press.

Tuma, E.H. 1981. Why problems do not go away: the case of inflation. *The Journal of Economic History*, 41(1):21–28.

Van Bueren, E.M., Klijn, E.-H. & Koppenjang, J.F.M. 2003. Dealing with wicked problems in networks: analyzing an environmental debate from a network perspective. *Journal of Public Administration Research and Theory*, 13(2):193–212.

Wentzel, A. 2006. Conjectures, constructs and conflicts: a framework for understanding imagineering. In: Pyka, A. & Hanusch, H. (eds), *Applied Evolutionary Economics and the Knowledge-based Economy*, Cheltenham: Edward Elgar, 13–39.

Wettersten, J. 2002. Problems and meaning today: what can we learn from Hattiangadi's failed attempts to explain them together? *Philosophy of the Social Science*, 32:487–536.

Willets, D. 1987. The role of the Prime Minister's Policy Unit. *Public Administration*, 65:443–454.

# 8 An instructional programme

Making original contributions, and not simply spotting gaps or replicating previous studies in a different context, is what allows researchers to have a greater impact on their discipline. The art of making an original contribution lies not in the analytical tools used to connect the contribution to existing knowledge (though no contribution can exist without this); but instead in reformulating problems, problematising and generating new questions and creating new ideas.

Yet, this skill is not taught within academic disciplines in the social sciences, and specifically not in economics, as explained in Chapter 1. Current approaches to generating original research contributions are unsatisfactory. The common approach of immersing oneself in a discipline relies mainly on serendipity and hope, while the less common approach of teaching generic creativity techniques does not start from within a particular discipline.

Chapters 3–7 proceeded to address this problem by developing a number of methodologies for generating original contributions from within the discipline. This chapter aims to bring all these insights together in an instructional programme that can be delivered to PhD students and novice researchers in economics, and with some adjustments to a similar audience in other social sciences. As with the immersion approach, this programme will teach techniques that are suitable to disciplines in the social sciences, while also being systematic in nature (as found in the approach of creativity techniques).

## Guiding philosophy

Given that this programme is designed for PhD candidates and novice researchers, it has to be guided by the principles of adult learning (also called andragogy). The differences between adults and children – in terms of experience, knowledge, aims and motivation – mean that they approach learning differently (Merriam, 2011), and the programme needs to reflect this. According to Johnson and Bragar, to be effective, adult learning should (1997:340):

- Involve transformation of the learner over time. As a result of the programme, participants will master new skills that will enable them to

improve their understanding of their field and to continue making new contributions.
- Follow a continuous cycle of action and reflection. This programme should take place over several sessions with time for practise and reflection.
- Address issues that are relevant to the learner. Every participant will either want to obtain a PhD or advance their academic career, and the ability to make original contributions is obviously relevant in attaining this purpose.
- Involve learning with others. Learning in this programme should take place in small group discussions and in collaboration with a supervisor or mentor.
- Occur in a challenging and supportive environment. The ability to make original contributions requires mastering unfamiliar conceptual tools, and this will be challenging to most participants. The programme should be structured to make the acquisition of these tools as easy as possible.

The view of knowledge – as created inside people's minds and through the interaction of those minds – taken in this thesis is aligned to the philosophy of constructivism. However, it is less aligned with radical constructivism, which is described in Chapter 2 as the construction model, and closer to the moderate version of constructivism, which is described in Chapter 2 as the hermeneutic model of scientific inquiry. According to constructivism, knowledge is created through collective meaning-making by humans with biases and filters such as mental models (Wilson, 1997:65). Constructivist philosophy can be made clearer by contrasting it with the more conventional objectivist understanding of knowledge and inquiry. This is shown in Table 8.1.

Constructivism currently also dominates our understanding of learning. Learning is seen as a process of meaning-making that occurs in a social context. For the instructional programme to be self-consistent, it has to facilitate learning that is constructivist in nature. It has implications for how the participants are evaluated throughout the programme and how they are encouraged to learn the skill of making an original contribution. The programme will need to be participative and authentic in its approach. All this will inform the process of designing the instruction to which we now turn.

## Instructional design

To guide the development of the programme, I follow a generally accepted systematic approach to instructional development. In its many guises, this approach is known as instructional design (ID).

There is a plethora of models from which to choose in this field. For the purpose of this thesis, and for designing the pilot version of the programme, one of the clearest approaches available will be followed: the simple

## 142  An instructional programme

*Table 8.1* Conventional view versus constructivist view

| Conventional view | Constructivist view |
|---|---|
| Truth can be determined by testing it in the real world | Truth is derived from the judgement of experts with different views |
| Facts do not depend on the beliefs and values of humans | Facts do not exist independently from beliefs and values: it is beliefs and values that make facts meaningful |
| Every effect has a clear cause and every cause has a clear effect | Causes and effects are complex and intertwined, so any isolation of causes and effects is a deliberate human act |
| The value of knowledge is judged on whether or not it allows us to predict and control | The value of knowledge is judged on whether or not it improves our understanding |
| Change is caused by outside forces and has to be managed | Change is inherent to, and ongoing in, any system and thus intervention may be useful |

*Source*: Adapted from Coleman, Perry and Schwen (1997).

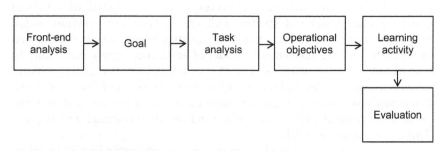

*Figure 8.1* The process of instructional design to be followed.
Source: Adapted from Ledford and Steeman (2000:8).

linear process of Ledford and Steeman (2000) presented here in Figure 8.1. Instructional design is a recursive and negotiated process, so instructors will find themselves returning to previous steps as they present programmes to new groups.

Ledford and Steeman (2000) unfortunately do not always provide sufficient guidance on the execution of each step. Throughout this chapter, when required, more detailed guidance will be drawn from Gagné, Wager, Golas and Keller (2005). The first author of this book, Robert Gagné, also developed many of the ideas that still form the foundation of instructional design today.

The development of the instructional programme will now be executed step-by-step and presented in the sections that follow.

## Front-end analysis

Before the programme is designed, an analysis is required to ensure that instruction is needed, will be feasible and will reach the correct audience. Gagné *et al.* (2005:22–26) recommend four kinds of analyses be done: (1) needs analysis; (2) instructional analysis; (3) learner analysis; and (4) condition and constraint analysis.

### *Needs analysis*

PhD students and researchers are required to make original contributions. They generally receive adequate instruction in the analytical techniques of the discipline, but very little in the act of conceiving an original contribution. It is this need that the programme will address.

The instruction needed in the skills of conceiving original contributions starts from within the discipline. To enable participants to benefit most from the programme, the skills should be taught and practised within an authentic context where participants work with subject experts in the field in which they intend to contribute new findings.

By mastering these skills, PhD students will be able to meet the most demanding condition for a PhD: that of finding an original contribution. Novice researchers will benefit in three further ways:

- They will produce original ideas for research that go beyond mere gap-spotting research and will therefore have a better chance of having an impact through publication.
- They will learn techniques that they can apply independently to their own research efforts throughout their career. and
- They will be able to use these techniques to guide their own (post)graduate students toward making more interesting contributions to their disciplines.

For participants to benefit from this programme, they need to have a working knowledge of their discipline, and a strong grasp of the specific area in which they wish to do research. They need to be competent writers and must also have a solid grounding in the basic analytical tools of the discipline, so that they will know what kind of work any research project will call for.

Advanced research methodology courses will benefit from this programme. Participants may realise that, to execute a certain kind of research, they need to improve their mastery of advanced analytical techniques. Since original contributions need to be communicated to subject experts, participants may also realise the need for more advanced research writing skills.

Other courses may also benefit from this programme. Participants will be able to practise the skill of conceiving original contributions on a smaller scale in some of the assignments they need to do as part of the coursework component of a PhD.

## Instructional analysis

Participants will leave this programme with a more sceptical view and a better understanding of the nature of scientific inquiry. In other words, they will realise that inquiry in economics and other social sciences is socially and politically constructed with many logical inconsistencies, and that it is exactly these characteristics that create the conditions for originality to emerge.

They will learn specific skills of: problem representation and reformulation; elicitation of mental models; question construction and analysis; question generation; and applying abductive reasoning to new ideas. These skills will also enable them to facilitate a structured group process to promote new learning and innovation within their field.

Participants need not write any tests, but will need to practise the discrete skills within their field in collaboration with the programme facilitator and a subject expert. There should be continuous and formative assessment as they receive feedback on their mastery of the discrete skills leading up to the final outcome. The final outcome should be a reasonable number of proposed original contributions conceived during the course of the programme, and these will be judged for originality by at least two subject experts.

The specific areas in which participants will need to develop are listed in the next table. The skill of facilitating dialogue involves all the skills listed and is therefore not shown as a discrete area of development.

The programme will consist of what Gagné *et al.* (2005:63) label "intellectual skills" aimed at problem solving (in this case, the problem of conceiving original contributions). Problem solving first requires the intellectual skill of discrimination – that is differentiating different kinds of originality, as well as objectivism versus constructivism – which leads to concepts, which are essentially ideas, questions and problems. Concepts are used in learning rules: such as problem representation, question analysis, assumption elicitation, question generation and abductive reasoning.

## Learner analysis

Given the techniques that will be applied in the programme, PhD students and novice researchers, in Economics and other theory-driven social sciences, would gain the most from it. The techniques are less suitable to the natural sciences and the more descriptive humanities disciplines.

Participants need to meet certain prerequisites in order to benefit from the programme. These prerequisites, and how it could be determined if participants possess them, are given in Table 8.3.

All the evidence should to be submitted at least a month before the commencement of the programme. This is to allow sufficient time to do the interviews (as referred to in Table 8.3) before the selection is made. In order to assess the motivational characteristics of participants, a commonly used method in instructional design, Keller's (1987) ARCS model, can be used to guide the interviews.

*Table 8.2* Main areas of development in the programme

| Skills | Tasks |
| --- | --- |
| Scientific inquiry | Understand the constructivist view of scientific inquiry<br>Recognise the role of ideas, problems and questions in science<br>Discriminate between different kinds of originality |
| Problem representation | Convert a trade-off into a logical conflict<br>Develop a logical conflict representation from a real-world problem<br>Convert a problematic question into a logical conflict |
| Question analysis | Conduct a Van Fraassen analysis<br>Identify and create problematic questions |
| Assumption elicitation | Elicit assumptions from a logical conflict<br>Elicit assumptions from a Van Fraassen analysis<br>Elicit assumptions from a relational analysis of a question<br>Elicit assumptions from the cross of creative questioning |
| Question generation | Generate questions from a logical conflict<br>Generate questions from a Van Fraassen analysis |
| Abductive reasoning | Reason towards new ideas from a logical conflict<br>Reason towards new ideas from a cross of creative questioning |

*Table 8.3* Prerequisites and evidence

| Prerequisite | Evidence required |
| --- | --- |
| Working knowledge of their discipline | Academic record<br>Recommendation by mentor |
| Strong grasp of the specific area of research | 15–20 page literature review of the intended area of research identifying main themes and approaches |
| Competency of basic analytical tools | Aspects of the literature review<br>Recommendation by mentor |
| Competency in writing | Quality of writing in literature review<br>Recommendation by mentor |
| Motivation to participate | Descriptions of five proposed original contributions<br>Interview with prospective participant and mentor |

## Condition and constraint analysis

For the programme to be most effective, the techniques need to be taught sequentially, while giving participants uninterrupted time for practice and reflection. The ideal format is therefore a five-day writing retreat attended by both the participants and their mentors. However, this is most likely not feasible given logistics, time and financial constraints.

A more feasible approach would be to conduct the programme as a series of five workshops and consultations over a three-month period. This will allow participants the time to practise the skills, consult with their mentor and programme presenter and produce the outputs on which the next workshop will build.

In the workshop format, besides a venue for every workshop, there needs to be a board on which the presenter can demonstrate the skills. Participants need to attend every workshop, but their mentors' attendance is voluntary. Most of the workshop time will be spent on practising the skills, so participants will need to bring with them writing instruments, paper and the most important texts in their field that they may need to consult. Ideally, there should be power plugs and Internet access in the venue so that participants can access these texts electronically.

The presenter will lecture for short periods combined with demonstrations. Most of the time, the presenter will engage with participants while they practise, so the venue should be large enough for people to work and move around comfortably.

## Goal, task analysis and objectives

The overall goal of the programme is for every participant to conceive of a predetermined and reasonable number of ideas for original contributions, judged to be original by subject experts in a particular discipline. The contributions can take the form of reformulated problems, problematised questions, new questions, previously unrecognised assumptions or new ideas. Each of these should be accompanied by a justification of significance from the literature and a proposed approach to the research. To achieve this goal, participants need to master the tasks of problem representation, assumption elicitation, question generation and abductive reasoning to new ideas. By analysing the tasks and determining the resulting interdependencies, one can map out the sequence in which the skills need to be developed (as shown in Figure 8.2).

Each of the skills in Figure 8.2 consists of systems of smaller tasks. Such a task analysis allows one to work out what the main units of the programme will be, what needs to be taught in each unit and in what sequence. Figures 8.3–8.7 below present the results of this analysis. The numbers in these figures indicate the order in which the content should be presented.

By the end of the first unit, participants will have a different attitude toward scientific inquiry. They will understand the constructivist or

*An instructional programme* 147

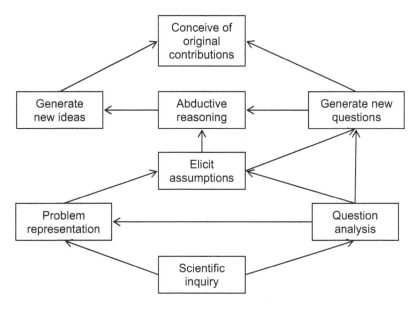

*Figure 8.2* Sequence of skills.

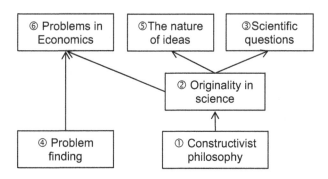

*Figure 8.3* Unit 1 – Scientific inquiry.

hermeneutic nature of social science and how this enables originality, as explained in Chapter 1. They will also understand that inquiry is driven by problems and questions. With this in mind, they will be able to find problems within their field based on the prerequisite literature review they submitted, and bring descriptions of these problems with them in preparation for the next unit.

The broken line in Figure 8.4 shows the content or skills from previous units that participants need to have mastered before engaging with the new unit.

148  *An instructional programme*

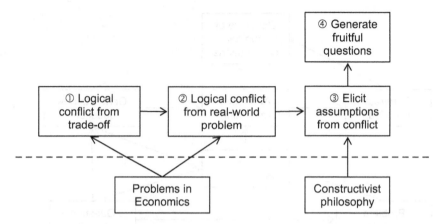

*Figure 8.4* Unit 2 – Problem representation.

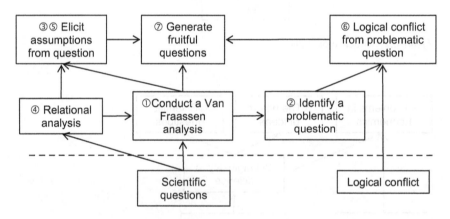

*Figure 8.5* Unit 3 – Question generation.

By the end of the second unit, participants will be able to construct a logical conflict representation from a trade-off and a real-world problem (as explained in Chapter 3). Using this representation, they will be able to elicit assumptions, and, from this, already derive possible questions that may lead to original contributions. During the session, they will be asked to practise all these skills on one of the problem areas they identified in preparation for this unit. They need to practise these skills independently and, in preparation for the next unit, derive a logical conflict with at least eight assumptions and two questions from each of their problem areas.

By the end of the third unit, participants will be able to analyse a question using Van Fraassen's method, and identify from this analysis if a

*An instructional programme* 149

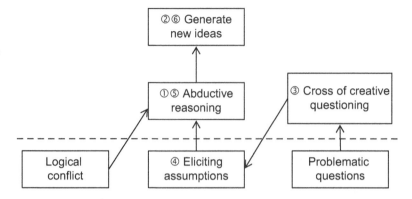

*Figure 8.6* Unit 4 – Idea generation.

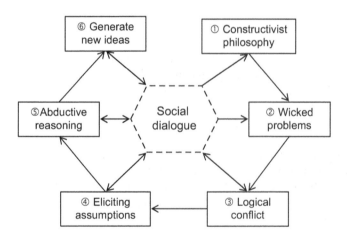

*Figure 8.7* Unit 5 – Facilitating dialogue.

question is problematic and what assumptions it is making, as explained in Chapter 4. They will also be able to elicit the assumptions of a question using relational analysis of a question. Using a similar method as the one learned in unit 2, participants will derive further possible questions that may lead to original contributions. During the session, they should be asked to practise all these skills on one or more of the questions they identified in preparation for this unit. They need to practise these skills independently and, in preparation for the next unit, identify three problematic questions in their field and generate at least two questions for original research from each problematic question.

By the end of the fourth unit, participants will be able to engage in two abductive reasoning processes, as explained in Chapter 5. First, using assumptions elicited from a logical conflict, participants will be able to use abductive reasoning to generate new ideas for research. Second, they will be able to construct a cross of creative questioning for a problematic question, and, from this, elicit assumptions and generate new ideas. During the session, they should be asked to practise setting up a process of abductive reasoning for one of the logical conflicts they generated after the second unit and also to construct a cross for one the problematic questions they identified in preparation for this unit.

After this unit, participants will have all the skills needed to individually conceive of original contributions. They need to practise these skills independently and, in preparation for the next unit, bring with them descriptions of five potential original contributions on which they would like to be assessed.

No new skills will be acquired in the fifth unit. Instead it will integrate the skills by showing how the process can be used to facilitate a dialogue around an economic problem between diverse stakeholders. This unit is therefore optional, and will be most useful to participants who plan to engage in multi-disciplinary research or with policy problems involving diverse stakeholders. By the end of the fifth unit, participants will understand that social dialogue around economic problems, if facilitated correctly, can lead to learning and innovation, and so generate further original contributions.

Based on the analysis thus far, it is possible to provide the programme outline. This is given as Table 8.4. The outline gives the estimated time to be spent on each skill and where guided practice will take place (marked by an asterisk).

If the programme occurs in a writing retreat format, there will be one workshop every day in the morning for five sequential days (except for the fifth session which should be in the early afternoon). If it is in workshop format, workshops will occur at more or less two-week intervals to allow sufficient time for independent work.

## Learning activities

Learning activities will follow the sequence as recommended by Gagné et al. (2005:10): (1) gain attention; (2) inform learners of the objective(s); (3) simulate recall of prerequisite capabilities; (4) present stimulus material; (5) provide learning guidance; (6) elicit performance; (7) provide feedback; (8) assess performance; and (9) enhance retention and transfer. The eighth step will occur out of sequence because it will involve the assessment of independent work after each session.

As mentioned before, the programme consists of the instruction of intellectual skills aimed at problem solving (the problem of conceiving original contributions). Problem solving first requires the intellectual skill of discrimination which leads to concepts. Concepts are used in learning rules: problem

*Table 8.4* Programme outline

| Event | Skills | Time |
|---|---|---|
| Workshop 1: Scientific inquiry (2–2½ hours) | Explain constructivist view of science | 20 min |
| | How this relates to originality | 20 min |
| | Distinguish between kinds of originality | 20 min |
| | The importance and nature of scientific questions | 10 min |
| | Find problems and show how they emerge from ideas* | 20 min |
| | Nature of ideas in science | 10 min |
| | Problems in Economics | 30 min |
| Independent work | From their literature review, find three real-world problems | |
| Workshop 2: Problem representation (2½–3 hours) | Recall: problems in economics | 5 min |
| | Derive logical conflict from trade-off* | 30 min |
| | Derive logical conflict from real-world problem* | 60 min |
| | Recall: constructivist view of science | 5 min |
| | Elicit assumptions from logical conflict* | 30 min |
| | Generate questions from the assumptions* | 20 min |
| Independent work | For each of their real-world problems, construct a logical conflict, derive eight or more assumptions and generate two or more questions | |
| Workshop 3: Question generation (3–3½ hours) | Recall: nature of scientific questions | 5 min |
| | Do a Van Fraassen analysis of a question* | 30 min |
| | Identify where a question may be problematic* | 30 min |
| | Elicit assumptions from a Van Fraassen analysis* | 30 min |
| | Do a relational analysis of a question* | 15 min |
| | Elicit assumptions from a relational analysis* | 15 min |
| | Recall: logical conflict | 5 min |
| | Derive a logical conflict from a problematic question and elicit further assumptions | 20 min |
| | Generate questions from the assumptions* | 20 min |
| Independent work | Identify three problematic questions in their field and what makes them problematic. Generate two or more questions from each problematic question. | |
| Workshop 4: Abduction to new ideas (3½–4 hours) | Recall: logical conflict and eliciting assumptions | 10 min |
| | Abductive reasoning to new ideas from a logical conflict | 60 min |
| | * Recall: problematic questions | 30 min |
| | Construct a cross of creative questioning* | 60 min |
| | Elicit assumptions of a question from the cross* | 30 min |
| | Abductive reasoning from a cross of creative questioning* | 30 min |
| Independent work | Produce ideas and questions and submit descriptions of their five best proposed original contributions | |

(*continued*)

152  An instructional programme

Table 8.4 (cont.)

| Event | Skills | Time |
|---|---|---|
| Workshop 5: Facilitating dialogue (2–2½ hours) | Recall: constructivist view and problems in economics | 10 min |
| | Explain wicked problems | 20 min |
| | Recall: logical conflict, eliciting assumptions, abductive reasoning to new ideas | 30 min |
| | Explain application to social dialogue | 60 min |
| Evaluation | Explained later in this chapter | 2–3 weeks |

\* Guided practice included.

representation, question analysis, assumption elicitation, question generation and abductive reasoning. Each kind of skill needs to be approached differently.

There are two areas in which participants should learn to discriminate. They should be able to discriminate between the constructivist view of science and the more conventional positivist view, and should be able to discriminate between different kinds of originality. To teach this discrimination, the programme will draw on the relevant content from Chapters 1 and 2 of this thesis. Gagné et al. (2005:65) recommend that instruction in discrimination should start with informing learners of the kind of discrimination to practise, then presenting examples and helping them notice the differences.

There are three defined concepts participants should learn the attributes and internal structure of: ideas, scientific questions and scientific problems. To teach the acquisition of defined concepts, Gagné et al. (2005:68) recommend that instruction in defined concepts should start by identifying the concept and presenting its definition, followed by showing examples and non-examples, and, finally, giving the opportunity to practise classifying examples and non-examples. To teach these concepts, the programme will draw on the relevant content from Chapters 2–4 of this book.

The bulk of the programme involves applying rules, that is: the various techniques of: problem representation and reformulation, question analysis, assumption elicitation, question generation and abductive reasoning. To teach the application of rules, Gagné et al. (2005:70) recommend first stating the skill to be learned, presenting a verbal description of the rule, demonstrating the rule and guiding learners in practising the rule. This will draw on the detailed explanations and examples of the techniques as presented in Chapters 3–7.

## Evaluation

According to Gagné et al. (2005), an instructional programme should be evaluated in five areas: (1) course material; (2) process; (3) participant reaction; (4) participant achievement; and (5) consequences. The first three are discussed below as part of the evaluation of the programme, and the last two as part of evaluation of participants.

Evaluation guided by a constructivist view of knowledge and learning will be led by an understanding that evaluation is collaborative, emergent and recursive. The outcomes of such evaluation are negotiated and this process has unpredictable outcomes, because evaluation changes the very reality it is trying to measure (Reeves, 1997:170). This is in contrast to the positivist view that sees evaluation merely as a description of an objective state of affairs. Application of constructivist principles needs to be evident in the evaluation of the programme and the participants.

## *Evaluation of the programme*

To determine the effectiveness of this programme, it needs to be tested in a pilot study with a small number of participants. After the pilot, participants and their mentors should be asked to complete a course evaluation in the form of a semi-structured interview. It should ask them to rate the value of the programme overall by considering the process and the clarity of the content and course materials and further discussion to explore their perceptions. The presenter should also engage in self-reflection. This feedback is then used to revise the programme. The revised programme can then be evaluated in the same way.

## *Evaluation of the participants*

The most appropriate kind of evaluation of participants in a programme that takes a constructivist view is authentic assessment (Wiggins & McTighe, 2005). Authentic assessment is the assessment of performance in real-life contexts. This kind of assessment has unpredictable outcomes and encourages intrinsic motivation, autonomy and participation in the learning process. Authentic assessment makes evaluation more complex and often happens collaboratively (McAlpine, 2000).

In this programme, researchers will be conceiving of original contributions for actual research they propose to do. It is these same contributions that will be assessed by the kind of people who would normally judge their research. Within the academic context, the assessment of each participant's achievement will therefore be authentic.

The value of the course will be evident from the qualitative change in the originality of the participants. Unfortunately, originality is hard to judge.

Originality has, as explained in Chapter 2, a hermeneutic nature in that it is a matter of interpretation by the intended audience. In academic research, the audience is comprised of subject matter experts, namely, the supervisors, examiners or reviewers. It can only be defined in terms of judgements of the audience, and may lead to diverging judgements. To alleviate this problem,

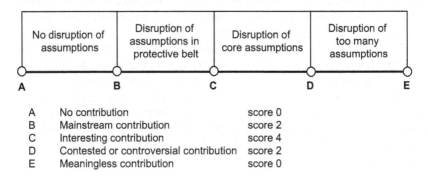

*Figure 8.8* Degrees of originality.

the programme facilitator should have discussions with the judges about the evaluation of originality prior to the assessment.

Any assessment has to take into account that there are degrees of originality. This was explained earlier and summarised in Figure 2.2 (reproduced as Figure 8.8). This continuum can be used to generate a provisional originality score for each contribution.

The participants will be deemed successful if their five (or whatever the predetermined number was) proposed original contributions after the programme are judged by two subject experts as more original than their five proposed original contributions before the programme. To avoid bias caused by knowing which contributions were generated after the programme, each participant's five pre-programme and five post-programme contributions should be judged as one group. The judges should be asked to classify each participant's ten contributions, without knowing which ones were generated before or after the programme, according to four criteria: (1) feasibility of the research; (2) novelty; (3) relevance to the discipline; and (4) potential significance to the discipline.

Proposed contributions that are not feasible or not relevant should be eliminated from the judgement process and given a score of 0. If a contribution is judged to be original, then judges should be asked to decide where, on the originality continuum in Figure 8.8, to place it. Since this is a continuum, scores may fall in between the intervals.

This placement will then determine the total score for the two groups of five contributions. The minimum total score is 0 and maximum score 20 (5 contributions × 4). This score is provisional since no quantitative measure can fully capture such a subjective, rich and multi-dimensional concept.

As a triangulation measure, judges can also be asked to place each contribution in one of Guetzkow *et al.*'s (2004) twenty-seven sub-categories (see Table 2.2) to see if it falls in the same range as the score. Discrepancies with the score should be explored in the interviews that follow.

*An instructional programme* 155

Since it is quite possible that the judgement of originality will be different from that reflected in the score, the final stage of assessment of the contributions will be unstructured interviews with the judges and participants. If the participant was successful, then his or her total originality score will have increased in all likelihood, but, more importantly, the participant's originality, as perceived by the judges, will have improved, as gathered from the interviews.

A follow-up study of all participants should be conducted at one-year intervals after they completed the programme. This is to establish if they were able to follow through with their proposed contributions and to judge the long-term effectiveness of the programme. After the first year one should contact the participants again and explore the questions such as the following with them:

- Did they continue using the techniques in their own research? In what ways? Did they find it useful? Did they adapt the techniques? Which techniques do they avoid or struggle with?
- Did they continue with the research contributions they conceived as an immediate result of the workshop? Did they find that they had more ideas for contributions or that the originality of their contributions changed after the workshop?
- Did they use the techniques in other ways (e.g. in supervision or teaching)? If so, how did they use it and how useful was it?

As a result of the interviews over this period, one's ideas about evaluation will probably undergo changes. This is consistent with the constructivist view of evaluation as a collaborative, recursive and emergent process that itself involves learning (Guba & Lincoln, 1989; Reeves, 1997).

## Some additional findings from the first pilot programmes

I presented the first pilot instructional programme (as explained in this chapter) in Colombia, to academics and PhD students from a range of social science disciplines at the Universidad Antonio Nariño in Bogotá in mid-2015, and then again a shorter version at the Universidad de Ibagué one week later. While time constraints did not permit me to present the programme exactly as anticipated, I did nevertheless learn from the pilot programmes, and incorporated the lessons into the design of the programme as presented in this chapter. Here I present some additional findings that I did not incorporate in the programme or that I wish to highlight for those who wish to implement the programme.

All participants found the workshops useful. The comments from feedback forms indicated that the programme changed most participants' understanding of research and originality. The main themes that emerged were:

## 156  *An instructional programme*

- The programme changed participants' views of originality because it provided relatively simple, practical and systematic methods for finding original contributions – something that they previously thought of as difficult. Some mentioned that they found this inspiring and that it motivated them to do research. This suggests that a programme such as this would be ideal for students who just finished the coursework part of their PhD studies and are about to embark on the research component.
- A number also commented that it widened their perspective on knowledge creation, and will enable to them to think more clearly about how they formulate their problems and questions. This suggests that this programme could also be a useful complement to existing philosophy of science or research methodology courses, and enhance the capability of PhD supervisors.

Participants were also asked to be critical and indicate where the programme could be improved. The most common comment is one that is already incorporated in the programme, but is worth mentioning again to emphasise its importance. Participants felt that, since these techniques are so new, they needed a lot more time to practise, first with examples provided by the facilitator, then with examples drawn from the participants and finally guided individual practice together with the facilitator. Participants made many mistakes the first time they tried the techniques individually, so examples and consultations with me were very valuable to them. Many found that they learned as much from these consultations, where we worked on their own research, than from the workshops themselves.

Participants found that examples improved their understanding of the techniques. I therefore created a fully worked out example on a topic with which I had limited familiarity (migration) but that could be understood by researchers from all social sciences (see the appendix to this chapter). The individual consultations with participants also enabled me to build a wider range of examples that can be used to explain the techniques.

I found that most preferred to use the logical conflict diagram, even when it was not appropriate, and neglected the question analysis techniques. I therefore found it useful to spend some time in the last workshop to discuss the appropriateness of different techniques. Participants should understand that the logical conflict is most useful for real-world problems about which there are different views. Why-questions and how-questions are usually not directly convertible into logical conflicts and for them it is better to use the question analysis techniques. As anticipated, the workshop on abductive reasoning was the most challenging to participants, and the cross of creative questioning was not used by anyone. Despite its difficulty it is a powerful technique for approaching unanswered questions and to derive more interesting questions from an apparently boring question.

## Appendix: a fully worked-out example

Since all the case studies thus far have been backward-looking, the benefit of hindsight made it easier to generate questions and ideas. To test the usefulness of the techniques and to generate more examples for future workshops, I chose a topic in which I have a basic knowledge – that of international migration of labour. I am familiar with the basic textbook analysis of the economic gains and losses from migration and co-authored two related articles on the economic effects of international students. I decided to base this exercise only on my rather limited prior knowledge combined with one recent article from the *Journal of Economic Literature* and generate potential contributions from it. This would place me in more or less the same position as a young novice PhD candidate starting out on the search for an original contribution.

The article chosen is a review essay by a leading economic researcher on migration, George Borjas, in which he critically looks at the argument that the lifting of migration restrictions will bring trillions of dollars of economic gains to the world economy. It is an argument that follows from most neo-classical economic models. In his review essay Borjas (2015) confronts the puzzle of why countries restrict migration when economic models show that large gains are there for the taking. Borjas employs mainly the invalidation strategy by showing that the models are based on questionable assumptions, but in this section I will show this research suggests many potential original contributions.

### *Deriving questions and ideas from the problem representation*

The easiest place to start is with problem representation and formulation. From this one can elicit assumptions to be questioned and generate possible new ideas. Figure 8.9A represents the puzzle as a logical conflict.

From this conflict representation we can derive assumptions by questioning each connective. Some of the assumptions are given in Table 8.5A.

Borjas (2015) makes many of the assumptions explicit by considering the assumptions of the orthodox economic models. He does so in order to invalidate connectives I and II. In the process he also reveals his own assumptions. Some of these assumptions lead to questions that may become original contributions. Taking only a few of the assumptions, or pairs of inconsistent assumptions, and questioning them suggest the following to me:

- What explains the wage differences between rich and poor regions – restrictions on immigration or productivity differences? Chang (2010) argues that productivity differences cannot explain the large wage gaps between countries which, if true, would substantially reduce the envisaged gains from migration.
- Following new growth theory (Romer, 1992) one may question whether the value of the ideas that migrants bring with them is underestimated

### 158  An instructional programme

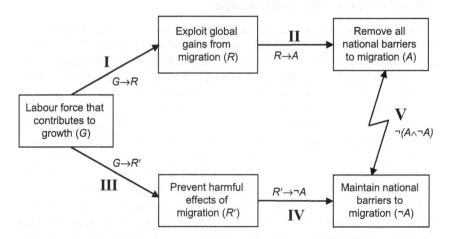

*Figure 8.9A* Representing the problem.

in neoclassical economic models due to the Cobb–Douglas production function focus on capital and labour as the main sources of growth. In fact, Romer (1994) argues that the losses of trade restrictions are underestimated because models do not take into account the value of ideas prevented from entering a country. This can be extended to restrictions on migration.

- Are tangible and intangible infrastructures (such as capital, institutions and governance systems) impervious to changes in the quantity and composition of the population? In cases where large scale migration took place, what effect did this have on the quality of institutions?
- Do global gains translate into national welfare? Drawing on the literature on the gains from free trade and capital flows, under what conditions do gains increase national welfare, and do these conditions exist in labour markets? (See for example Lall and Pietrobelli, 2002.)
- To what degree is migration policy determined by national interest? Drawing on the field of ideational scholarship (cf. Béland & Cox, 2011) one may track the evolution of the idea of migration restrictions to determine what factors played a role in arriving at the current state, especially to identify how contextual factors and attempts to shape perceptions influenced current policies.
- Factor price elasticities are different between countries in different segments of the labour market. What difference does this make to the model?
- In cases where large scale migration took place, what kinds of externalities (if any) emerged, and how were they dealt with? Are such cases sufficient to be extrapolated to the much larger numbers expected to migrate when restrictions are completely relaxed?

*An instructional programme* 159

*Table 8.5A* Assumptions that structure the problem

| | |
|---|---|
| Connective I | Net global gains from migration exceed national losses, gains are not being exploited, migration will raise output and returns on capital in rich regions and raise labour income of workers in and from poor regions (this is based on further assumptions: differences in tangible and intangible infrastructures exist and are fixed, these infrastructures determine relative labour productivity between regions, wage depends on marginal labour productivity, Cobb–Douglas production function is fixed, factor price elasticity is negative and the same in all regions, all labour is homogenous and inelastically supplied, mobility will equalise wages, no externalities in host country due to inflow, losers in the host country can be compensated, migrants will increase demand for output in the rich regions) |
| Connective II | Barriers are self-imposed and based on ignorance or narrow interests, migration restrictions limit gains, lifting restrictions will cause labour to migrate from rich to poor regions and materialise the gains |
| Connective III | National growth more important than global gains, global gains don't translate into national welfare, migration will not raise output in rich regions (this is based on further assumptions: tangible and intangible infrastructures are not fixed and migration will reduce their quality, migrants will remit income, negative externalities such as congestion, politically infeasible to redistribute from winners to losers, losers can be economically disruptive), poor regions will suffer losses (brain drain, lower quality of tangible and intangible infrastructures), wages determined by restrictions more than by productivity differences |
| Connective IV | Countries know what is in their best interest and design policies accordingly, context determines a country's interests, lifting restrictions will cause labour to migrate from rich to poor regions |
| Connective V | Restrictions have to be relaxed in the same place, no differentiation between restrictions, restrictions are all-or-nothing |

The conflict representation can also be used to formulate three main groups of questions designed to generate new ideas or assumptions as shown in Figure 8.10A.

The questions that follow are:

- $R \rightarrow \neg A$: How can countries exploit the gains of migration while maintaining national barriers to migration?
- $R' \rightarrow A$: How can countries prevent the harmful effects of migration while removing national barriers to migration?
- $A \wedge \neg A$: How can national barriers to migration be removed while maintaining such barriers?

160  *An instructional programme*

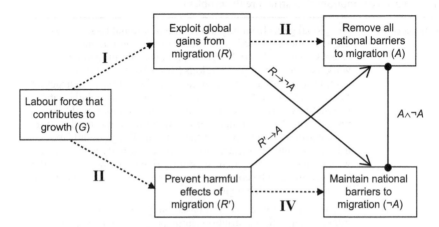

*Figure 8.10A* Questions designed for synthesis.

New ideas for research can be generated directly by these questions, or indirectly through the negation of assumptions. The following emerged for me:

- $R \rightarrow \neg A$: How can countries exploit the gains of migration while maintaining national barriers to migration? Central to answering this question is the issue of how much barriers to migration are worth to the host country. All ideas that are generated from this question rely on this kind of valuation. Further ideas followed from this:
    - Are there methods to force governments to reveal what certain barriers (or lack thereof) are worth to them? There is a strong tradition in Economics that argues that preferences are revealed through market actions. Can a market for migration barriers be designed?
    - Can host countries play a larger role in improving source countries' tangible and intangible infrastructures or raising the labour income in source countries? This suggests the design of economic aid or other forms of cooperation linked to labour market outcomes in the source countries.
    - Is there a way to force migrants to internalise the externalities caused by large inflows? Or is this the wrong question, as Coase might have suggested, because there is reciprocal harm from discouraging migration? Is it not better to create conditions where host country workers can bargain with source country workers?
    - Are there hidden gains from migration (not recognised in economic models) that are created by maintaining barriers?
- $R' \rightarrow A$: How can countries prevent the harmful effects of migration while removing national barriers to migration?
    - Can source countries or their migrants be involved in raising the quality of the tangible or intangible infrastructures of the host country?

*An instructional programme* 161

It suggests researching the current Chinese strategy of building cities in host countries.
- It could also suggest new ideas such as host countries establishing pre-migration centres in the source countries. In such centres the host country finances the development of potential migrants which will make it easier for them to succeed in the host country. Potential migrants are not under any obligation to migrate and may elect to stay if due to their development they are offered more attractive opportunities in their home country.
- In host countries with a sovereign fiat currency and a flexible exchange rate, an unexplored idea for compensating those who lose jobs due to migration are an adapted version of the employment guarantee schemes that have proven to be effective in Argentina (Tcherneva, 2012).
- $A \wedge \neg A$: How can national barriers to migration be removed while maintaining such barriers?
  - This is possible if barriers are segmented and leads to research on the idea of differentiated migration restrictions (allowing some migration while placing restrictions on the current or potential migrants) in place in many countries. Research could explore and develop a taxonomy of differentiated restrictions applied by countries and identify the conditions under which they may be effective.
  - The labour market may be segmented either geographically (designing the equivalent of EPZs (export processing zones) for labour markets) or by degree of human capital (freeing up flows in certain skill areas).
  - The time horizon can also be extended to allow for gradual relaxation of restrictions, but with the restriction relaxation being guided by Coasean market signals.

*Deriving questions and ideas from a Van Fraassen analysis*

Suppose the core question is: 'Why do countries resist the net gains they can obtain from unrestricted migration?' The topic of the core question is: 'countries resist the net gains they can obtain from unrestricted migration' and if this were not true, the question would be problematic. Table 8.6A shows some of the contrast classes and relevance relations that may follow from the core question and each of these present opportunities to problematise the question and raise other questions.

Exploring the different contrast classes gives rise to some of the following questions that problematise the core question:

- 1a: Is the infeasibility of restricting national migration the main reason governments do not impose the same restrictions as they do on international migration? Is restricting international migration not equally

162  *An instructional programme*

*Table 8.6A* Contrast classes and relevance relations

| | Question | As opposed to… (contrast class) | Answers will focus on… (relevance relation) |
|---|---|---|---|
| 1a | Why do *countries* resist the net gains they can obtain from unrestricted migration? | …provinces/states, cities | Reasons why national migration cannot or should not be restricted in the same way as international migration. |
| 1b | Why do *countries* resist the net gains they can obtain from unrestricted migration? | …other authorities or institutions | Reasons why national governments restrict migration. |
| 2 | Why do countries *resist* the net gains they can obtain from unrestricted migration? | …ignore, allow, encourage | Explanation of why countries actively resist gains possible from migration. |
| 3 | Why do countries resist the *net gains* they can obtain from unrestricted migration? | …net losses | Identifying the net gains that exist and how they come to be. |
| 4 | Why do countries resist the net gains *they can obtain* from unrestricted migration? | …others obtain | The mechanisms by which countries can appropriate the gains from migration. |
| 5 | Why do countries resist the net gains they can obtain from *unrestricted* migration? | …restricted, prohibited | Arguments that net gains mainly follow when there are no restrictions. |
| 6 | Why do countries resist the net gains they can obtain from unrestricted *migration*? | …trade, capital flows, idea flows | Why net gains from migration are more important than those from other forms of economic integration. |

infeasible? Can the non-coercive instruments used to influence national migration be adapted to influence international migration?
- 1b: Why do multilateral organisations have a different view on the economics of labour migration than national governments? Are they using different models or select different data?
- 2: What non-economic factors contribute to the resistance? To what degree do biases (from behavioural economics) play a role? Or is there a public choice kind of explanation?
- 3: Are economic models accurate depictions of the net gains from migration or are these net gains sensitive to the assumptions of the models? Borjas (2015) attempts to answer this particular question.

*An instructional programme* 163

- 4: Is it possible for countries to appropriate the gains from migration? Do these gains have characteristics of public goods or positive externalities that make it difficult to capture the gains? Or might it be the case that these gains are simply too difficult to measure?
- 5: Are the net gains dependent on the lack of restrictions, or do restrictions generate gains not recognised by economic models?
- 6: Can the gains from migration not be achieved through other forms of economic integration? What is the relationship between gains from migration and free trade, aid, capital flows or sharing of intellectual property?

*Deriving questions and ideas from a relational analysis*

The relational analysis reveals many of the same assumptions that become evident from the other techniques. The analysis is based on the question: 'Why do countries resist the net gains they can obtain from unrestricted migration?' Questioning the assumptions leads to possible areas for original research.

Some of the assumptions derived from Figure 8.11A appear in Table 8.7A below. Each one can be converted into a question and some may trigger original research:

- A2: Whose interests are served by restricting international migration of labour? Are these interests representative of national interest, and if not, what biases cause these interests to be dominant?
- B1: What undermines pursuit of gains? As already mentioned, this leads to research on the interests and perceptions that influence migration policy, or on the potential public good nature of these gains.
- D1/D2: How binding are restrictions on migration really? Is it true that migration will still happen regardless of the severity of the restrictions? What is the economic cost of these restrictions and at what point do these costs become unjustifiable?

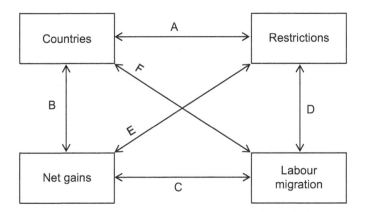

*Figure 8.11A* Relevance relations in a question.

164  *An instructional programme*

*Table 8.7A* Assumptions derived from relational analysis

| Relation | Assumptions |
|---|---|
| A | A1: Countries place restrictions on economic activity |
|   | A2: Restrictions serve the interests of a country |
| B | B1: Countries pursue net gains to themselves if available |
|   | B2: Net gains are more important than the composition of gains and losses |
|   | B3: Global gains become national gains |
| C | C1: There are net gains for all countries from labour migration |
|   | C2: There are winners and losers when migration takes place |
| D | D1: Countries impose restrictions on labour migration |
|   | D2: Labour migration would take place in the absence of restrictions |
| E | E1: Restrictions reduce the gains from labour migration |
| F | F1: Migration takes place between countries |
|   | F2: Countries have different levels of attractiveness for migrants |

- E1: Are there hidden gains from maintaining barriers to migration? (already mentioned).
- F2: Is it possible to construct an 'attractiveness indicator' that identifies whether a country is becoming more or less attractive to migration? If the indicator can distinguish bilateral attractiveness levels or between skill levels it would be even more useful for policy purposes.

### Cross of creative questioning

The cross technique of creative questioning guides the interplay of negation and affirmation and directs the process by defining the starting point (a problematic question: 'Why do countries resist the net gains they can obtain from unrestricted migration?'), the mid-point (a conjunction of an affirmation and a negation) and the end point is a solution that satisfies the conjunction and solves the problem.

The topic of the problematic question should have a noun-phrase (*NP*) containing the subject, another noun-phrase containing the object and a verb-phrase (*VP*) describing the interaction between subject and object. This topic is a compound sentence which complicates matters because it allows for more than one way to set up the cross diagram. There is an inner sentence 'countries can obtain net gains from unrestricted migration' with a subject *NP* ('countries'), an object *NP* ('unrestricted migration') and a *VP* ('gain'). Around this is an outer sentence where the subject *NP* is 'countries', the *VP* is 'restrict' and the object *NP* is the inner sentence. Figure 8.12A shows the simple grammatical mapping.

In this case the two *NP*s that are of the inner sentence are placed in the vertical bar of the cross. The affirmation (labelled *NP* in Figure 8.13A) is the

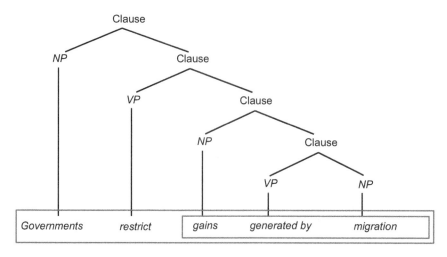

*Figure 8.12A* Simplified grammatical mapping of the question.

relation between these two *NP*s and the negation is simply the opposite of the affirmation (labelled ¬*NP* in Figure 8.13A).

The *VP* is placed in the horizontal bar of the cross. The affirmation (labelled *VP* in Figure 8.13A) captures the interaction between the subject ('countries') and object (the inner sentence) and the negation is simply the opposite of the affirmation (labelled ¬*VP* in Figure 8.13A). The verb is 'restrict' and this needs elaboration – the kind of restriction implied is governments' restriction of migration. As shown in Figure 8.13A *VP* in this case is 'government restricts migration' and ¬*VP* is 'government does not restrict migration'.

Now the midpoint of the cross can be generated by conjoining an affirmation from one bar of the cross and a negation from the other bar of the cross. It makes us search for answers to the question: how could *NP*∧¬*VP* or ¬*NP*∧*VP* be true? They are deliberate provocations of anomalies aimed at disrupting existing knowledge and forcing a search for new assumptions.

To use the creative power of negation one takes each negation and asks: what are the possible forms this negation may take (and so populate the contrast classes). Table 8.8A shows these negations which open up creative possibilities.

For the creative potential of negation to be utilised, it needs to be constrained by an affirmation. This is done by conjoining the negations on one bar of the cross to an affirmation on the other bar of the cross, as given in Table 8.9A.

Conjoining the negations in every column with their relevant affirmation gives us several possible conjunctions to explore. The purpose is to generate statements that will disrupt the system of ideas that maintain the problem.

166   *An instructional programme*

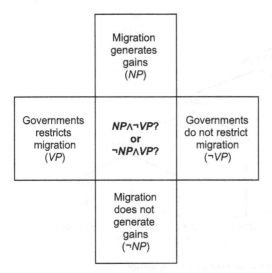

*Figure 8.13A* Cross of questioning.

*Table 8.8A* Possible negations

| ¬*NP: migration does not generate gains* | ¬*VP: government does not restrict migration* |
|---|---|
| ¬$NP_1$: migration generates net losses<br>¬$NP_2$: migration is welfare neutral<br>¬$NP_3$: something else generates gains | ¬$VP_1$: government encourages migration<br>¬$VP_2$: government does nothing about migration<br>¬$VP_3$: government prohibits migration<br>¬$VP_4$: some other group restricts migration<br>¬$VP_5$: government restricts something else |

Negation

Some of the more disruptive conjunctions that lead to possible areas for research are:

- $VP \land \neg NP_3$: This suggests the possibility that there are other, more desired ways to generate the gains from migration. It leads to the question of whether the proposed gains from migration can only be brought about by migration. Are these gains uniquely generated by migration or is migration the most efficient way to generate these gains?
- $NP \land \neg VP_2$: This would be true if government felt indifferent towards the gains from migration, perhaps because it cannot appropriate the gains. Again this suggests exploring the possible public goods nature of the

*Table 8.9A* Possible conjunctions

|  | Conjunctions 1–3 (¬NP∧VP) | Conjunctions 4–8 (NP∧¬VP) |
|---|---|---|
| Negation | ¬$NP_1$: migration generates net losses<br>¬$NP_2$: migration is welfare neutral<br>¬$NP_3$: something else generates gains | ¬$VP_1$: government encourages migration<br>¬$VP_2$: government does nothing about migration<br>¬$VP_3$: government prohibits migration<br>¬$VP_4$: some other group restricts migration<br>¬$VP_5$: government restricts something else |
| Conjoin with… | VP: government restricts migration | NP: migration generates gains |

gains, and if it is found to be true, it would suggest research into how government could be made less indifferent through methods of appropriating some of the gains.
- $NP∧¬VP_3$: If this conjunction were true, it would be a stronger version of the previous conjunction ($NP∧¬VP_2$) and suggest that the gains from migration undermine government power.
- $NP∧¬VP_4$: Again, this suggests research into whether or to what degree migration policy is captured by special interests.
- $NP∧¬VP_5$: The question raised here is whether the gains from migration are conditional on the restriction of something else. It would lead to a search for possible variables that mediate the relationship between migration and its economic gains and whether it might be more fruitful to restrict or relax restrictions on these variables.
- ¬$NP_1∧¬VP_5$: This conjunction suggests a search for possibilities that migration is not the reason for the losses ascribed to it. Losses may be due to some deeper underlying institutional problem in the host country that converts migration gains into losses.

*Reflection on the process*

I found this process useful because it enabled me to identify potential directions for research. It provided purpose to my reading which followed after I completed this process. Some researchers recommend a process similar to this one – they argue that it is better to explore a field after gaining some basic knowledge since creativity can be stifled by too much prior reading. As expected, it also made me more interested in it. I also realised that it would be useful approach to generate topics for graduate students below doctoral level, or even undergraduate research projects.

# References

Béland, D. & Cox, R.H. (eds). 2011. *Ideas and Politics in Social Science Research*. Oxford: Oxford University Press.

Borjas, G.J. 2015. Immigration and globalization: a review essay. *Journal of Economic Literature*, 53(4): 961–974.

Chang, H.-J. 2010. *23 Things They Don't Tell You About Capitalism*. London: Penguin.

Coleman, S.D., Perry, J.D. & Schwen, T.M. 1997. Constructivist instructional development: reflecting on practice from an alternative paradigm. In: Dills, C.R. & Romiszowski, A.J. (eds), *Instructional Development Paradigms*, Englewood Cliffs, NJ: Educational Technology Publications, 269–282.

Gagné, R.M., Wager, W.W., Golas, K.C. and Keller, J.M. 2005. *Principles of Instructional Design*. Belmont, CA: Wadsworth.

Guba, E.G. & Lincoln, Y.S. 1989. *Fourth Generation Evaluation*. Newbury Park, CA: Sage.

Guetzkow, J., Lamont, M. & Mallard, G. 2004. What is originality in the humanities and the social sciences? *American Sociological Review*, 69(2):190–212.

Johnson, K.A. & Bragar, J.L. 1997. Principles of adult learning: a multi-paradigmatic model. In: Dills, C.R. & Romiszowski, A.J. (eds), *Instructional Development Paradigms*, Englewood Cliffs, NJ: Educational Technology Publications, 335–349.

Keller, J.M. 1987. The systematic process of motivational design. *Performance & Instruction*, 26(9):1–8.

Lall, S. & Pietrobelli, C. 2002. *Failing to Compete: Technology Development and Technology Systems in Africa*. Northampton, MA: Edward Elgar.

Ledford, B.R. & Steeman, P.J. 2000. *Instructional Design: A Primer*. Greenwich, CT: Information Age Publishing.

McAlpine, D. 2000. Assessment and the gifted. *Tall Poppies*, 25(1):4–7.

Merriam, S.B. 2011. Adult learning. In: Rubenson, K. (ed.), *Adult Learning and Education*, Amsterdam: Elsevier, 29–34.

Reeves, T.C. 1997. Established and emerging paradigms for instructional design. In: Dills, C.R. & Romiszowski, A.J. (eds), *Instructional Development Paradigms*, Englewood Cliffs, NJ: Educational Technology Publications, 163–178.

Romer, P.M. 1992. Two strategies for economic development: using ideas and producing ideas. Proceedings of World Bank Annual Conference on Development Economics 1992, 63–91.

Romer, P.M. 1994. New goods, old theory, and the welfare costs of trade restrictions. *Journal of Development Economics*, 43:5–38.

Tcherneva, P.R. 2012. Beyond full employment: what Argentina's Plan Jefes can teach us about the employer of last resort. In: Murray, M.J. & Forstater, M. (eds), *Employment Guarantee Schemes: Job Creation and Policy in Developing Countries and Emerging Markets*, New York: Palgrave MacMillan, 79–102.

Wiggins, G.P. & McTighe, J. 2005. *Understanding by Design*, expanded 2nd edition. Alexandria, VA: Association for Supervision and Curriculum Development.

Wilson, B.G. 1997. Reflections on constructivism and instructional design. In: Dills, C.R. & Romiszowski, A.J. (eds), *Instructional Development Paradigms*, Englewood Cliffs, NJ: Educational Technology Publications, 63–80.

# 9 Next steps

This book developed a systematic approach to teach researchers in economics (and other social sciences) how to conceive of original contributions, while also aiming to bring the scholarship of intellectual creativity by economists within the domain of economics. It argued that most economic researchers hold rather unsophisticated ideas about intellectual creativity that are not informed by the actual research on the topic. This hampers not only the pedagogy of economics but also closes off an area with great potential for further research. This chapter will explore some of these possibilities.

There is sufficient evidence today that new insight is not the result of erratic inspiration, but rather of analytical thinking. By extension, the act of generating the original research contribution similarly results from analytical thinking. With this book I argued that understanding originality in this way helps researchers not only to gain greater insight into the development of their field, but also to generate original contributions more systematically and frequently and to instruct others in this art.

This book offered theoretical arguments for, and demonstrations of, a variety of techniques that can be used to reformulate problems, expose assumptions, generate interesting questions and discover new ideas in economics. I am not suggesting that readers will suddenly generate ground-breaking theories, and in fact this may not be desirable as I explained in the second chapter. In fact, in order to advance, a discipline does not need a major breakthrough in every paper written, it merely needs a steady accumulation of papers that go only slightly beyond the boundaries of what is assumed. The techniques in this book will simply help researchers to generate and discover ideas and interesting questions that they may not have thought of normally.

There is much dissatisfaction with the current graduate training in economics. One anonymous reviewer summarised it: "We have all seen too many job candidates whose job market paper proposes to see what happens when we relax assumption x. Often this involves adding new (and very unhelpful) assumption y. When the candidate is pressed to explain why they chose this line of research or why it matters they have no answer beyond, 'I can mathematically solve the resulting problem.' Clearly such work isn't very useful." With this book I am not calling for a transformation of the discipline, it is much more modest – it aims to make a contribution by addressing this dissatisfaction. Recognising the importance of creativity in economic research does not require a transformation, but it does suggest that economists should reconsider their role in society and the way they educate their researchers.

Economics is a discipline that has much potential for creative research and economists can be taught to conduct more of this. Again I want emphasise that the systematic approach developed in this book does not guarantee that original contributions will automatically follow, in the same way that knowing how to construct econometric or mathematical models cannot guarantee that good results will follow. The approach does make it more likely that more original research, of the interesting kind, will be conceived, but it still requires a strong grasp of the theory and analytical techniques that will make these contributions meaningful. This implies that the education of graduate students in Economics could, and should, include training on how to conceive of original contributions. The techniques developed in this thesis can form part of a larger reformed approach to graduate development as explained by Colander (2011).

If we accept the possibility of intellectual creativity in economics, economists should take a broader view of their role in society. They should shift away from seeing themselves as describing, predicting or controlling economic reality, and also embrace the creative role they can play in the shaping of this reality, as confirmed by recent work on the performativity of economic theory (Colander, 2008; Ferraro, Pfeffer & Sutton, 2005; MacKenzie, 2006; Muniesa, 2014). The systematic approach developed in this book offers an approach for economists to become more creative participants in the social argumentation process that moulds economic reality, and will enable economists to take a more active role in dialogue with other groups. Instead of focusing on only trying to control or predict, they should recognise that they help to create the very economic reality they try to describe and control. The most important neglected role of economists may well lie in facilitating collective learning and innovation within economic reality.

## Direct uses of this research

As already argued in previous chapters, this work offers ways to complement existing research methodology and philosophy of science courses in economics. It would be an ideal component of the preparation of graduate students and specifically doctoral candidates. It would also complement philosophy of science or research methodology courses given that it offers a different set of tools by which to analyse knowledge creation in the discipline.

Supervisors of graduate students can use the techniques to generate new problems and questions for their students. Researchers pursuing larger research programmes will find the techniques useful for opening up new avenues for interesting research. PhD candidates and post-docs should find sufficient guidance in this book to apply the techniques to search for original contributions, even without the assistance of a supervisor.

## Obvious extensions

It would be useful to apply the techniques to a wider range of case studies in economics. One such extension may be to apply the ideas in this book to explore in detail why highly creative economists such as Kenneth Boulding had a minor impact on the mental model of the discipline, while relatively less creative economists, such as John Muth, had a much larger impact. Combined with existing research on the spread of economic ideas and the sociology of economic knowledge (Colander & Coats, 1989; Steiner, 2001; Alkire & Ritchie, 2007) this research would give us a fuller understanding of the role of ideas within the discipline of economics.

Additional obvious areas for exploration would be the development of new techniques, or improvements on these techniques as they are applied more widely. Since the first workshops showed that researchers from other social sciences found the techniques useful, one could also extend the research into disciplines such as management, psychology and sociology, to name a few.

The collaborative creative process as explained in Chapter 7 can be applied beyond dialogue on policy issues. With some adjustments, it would be useful for guiding collaborative research within economics, and probably more effectively for guiding multi-disciplinary research.

## Less obvious extensions

One minor, and less obvious, extension of this research might be as a tool to improve the writing of literature reviews. Literature reviews aim to consolidate our understanding of an issue, to explain how we arrived at this understanding and what the future developments might be. The technique of problem formulation is well-suited to understanding the often hidden assumptions that guided the understanding of an issue up to the present, and by revealing the current substance constraints, it also suggests the most fruitful areas for further exploration. As I have explained in detail elsewhere (Wentzel, 2016) a literature review informed by the underlying assumptions of a problem or a question is likely to lead to literature reviews that are more coherent and argumentative.

Hattiangadi (1979) argued that most disciplines can be told as a history of intellectual problems, and that knowing the structure of problems also provides us with a thinking framework within which to reconstruct past problems and improve our understanding of how progress occurs in a discipline. He explained that a discipline emerges from a fundamental problem (or logical conflict), which in turn creates further logical inconsistencies as previous problems are solved. Not only does this suggest that the techniques in this book will allow researchers to write better literature reviews, but that it can also enrich the teaching of economic thought. In fact, the value of teaching economics through controversies and conflicts has been recognised by economists across a range of ideological positions (Moseley, Gunn & Georges, 1991; Raveaud, 2001; Rothbard, 2011).

Following from this, possibly the biggest potential for extension of this research lies in pedagogy. Some of the most innovative methods of instruction that have been recognised in economics are problem-based learning (Forsyth, 2010), Socratic teaching (Elzinga, 2012) and inquiry or discovery learning (Frank, 2014) or a combination of such approaches (Becker & Watts, 1995; McGoldrick & Garnett, 2013). While all of these approaches aim to get the student to think like an economist, they are rarely informed by an understanding of the structure of problems, question and ideas in economics. Understanding the logical structure of a problem offers a framework within which students can formulate economic problems, identify assumptions, pose questions and discover solutions, and so scaffold learning. The question formulation techniques provide the means by which instructors can generate the kinds of questions that provoke insight, or teach students to generate their own questions. Knowing how to discover meaningful new questions is a skill that is more valuable than reproducing old answers in a changing economic reality. Finally, the logical (abductive) approach to generating ideas may guide students in a process of rediscovering the ideas of great economists for themselves, an act of insight that makes learning deeper and more permanent.

Admittedly, these methods of teaching take more time, though Davies (2012) and Frank (2014) argue that it is more productive for economics students to really learn a few concepts really well, rather than being able to reproduce a large volume of content without understanding. And by teaching students in this way, I believe we increase the chances that they will be more interested in economics, and some become more critical and creative researchers in the future.

## References

Alkire, S. & Ritchie, A. 2007. Winning ideas: lessons from free-market economics. Working Paper No. ophiwp007. Queen Elizabeth House, University of Oxford.

Becker, W.E. & Watts, M. 1995. Teaching tools: teaching methods in undergraduate economics. *Economic Inquiry*, 33(4):692–700.

Colander, D.C. 2008. Review of 'Do Economists Make Markets? On the Performativity of Economics'. *Journal of Economic Literature*, 46(3):720–724.

Colander, D.C. 2011. Adding a bit more creativity to the graduate economics core. Paper presented at Allied Social Science Associations, 6–9 January 2011, Denver. https://www.aeaweb.org/aea/2011conference/program/preliminary.php, accessed 19 October 2011.

Colander, D.C. & Coats, A.W. 1989. *The Spread of Economic Ideas*. Cambridge: Cambridge University Press.

Davies, P. 2012. Threshold concepts in economics education. In: Hoyt, G.M. & McGoldrick, K. (eds), *International Handbook on Teaching and Learning Economics*, Cheltenham: Edward Elgar, 250–256.

Elzinga, K.G. 2012. Teaching economics Socratically. In: Hoyt, G.M. & McGoldrick, K. (eds), *International Handbook on Teaching and Learning Economics*, Cheltenham: Edward Elgar, 129–136.

Ferraro, F., Pfeffer, J. & Sutton, R.I. 2005. Economics language and assumptions: how theories can become self-fulfilling. *Academy of Management Review*, 30:8–24.

Forsyth, F. 2010. Problem-based learning. In: *The Handbook for Economics Lecturers*, revised edition. Available from https://www.economicsnetwork.ac.uk/handbook/pbl/, accessed 25 May 2016.

Frank, R. 2014. Do we try to teach our students too much? In: Lanteri, A. & Vromen, J. (eds), *The Economics of Economists: Institutional Setting, Individual Incentives, and Future Prospects*, Cambridge: Cambridge University Press, 243–255.

Hattiangadi, J.N. 1979. The structure of problems (Part II). *Philosophy of Social Science*, 9:49–76.

McGoldrick, K. & Garnett, R. 2013. Big think: a model for critical inquiry in economics courses. *The Journal of Economic Education*, 44(4):389–398.

MacKenzie, D. 2006. Is economics performative? Option theory and the construction of the derivatives market. *Journal of the History of Economic Thought*, 28(1):29–55.

Moseley, F., Gunn, C. & Georges, C. 1991. Emphasizing controversy in the economics curriculum. *The Journal of Economic Education*, 22(3):235–240.

Muniesa, F. 2014. *The Provoked Economy: Economic Reality and the Performative Turn*. London: Routledge.

Raveaud, G. 2001. Teaching economics through controversies. *Post-autistic Economics Newsletter*, 5(6). Available at www.paecon.net/PAEReview/wholeissues/issue5.htm, accessed 25 May 2016.

Rothbard, M.N. 2011. *Economic Controversies*. Auburn, AL: Ludwig von Mises Institute.

Steiner, P. 2001. The sociology of economic knowledge. *European Journal of Social Theory*, 4(4):443–458.

Wentzel, A. 2016. Creating the literature review: research questions and arguments (Part 1 of 4). Available at https://doctoralwriting.wordpress.com/2016/02/23/creating-the-literature-review-research-questions-and-arguments/, accessed 25 May 2016.

# Index

abductive reasoning 73–5; central banking *see* central banking ideas (Kydland and Prescott); creative research as systemic process 3–4; new ideas *see* new ideas' generation by reasoning; synthetic-abductive dialogue 132–4
Aliseda, A. 73
Allais, M. 1
Alvesson, M. 19–20, 61
Amabile, T. 5
American Economic Association's Commission on Graduate Education in Economics (CoGEE) 1
argument construction *see* economic problem solving
Arrow, K. 1
Arrow's Impossibility Theorem 92–3
artificial intelligence 4–5
assumption identification 55–7
authentic economic problem solving *see* economic problem solving

BACON programme 4
banking ideas *see* central banking ideas (Kydland and Prescott)
Belnap, N.D. 65
Beveridge curve 37
Bisseker, C. 128
Blinder, A.S. 106
Borjas, G. 157
Boulding, K. 171
brainstorming *see* new ideas' generation by reasoning
Bromberger, S. 65–6

capability approach (Sen) 91–8; Arrow's Impossibility Theorem 92–3; background/summary 1–2, 97–8; developing questions 95–7; formulating problems 92–5; impact of approach 97–8; invalidation approach 95; liberal paradox 92–5; summary of approach 92; synthesising approach 95–7
central banking ideas (Kydland and Prescott) 98–106; abductive reasoning application 101–6; contrast classes and relevance 105–6; discretion rules 98–9; end point derivations 101–2; formulating problems 98–101; generating idea by making connection 103–4; generating questions 104–6; reformulation of the rules-discretion problem 98; starting point derivation 102–3; summary 106; time-inconsistency problem 98–101; Van Fraassen analysis 105
Cherniak, C. 89
Coase, R.H. 9, 89, 106
Coase's Theorem 106–12; assumptions eliciting 110–12; contrast classes and relevance 107; creative questioning cross 107–12; discouraging externalities 106; negations/conjunctions 109–11; summary 112–13; Van Fraassen analysis 106–7
cognitive science research *see* creative research as systemic process
Colander, D.C. 170
computational modelling *see* creative research as systemic process
conflict representation *see* problem representation
confrontational-empirical dialogue *see* economic problem solving
construction model *see* originality in social science research

contrast classes and relevance: central banking ideas (Kydland and Prescott) 105–6; Coase's Theorem 107
Copernicus, N. 81–2
creative mathematics *see* new ideas' generation by reasoning
creative process *see* new ideas' generation by reasoning
creative questioning cross *see* new ideas' generation by reasoning
creative research as systemic process 3–5; cognitive science research 4–5; computational modelling 4; deductive/inductive/abductive logic 3–4; overview of book 8–9; reasoning in science 4; trial-and-error approach 5, *see also* scientific creativity
creativity, scientific *see* scientific creativity
creativity studies 5–8; books for economic researchers 7–8; disciplinary context 6; domain-specific creativity 5–6; economic influences on/of creativity 6–7; exposure to scientific papers 7; on systematic approach 8
Cross, C. 66

Darden, L. 91
Davies, P. 172
Davis, M.S. 18–19
Denzau, A.T. 23
destructive dilemma 39
Dewey, J. 34
disciplinary context: creativity studies 6; originality in social science research 23–4
discretion rules *see* central banking ideas (Kydland and Prescott)
domain-specific creativity *see* creativity studies

economic problem solving: argument construction 127–30; authoritative strategies 121–2; confrontational-empirical dialogue 132; creative dialogue 131–2; group selection/preparation 125; inconsistent beliefs 117; key issues/summaries 115–16, 124, 136; Knightian uncertainty 115; less confrontational approach 137; logical conflict elicitation 126–7; maximally consistent subset (MCS) 137; mental models 126–31; participative approach 124–5, 135–6; policy games 118; political nature 117–18; preparation of mental models 130–1; problem of authentic problem solving 116; social nature 116–17; synthetic-abductive dialogue 132–4; taming strategies 122–4; Taylor's monetary policy trade-off 126, 134–5; Toulmin model of argumentation 128–9, 137; trade-off infertility for dialogue 134–5; unstructured nature 118–20; wicked problems 120–4, 135–6
Edwards, L. 122
Einstein, A. 24–6
end point derivations: central banking ideas (Kydland and Prescott) 101–2; new ideas' generation by reasoning 79–80
erotetic logicians 28, 60, 65
Ethridge, D.E. 7
Euclidian proofs 76
EURISKO programme 4
*ex falso quodlibet* principle 39

feasibility *see* originality in social science research
Forder, J. 106
Frank, R. 172
Friedman, M. 2, 5
future use of techniques: aim of techniques 169; collaborative creative process 171; current training dissatisfaction 169–70; direct uses 170–1; less obvious extensions 171–2; major extensions 171; obvious extensions 171; role in society 170; worked-out example 157–67

Gagné, R.M. 150, 152
gap-spotting research 20–1
global financial crisis 1
Golden-Biddle, K. 22
Goodfriend, M. 116
Greenlaw, S.A. 7
Grieve, R.H. 1
Guetzkow, J. 22, 28

Hammersley, M. 15–17
Hamming, R.W. 78
Hattiangadi, J.N. 28, 38–9, 118, 171–2
Haubrich, J.G 102
hermeneutic model 17

# Index

ideas generation *see* new ideas' generation by reasoning
instructional programme: background/reflection 140, 167; condition/constraint analysis 146; constructivist v conventional view 141, 142 *Table*, 152; degrees of originality 153–4; design process 141–2; development areas 145; evaluation 152–5; front-end analysis 143–6; goal of programme 146; guiding philosophy 140–1; instructional analysis 144; Keller's ARCS model 144; learner analysis, prerequisites/evidence 144–5; learning activities 150–2; needs analysis 143; objectives 147–50; outline of programme 150–2; participants' evaluation 153–5; pilot programme findings 155–6; programme evaluation 153; task analysis 145 *Table*, 146–7; Units 147–9; interesting research *see* originality in social science research

Jardine, N. 29

Keller, J.M., ARCS model 144
Keynes, J.M. 4–5, 7
Knightian uncertainty 115
Krugman, P. 20, 66
Kuhn, T.S. 9, 23, 34, 38, 91
Kydland, F.E. 9, 33, 42, 89; case study *see* central banking ideas (Kydland and Prescott)

Laffer curve 37–8
Lakatos, I. 19, 21, 24, 91
Ledford, B.R. 142
Lenat, D.B. 4
liberal paradox *see* capability approach (Sen)
Locke, K. 22
logical conflict structure *see* problem representation
logical/creative activities, differences *see* new ideas' generation by reasoning
Lohmann, S. 101–2
Lucas, R. 1

McCloskey, D.N. 5
McKinnon, L.A.K. 7
Malthus, T 38

Mann Gulch disaster 84–5
Manor, R. 137
Mason, R.O. 137
mathematics, creative *see* new ideas' generation by reasoning, creative mathematics
Mauritius 33, 44–7; development of island 45; formulation of problem 49–50; labour market innovations 46–7; meaning of development 45; problem as logical conflict 45–6; as scarcity problem 44; trade-off representation 44–5
maximally consistent subset (MCS) *see* economic problem solving
Meade, J.E. 33, 44–7, 49–50
Medawar, P. 8–9, 18, 22, 26, 78
mental models: economic problem solving 126–31; new ideas' generation by reasoning 74–5; originality in social science research 24–6
Minsky, H.P. 35
Mishkin, F.S. 116
Mitroff, I.I. 131, 137
Muth, J. 171

negation's creative power *see* new ideas' generation by reasoning
negations/conjunctions *see* Coase's Theorem
new ideas' generation by reasoning: abduction connecting S and E 82–8; abduction and logical conflict 78–82; abduction and questions 82–8; abductive reasoning 4, 73–5; assumption finding 78–9; background/summary 71, 88–9; brainstorming 83; creative mathematics 76; creative process 71–2; creative questioning cross 84 *Fig.*, 85–6; deductive reasoning 74–5; end point (E) derivation 79–80; Euclidian proofs 76; logical/creative activities, differences 71–2; mathematical proof 76–8; meaning of new ideas 73; mental models 74–5; negation's creative power 83, 86–8; problem's logical structure 79; shared mental models (abduction/deduction) 74–5; starting point (S) derivation 80–2; strategic constraints 72–3; substance constraints 71–3

next steps *see* future use of techniques
Nickles, T. 62
North, D.C. 17, 23

originality in social science research: background 15; break-out/leap of conjecture 24–6; conceptions/ideas identified 27–9; construction model 16; defining originality 15–17; degrees of originality 21–2; disciplinary origin 23–4; Einstein's approach 24–6; evaluation of product of originality 22; feasibility 21–2; gap-spotting research 20–1; hermeneutic model 17; interesting research 18–21; judging originality 23 *Table*; leap of conjecture 26–7; meaningfulness of contribution 18; mental models 24–6; novelty of contribution 17; performativity 16; process of conceiving 27; systematic approach requirements 30
Osborn, A. 83

performativity 16
Phillips curve 37, 98
Pólya, G. 78
Popper, K.R. 3–4, 28, 48–9
Posner, R.A. 112
Prescott, E.C. 9, 33, 42, 89; case study *see* central banking ideas (Kydland and Prescott)
problem representation: assumption identification 55–7; background/summary 33, 57; Beveridge curve 37; comparison of conflict/trade-off representations 44, 47–8; conflicts representation 38–44, 48–55; constraints on the solution 42–3; constructing problem as conflict 48–55; destructive dilemma 39; *ex falso quodlibet* principle 39; importance of problems 33–5; Laffer curve 37–8; logical conflict structures 39–44; meaning of problem 34; Phillips curve 37; Sraffa's dilemma 43; trade-off convertibility 49–50; trade-off representation 36–8; trade-off/dilemmas, conversion into logical order 50–2; undesirable effect, conversion into logical order 52–5; valuation solution 48; Williamson model 37; World I/World III problems 48–9, *see also* Mauritius
Pullen, J. 38

questioning techniques: assumptions 62–4; classes/relevance relations 66–7; conflict representation 60, 61 *Fig.*, 62; creative questioning cross 164–7; critical confrontation 62–4; elements of a question 66–7; erotetic logicians 28, 60, 65; generating interesting questions 60–1; interrogating the questions 65–6; key issues/summary 60, 70; p-predicaments/b-predicaments, distinction 65; problem representation, questions/ideas from 157–61; problematising questions 65–9; relational analysis 68–9; relational analysis, questions/ideas from 163–4; synthesising approach 64–5; Van Fraassen analysis 161–3; ways of generating 61; why-questions 66–8

rational reconstruction: case studies 91–2; Coase's Theorem case study *see* Coase's Theorem; definition 91; Kydland and Prescott case *see* central banking ideas (Kydland and Prescott); Sen case study *see* capability approach (Sen); summary 112–13
Rescher, N. 137
Rittel, H.W.J. 118–20, 135
Ritter, J.A. 102
Robbins, L. 36, 38, 48
Rogoff, K. 101–4, 106
Romer, P 6–7, 39
Rosenhead, J. 122

Sandberg, J. 19–20, 61
Sargent, T. 123
Schumpeter, J.A. 45
scientific creativity 1–3; ability of economists questioned 1–2; definition 1; double transformation 2–3; guidance from economists 2; originality expectation 1; role of creativity 2
Seely-Brown, J. 4
Sen, A. 9, 33, 89, 91; case study *see* capability approach (Sen)
Simon, H. 4, 34, 119
Smith, A. 19

Sraffa's dilemma *see* problem representation
starting point derivations: central banking ideas (Kydland and Prescott) 102–3; new ideas' generation by reasoning 80–2
Steeman, P.J. 142
Stigler, G.J. 34
Stiglitz, J. 1, 123
synthesising approach: capability approach (Sen) 95–7; questioning techniques 64–5
synthetic-abductive dialogue *see* economic problem solving

taming strategies *see* economic problem solving
Taylor, J. 37
Taylor's monetary policy trade-off *see* economic problem solving
techniques' use *see* future use of techniques
Thaler, S. 4, 19, 88
Thomson, 7
Thurow, L. 16
time-inconsistency problem *see* central banking ideas (Kydland and Prescott)
Tinbergen, J. 34
Tobin, J. 35
Toulmin model of argumentation *see* economic problem solving
trade-off issues *see* economic problem solving; problem representation
trial-and-error approach *see* creative research as systemic process

use of techniques *see* future use of techniques

valuation solution *see* problem representation
Van Fraassen analysis: central banking ideas (Kydland and Prescott) 105; Coase's Theorem 106–7; instructional programme 161–3
Van Fraassen, B.C. 66–8, 70
Viner, J. 35

Walsh, C.E. 101–2
Webber, M.M. 118–20, 135
Weick, K.E. 16, 29, 84
Weisberg, R.W. 4–5, 20
White, P. 29
why-questions *see* questioning techniques
wicked problems *see* economic problem solving
Willets, D. 122
Williamson model *see* problem representation
World I/World III problems *see* problem representation